WORKERS IN A LABYRINTH
Jobs and Survival in a Bank Bureaucracy

Based on extensive interviews of clerical workers in a large international commercial bank, this book illuminates in great detail the actual workings of corporate bureaucracy and the ways it affects people. Specifically, the volume analyzes the intricacies of bank organizational structure and the standardization, isolation, friction, and status deprivation that bureaucratic work produces for those at the bottom of the hierarchy.

The book's central concern is with the ambiguous tangle of workers' experiences as they try, because they have few other choices, to come to terms with their bureaucratized work. It shows how workers shape armed truces with alienation by excusing and justifying even the most despised aspects of their jobs. Further, it records their struggles to find positive rationales for working in the same bureaucratic structure which thwarts their autonomy and narrows their visions of the world and of themselves.

Workers In A Labyrinth

Jobs and Survival in a Bank Bureaucracy

by
ROBERT JACKALL

LandMark Studies
ALLANHELD, OSMUN   MONTCLAIR
UNIVERSE BOOKS   NEW YORK

ALLANHELD, OSMUN & CO. PUBLISHERS, INC.
Montclair, New Jersey

Published in the United States of America in 1978
by Allanheld, Osmun & Co., 19 Brunswick Road, Montclair, N.J. 07042,
and by Universe Books, 381 Park Avenue South, N.Y., N.Y. 10016
Distribution: Universe Books

LIBRARY OF CONGRESS CATALOGING IN PUBLICATION DATA

Jackall, Robert
  Workers in a labyrinth.

  (Landmark studies)
  Bibliography: p.
  Includes index.
  1. Bank employees—United States—Case studies.
2. Industrial sociology—Case studies.   I. Title.
HD8039.B27U55   331.7'61'33210973   77-84347
ISBN 0-87663-817-5

Printed in the United States of America

For Janice Michiko

Preface

This book is about bureaucratic work and about how people come to terms with it. It is not an abstract treatment of the subject. Rather, it studies one group of workers in one large organization—that is, clerks in the domestic branches of an international bank to which I have given the fictitious name of First Bank of Columbia. By analyzing in detail the experiences of these bank workers, the book tries to address some of the central issues emerging from bureaucratic work in our society, issues which a great many men and women face.

Much modern literature on work focuses on workers' alienation from their jobs, and alienation is one theme which runs through bank workers' experiences. However, the focus of this book is not on workers' alienation, but on how they try to resolve it or at least come to live with it. It is an analysis of how bank workers *legitimate* their work—how they explain it to themselves and to others and how, when they experience it as alienating, stressful, or unrewarding, they account for it through excuses and justifications. The book argues that it is precisely through such legitimations that workers join themselves to their work even when they find it alienating. In doing so, they help create and renew one of the central institutions in their own lives and in the social structure as a whole. The book is therefore a study of ambivalence rather than of alienation. Also, because the book examines how workers construct legitimating meanings for their work, it is inescapably a study of the power contexts within which such meanings are formed and asserted. Here this means especially an analysis of how the bureaucratic structure of the First Bank of Columbia affects workers' consciousness.

The material in Chapter 4 was published in a somewhat different form in "The Control of Public Faces in a Commercial Bureaucratic Work Situation," *Urban Life* Vol. 6, No. 3 (October, 1977), pages 277-302, and appears here by permission of the publisher, Sage Publications, Inc.

Many people have contributed to the making of this book, and it is a pleasure to acknowledge their help here. The book would not have been possible without the generous and open cooperation of First Bank of Columbia workers. Their statements of their experiences constitute the core of this work, and I only hope that I have adequately captured the difficulties, complexities, and ambiguities of their situations. I also want to thank the bank's management for allowing me to do this study; several other large corporations would not. One official in particular, who must remain anonymous, was instrumental in helping me gain access to several bank branches, and I am grateful for his assistance.

I am also indebted to many people for their ideas and scholarly example. My teachers and advisers at the Graduate Faculty of the New School for Social Research, where this book was originally a dissertation, helped me in many ways. I found Stanford M. Lyman's ideas consistently fruitful throughout this project, and I have also been deeply influenced by Arthur J. Vidich's work in both sociology and anthropology. Their emphasis on the importance of field work and their insistence on standards of excellence contributed immeasurably to whatever quality this work possesses. I appreciate as well the advice, direction, and sustaining encouragement that I have received over the years from Trent Schroyer and Robert L. Heilbroner. Finally, although I never knew him, my intellectual debt to C. Wright Mills is considerable.

I owe a special thanks to my many students over the years, particularly at the University of San Francisco, Evening College. They listened very patiently and responded creatively to my grapplings with the data. Often by recounting their own work experiences, they illuminated the material. Ronald S. Berlin carefully read the entire text and made many helpful criticisms of it; I have profited greatly from our discussions and arguments.

My parents George and Mary Jackall taught me a great deal about the importance of work in people's lives, and I am grateful for that awareness. Finally, my deepest thanks go to Janice Hirota Jackall for her generous and sustained help throughout this work. The field work for the study and the preliminary analysis of the data were made possible only because she largely supported us through her own work. Even more important, her many insights into the material, her critical suggestions, and her very considerable editorial abilities made the book both more substantive and readable. I am very happy to dedicate this work to her.

Contents

part four
CONCLUSION

part one

THE STUDY AND ITS
THEORETICAL BASIS

1 Introduction

This book studies clerical workers in a large, branch banking system. It analyzes their experiences of work and the meanings they give to those experiences. Specifically, it focuses on how these workers legitimate* their work—that is, how they explain it and, where they experience it as problematic, how they account for it to themselves and to others. In legitimating their work, these workers construct and affirm a critical part of their lives.

Why Clerical Workers?

Both in numbers and functions, clerical workers are increasingly a crucial part of the American economy; hence their legitimations for work assume special importance for understanding how social order is achieved within the United States's political economy. Since 1900, the American economy has changed drastically. Workers have shifted from the farm, through the factory, and into white-collar service occupations.[1] This burgeoning white-collar sector constituted 46 percent of all American workers in 1973 and will constitute 50.8 percent of the labor force by 1980.[2] In 1973, clerks were 16.9 percent of all workers and 36 percent of all white-collar workers.[3] By 1980, clerical workers will be 18.2 percent of the work force, more than 17½ million workers, and, for a time, the largest numerical category of all workers.[4] Even though clerks do not produce value in the classical sense of political economy, their labor is indispensable. The bureaucratization of the American economy has produced ever growing amounts of paperwork, computer audits, and demands for interpersonal links within and between corporations and between corporations and

---

*This sociological term is used throughout the book. To legitimate some aspect of reality is to construct a special meaning for it which makes it more intelligible and more acceptable both to others and to oneself. Legitimations can be positive motives or explanations, or defensive accounts for something; most often positive and defensive legitimations are entangled. The term and its uses are explained in detail in chapter 2.

3

their customers. It is no exaggeration to say that without the clerks who process the mountains of paper, make up payrolls, type letters, answer phones, greet visitors or customers, and perform the bulk of the enormously detailed tasks that underpin production, the American economy would disintegrate into a maze of confusion. How clerical workers legitimate their work is then a sociological problem with wide ramifications. Because of clerks' key position in the economy, their continuing assent to what they do is crucial not only for their own lives, but for the work and lives of many other people.

The growing numerical strength and functional importance of clerical workers have been matched by the rationalization of their work. This rationalization—the standardization, segmentation, and mechanization of clerical work to produce the greatest efficiency—has followed the same patterns which shaped blue-collar labor in this country.[5] Modern societies tend to streamline those areas of work necessary for their economic well being. In this, the rationalization of clerical work may presage similar developments, in fact already well begun, in other white-collar sectors—specifically, in the managerial, technical, and professional work force.[6] Clerks' legitimations for their work, therefore, can give us clues to the meaning of one of the dominant social processes in American society.

Another reason for studying clerical workers and their legitimations for work is the paucity of sociological research on the subject. Some studies in other countries which select clerks as a focal point for an analysis of the white-collar strata are, however, particularly germane to this work.[7] In contrast to these studies, sociologists in America either have not focused on clerks as a representative white-collar group or, because of narrowness of focus or of methodology, have not shed much light on clerks' legitimations for their work.[8] The most notable exception is Chris Argyris's *Organization of a Bank*.[9] Argyris is not principally concerned with clerks as such nor with their legitimations for work, but rather with the process of "fusion" between individuals and a work organization. However, because he chooses a bank for his investigation, most of his subjects are clerks. Moreover, in his search for factors which cause or retard fusion, he examines virtually every area of these workers' experiences. His data are rich and complex, especially his interview materials, and they parallel, at times almost exactly, data in this study. Argyris's interpretation of how fusion occurs, however, is at best specific to his own materials. Briefly, he explains the social integration of the bank which he studied through the organization's adroit and successful selection of workers who have acquiescent personalities and who smoothly fit into the preexisting organizational framework and perpetuate its order. This schema is far too static to explain the materials or to address the problem of the present study and, in my view, is inadequate even for Argyris's study. Still, Argyris has written one of the few in-depth studies of clerks, and aspects of it will be discussed in later chapters.

Field Work in the First Bank of Columbia

Among the many possible explanations for the paucity of in-depth studies of American clerical workers is a practical obstacle: many American corporations are unwilling to allow independent field research on their clerks within the work situation. To gain a secure basis for sociological generalization, I sought access to typical clerical work situations: that is, large offices in urban settings where the work was highly mechanized and bureaucratized. Seven major corporations with these structural features all refused permission for this study; these included a bank, a brokerage house, some insurance companies, a utility company, and a telephone company. Underlying the bureaucratic excuses, there seemed to have been two critical reasons for refusal. First, ethnographic field study, involving great amounts of time observing and interviewing clerks, was thought likely to disrupt work processes. Second, it was feared that I might discover, or unleash, latent worker resentments. A regional executive of one corporation (in a memo which was not intended for me, but which I received through a sympathetic contact in the organization) partially documents these explanations:

General Administration is cool to the idea of [the author's] study because:
1. the disruptive or nuisance effect of his intervention in the job for up to 6 weeks;
2. the possibility of having unfavorable Service Representative attitudes published.

Such organizational reluctance can and, I suspect, has discouraged many potentially fruitful investigations of clerks and their work.

Given this type of corporate attitude, my admittance to several large, urban branches of the First Bank of Columbia, where I was permitted to do the field work for this study, was rather fortuitous. It was accomplished, in fact, only through a friendly institutional connection between the bank and an organization where I was working. Even then, the understanding was that my stay would be brief. However, when it became apparent that my methods for collecting data did not unduly disrupt the bank's work flow, the officials who had allowed my entrance in early July of 1973 renewed my stay several times over until I completed the study in late December, 1973. Even more fortuitously, the setting turned out to be ideal for the study of clerical workers. Not only did the bank's branches correspond to my initial, rough selective criteria for generalizable work settings, but the clerical work in these branches is typical of much clerical work in the United States.

BRANCH BANKING AND THE STRUCTURE OF CLERICAL WORK

Clerical branch work in the First Bank of Columbia is typical of clerical work as a whole because of the close interconnection of its central features: it is commercial, it is mechanized, and it is bureaucratic. The commercial purpose of the bank's branches determines the ambiance and shape of branch clerical work. Branches are essentially the retail outlets of large banks like the First Bank of Columbia; the purpose of branches is to provide total banking services to as many customers as possible. As their branches sell checking accounts, credit cards, savings accounts, travellers' cheques, a host of other services, and, most important, consumer and business loans, large commercial banks not only make immediate profits, but they are also able to pool some of the capital necessary for larger financial transactions with big businesses. Such a commercial design makes bank branches financial department stores, and every clerk is actually or potentially a salesperson who must orient herself° to pleasing customers. To insure success for the bank in these transactions, the First Bank of Columbia imposes on its clerks stringent requirements of appearance, demeanor, and approach. All of these regulations have important consequences for their work. One of the principal jobs of clerks, especially those in the public view, is to arrange their presentations of themselves to sell the bank most effectively to customers. Such a commercial ambiance typifies the situations of many other American clerical workers who are expected to convey favorable corporate images to potential buyers of goods and services.

The commercial thrust of branch banking has other consequences for its clerical workers which also typify developments in the modern office. Because branch banks are structured to sell banking services primarily to individuals, the sheer volume of business necessary to make desired profits and to gather capital has demanded increasing mechanization of the workplace. For instance, the key to successful retailing of bank services has historically been the demand deposit, or checking account. Large commercial banks view checking services as the important initial contact with a customer. A checking account, on one hand, facilitates selling a customer other services more profitable to the bank; and since, in most states, money in checking accounts collects no interest, these accounts become in themselves important sources of free capital for other uses. However, checking services involve staggering amounts of paperwork. Between 1939 and 1970, the total number of checks cleared through American commercial banks went from 3.5 billion to 22 billion; by 1980, the latter figure will double.[10] The First Bank of Columbia alone processes an average of two million checks each business day. Increasing reliance on the computer is the only way that branch banks can begin to handle this volume of checks while maintaining efficiency and low costs. Such cost and efficiency mechanization, which most of all affects the shape of branch clerical work, is typical of the modern office since not only banks but virtually all corporations have become, as one bank worker put it, "paper mills."

Finally, despite the seeming decentralization of branch banking, retail

°Since between 85% and 90% of First Bank of Columbia clerical personnel are female, the feminine pronoun is appropriate for general use throughout this book except where specific instances involving male workers dictate the use of the masculine form.

banking enterprises like the First Bank of Columbia are actually thoroughly centralized and bureaucratically structured. The bank's hundreds of branches are controlled by both a regional and central administration. Hierarchical, overlapping authority structures govern the branch network with systematic thoroughness. Few, if any, decisions about details of policy, work structure, marketing strategies, or external appearances of the workplace are left to local authorities. Similarly, in an effort to gain system-wide uniformity, maximum efficiency, and strict control of funds, branch work is completely standardized and segmented into discrete, hierarchical arrangements accompanied by carefully defined, differentiated rewards. Such centralized, bureaucratic structures are the hallmark of the American corporate economy;[11] as such, they are the frameworks within which the bulk of clerical work in the United States takes place.

QUALITATIVE RESEARCH AND BUREAUCRATIC PRESSURES

From a structural standpoint, then, the First Bank of Columbia was an ideal field setting for a study of clerical workers. Once I gained entrance to the bank, my problem became how to gather the qualitative material I needed from a representative sample of workers and, at the same time, not jeopardize my continued presence in the bank. Each aspect of this general problem and its resolution needs discussion.

An initial, but principal, methodological issue was to establish some criteria to insure that I interviewed a representative sample of the bank's urban branch workers. This meant, first of all, doing research in several field sites which were as diversified as possible. During my six months of field work, I was able to do research in five sites in three of the bank's large urban branches. While the overall structure and purpose of clerical work in these sites were much the same, there were important differences between them which affected workers and provided bases for analytical comparison. The key variables in differentiating sites were size, types of clientele, and types of authority. The first field site was a moderately sizable branch of 64 employees, all of whom worked on the main banking floor. While the segmentation of work among these workers was considerable, they had a more flexible work structure than did the workers in larger branches. The branch itself primarily serviced a clientele of law students, government workers, pensioners, and street people from the nearby red light district. The wide variety of customers produced what were called "problems of predictability" for workers, and this branch had a very high money-loss rate and, because of that, a high rate of employee turnover. Types of authority varied, even within this branch's small number of managerial personnel, but the dominant managerial style was marked by a functional mentality—that is, a workaday orientation directed at the accomplishment of the bank's work, as the bank wanted it done, but without the pressures on workers created by extreme managerial career-mindedness.

The second and third field sites were located in a large First Bank of Columbia complex of several hundred workers. It contained a wide range of bank operations. Within the complex was a large branch of 96 employees, of whom two-thirds worked on the main banking floor; the remainder did specialized branch work in an interior office several floors away. The size of this branch, one of the largest in the city, produced much more rigorous compartmentalization of work both on the main floor and in the interior office than the first field site evidenced. There were, moreover, differences in clientele. The main banking floor catered basically to local businessmen and to office workers from nearby corporations. Although the social basis of the clientele made customer contact more predictable here than in the first branch, the large volume of business made the main floor a very harried work and research site. The interior office principally handled automobile financing, union accounts, and military banking; its specialization isolated this site from the banking floor, creating the material conditions for sharp social differences between them. However, the interior office also did regular branch work in servicing the banking needs of many of the First Bank of Columbia workers in the same building. All types of authority that I found throughout the bank were present in these two sites, but the dominant style here was aggressively authoritarian—that is, authorities exhibited a dominating, frequently harsh approach to workers, especially when a worker's performance threatened their own career goals. To some extent, this tone was fostered by both the branch's size and its position in the First Bank of Columbia's hierarchy. It was near, but not quite at the top of that hierarchy, and only the most successful managerial personnel, in the bank's terms, went beyond this level.

The last two field sites in the study were located in the largest First Bank of Columbia branch, a multi-floored, highly compartmentalized operation of more than 200 employees. Here I studied a note division of 30 workers and a commercial interior office of 35 workers. Because of this branch's great size, each of its departments was totally segregated from every other department, and the work within each was highly segmented, more so than in any other site. Competition for prestige was also more evident in this branch, and such status-consciousness was closely related to the work done and the clientele served. The note division handled only loans and their documentation, prestigious work in itself because of the amounts of money involved. Moreover, since this branch was located in the heart of the city's business district, most of its clientele were relatively well-off business people. These factors set this site apart from the other work situations studied. The commercial interior office had no customer contact at all; its work consisted entirely of processing the paper from all the other departments of the branch. It was located in the branch's basement. Its windowless, airless atmosphere and its relatively poor appointments were tokens of the low prestige such work had within the branch. In both sites, the style of authority was one of enlightened management with an emphasis on human relations approaches to workers, although there were also strong tendencies towards the previously mentioned "functional" managerial mentality, especially in the commercial interior site. The enlightened management style, with its emphasis on "understanding workers," contrasted sharply with the other types of authority discovered in the field research.

While these several sites differed enough in size, types of clientele, and types of authority to give the study a diverse base, I still had to select for interviewing a representative cross section of clerical workers within each site. The classical method of selection—random sampling—did not seem appropriate since, in urban areas, the social backgrounds of the bank's personnel vary considerably. I wanted to guard against any possible bias that outside status characteristics might introduce into the data.[12] In addition, work tasks in large branches are, as I have emphasized, highly specialized and segmented, one from another; previous study has indicated that the type of work tasks performed influences work attitudes.[13] I opted, therefore, for structured samples of workers from each work site—that is, I took into account and tried to hold constant the social factors of age, sex, ethnic background, education, and marital status, as well as work specialization. Table I shows the demographic

Table I

Demographic Characteristics of First Bank of Columbia Workers Interviewed
(Complete Interviews Only N = 50)

Category	Number	Percentage of Total
Ethnic Origins		
Caucasian	34	68
Minority	16	32
Asian	10	20
Black	3	6
Spanish-speaking	3	6
Sex		
Female	45	90
Male	5	10
Education		
Completed high school	36	72
Some college	14	28
Marital Status		
Married	26	52
Single	20	40
Divorced	4	8
Age		
18–29	36	72
30–49	8	16
50+	6	12

distribution of the sample. The statistical proportions of each category, on the whole, accurately represent the demographic structure of the five field sites. Indeed, based on statistics obtained from the First Bank of Columbia, this sample is a fairly accurate picture of branch clerical workers throughout the bank's state-wide system. The only significant difference is that minority workers are somewhat overrepresented in this sample as compared to minorities in the bank as a whole, although not in the urban branches studied. In the bank's entire system, only 23 percent of all employees belong to minority groups. More particularly, Asian workers — mostly Chinese and Filipinos—constitute 20 percent of my sample whereas they are only 5 percent of the entire population of First Bank of Columbia employees. Again, this is a function of the metropolitan location of this study. In addition to controlling for these demographic variables, I systematically interviewed workers at every level of the clerical work hierarchy. Certainly, every *type* of clerical work done in the bank's branches, if not every specific task, is represented and controlled for in this sample. In addition to complete interviews, I conducted partial interviews with a score of other workers, divided about equally between the several field sites. In these discussions, I was interested either in corroborating specific facts or, more often, in exploring more extensively specific attitudes which emerged in the interviews with my major respondents. Some of the partial interviews, however, turned out to be quite substantial, and I have occasionally used illustrative materials from them.

A second methodological problem was how to establish the rapport with workers which would enable me to gather the requisite interview material. Apart from the niceties of personal approach, such rapport required most of all a clear definition of my own status in the workplace: first, that my presence was approved by bank authorities, and second, that my research was entirely independent of the bank. This was especially important because the First Bank of Columbia constantly conducts efficiency studies of its workers. In all but one field site I was able to arrange a general introduction to workers through their managers, operations officers, or supervisors. I followed such general introductions with personal, informal visits with each worker. During the personal visit, I carefully described the independent nature of my inquiry, emphasizing that I was in no way connected with the bank; in addition, I described the purposes and methodology of the study. In the single case where I was not introduced by an authority figure, I had to make considerable efforts to assure workers that, on the one hand, they had permission to talk with me and, on the other, that I was not conducting a time and motion study for the bank. I did not, except in the instance described and in a few isolated conflicts of personality, encounter any notable suspicion from workers.

The interviews themselves were aimed at obtaining detailed data in three general areas. My first concern was to grasp workers' experiences of their work situations. To do this, I probed for their likes and dislikes in their jobs, and for their perceptions and definitions of the following dimensions of their work situations: the technological environment, the structure of authority, the work tasks themselves, the bank's organizational demands, the rank and status hierarchy, relationships with co-workers, pay and benefits, mobility, and the absence of a union. Second, I was concerned with workers' legitimations for those work situations and for work itself. Legitimations of work situations were most often revealed in and intermeshed with workers' descriptions of their experiences. However, to understand their feelings about work itself, I explored the following areas: why workers saw themselves working, whether they would work if they had other sources of money, the meaning of the concept "work," and finally their perspectives on a range of factors related to the traditional work ethic—savings, investment, the restriction of consumption, the use of credit, the concept of success, their goals, and their perceptions of the future. Finally, I wanted to explore the relationship between work and the rest of workers' lives. To do so, I asked them about what they considered important in their lives outside of work, about their lifestyles, their use of free time, their perceptions of themselves both at work and outside of work, and how, if at all, they saw their work and life interrelated.

The initial key to successful qualitative field research in a pressured, bureaucratic work situation is to be as unobtrusive as possible. This means, first of all, adapting oneself thoroughly to the work pace and rhythm of the office under study. I learned to work with the daily, weekly, and monthly cycles of branch work. Mornings before the 10:00 A.M. opening were generally good times for interviewing; the middle of the week was always better than the chaotically busy Mondays and Fridays; and interviews were virtually impossible at the beginning, midpoint, and holiday periods of a month. Second, remaining unobtrusive also requires familiarizing oneself with the routines of those workers to be interviewed. For instance, I found I could best approach tellers in the early morning before customers arrived, or proof-machine operators in the late morning after they had finished reviewing the computer's mistakes from the previous day and before the afternoon's flood of work began. Adapting to branch cycles and familiarity with individuals' work rhythms enabled me to be alert for opportunities to talk to workers when my presence would not interfere with their work and, because of the interconnected work structure, with the work of others. This strategy generally enabled me to remain both inconspicuous and nondisruptive of work processes; I was able to avoid the attention of bank authorities and so remain in each field site for up to five weeks to gather the requisite data. The validity of this strategy was confirmed in a negative way in one field site. In one very busy branch the work was so tightly pressured that there were very few slack periods for interviewing. This time-scarcity was further complicated by an unannounced internal audit by bank investigators. Since I had already invested a considerable amount of time gathering parts of interviews, I pressed to finish my work there. A few workers, aware that I wished to talk with others, helped by trying to take over some of the interviewees' work chores. Despite their kindnesses, which enabled me to finish some of my work, my new obtrusiveness drew unfavorable notice from authorities and, in order to avoid jeopardizing the possibility of further field work in other branches, I was forced to leave the site.

With only a few exceptions, each complete interview took at least three hours, recorded verbatim by hand during the interview or, if necessary, reconstructed immediately afterwards.* Interviews with some workers took much longer; I spent, for example, six hours with one worker and eight with another to get the material I needed. Obviously I could not gather all the necessary material from a worker at one time and expect to remain inconspicuous. I therefore broke the interviews into three sections, rarely taking more than an hour with one worker at a time. This meant that I often had to stay longer at a site than I wanted, because, for example, an interviewee's time schedule might allow an interview period only once or twice a week. However, although the need for unobtrusiveness dictated patience in the field, the patience itself had its own rewards. In breaking interviews into hour segments, sometimes set apart by several days, I had to have several interviews in process simultaneously in order to finish the research at all. Viewpoints which emerged in one worker's interview could often be tested immediately against the views of another worker. Also, during the respites in a single interview, I could formulate clarifying questions to ask when the interview resumed. Finally, collecting data from the same person at different times served as a control on that person's moods or possible weariness at being questioned.

SUPPLEMENTARY FIELD DATA

While the interviews with workers are the core of this study, I also gathered complementary primary and secondary data to help me interpret the interview material. First, it was important to become thoroughly familiar with the particular culture of each work site. I therefore attended and made observations of all the staff meetings, celebrations for officers' promotions, and office parties which occurred in a branch while I was there. I also spent a good deal of time in lunchrooms or cafeterias chatting with workers. Besides giving me a sense of the ambiance of the workplace, these observations and conversations often provided material which illuminated the interview data.

Second, it became apparent very early in the field work that the organizational framework of the First Bank of Columbia, particularly as mediated by local authorities, was a crucial factor in shaping the meanings that many clerks gave to their work. I therefore interviewed 15 managers, operations officers, and supervisors in the field sites which I

*I decided that tape-recording the interviews was too obtrusive a method. Even my spiral notebooks occasionally drew unfavorable attention from workers whom I did not interview and from some managers.

studied. These data are fragmentary in comparison with the data from workers, although I did obtain some useful material. Even though my study had higher managerial sanction, and quite possibly because of that sanction, many local officials were deeply suspicious and some put obstacles in my way. Their points of view regarding workers' situations, backed as they are by authority, are, however, crucial slices of data to be matched with the corresponding and often opposing perspectives of workers.

Finally, it also quickly became apparent that the bank's gigantic bureaucratic apparatus was a decisively important factor in shaping meaning in the workplace. With its considerable power over local authorities, the bank dictates the policies to be followed with regard to workers. Many of these directives are formalized in internal management publications which document to some extent the aims, purposes, and methods of the bank's business structure and its concomitant policies towards workers. Moreover, the bank tries to shape workers' images of their work, of themselves as workers, and of the bank itself through internal publications directly aimed at workers, such as training manuals, circulars for posting, the monthly employee magazine, and orientation literature for new workers. These materials helped me understand the shape and meaning of clerical work in the bank.

The following chapter suggests a theoretical framework to look at these field data—a framework which does not suppress the ambiguities of workers' experiences, but does offer, at the same time, the conceptual tools to fashion a sociological understanding of their work legitimations.

References

1. Robert L. Heilbroner, *The Economic Problem* (Englewood Cliffs, N.J.: Prentice-Hall, 1968), p. 349.

2. Daniel Bell, "Labor in the Post-Industrial Society," in *The World of the Blue Collar Worker*, edited by Irving Howe (New York: Quadrangle-New York Times, 1972), p. 172.

3. *Ibid.* Sales personnel are not considered clerical workers in these figures.

4. *Ibid.* The temporary element is stressed here since professional and technical workers are growing even more rapidly than clerical workers. According to Bell's figures, the former were 13.6% of the work force in 1968 and will be, by 1980, 16.3% of all workers.

5. C. Wright Mills, *White Collar* (New York: Oxford Univ. Press, 1951), pp. 65 f.

6. Alfred DeMaria, Dale Tarnowieski, and Richard Gurman, *Manager Unions?* (New York: American Management Association, 1972); also, Harold Wilensky, "Work, Careers and Social Integration," *International Social Science Journal*, 12 (Fall 1960), 557.

7. I shall mention only the most important of these studies. David Lockwood in *The Black-Coated Worker* (London: George Allen and Unwin, Ltd., 1958) analyzes the economic and social position of clerks in Great Britain and provides some valuable perspectives, especially on their shaky status situation. However, Lockwood is not concerned with workers' subjective attitudes but rather with more collective indices of class consciousness, such as unionization statistics. Michael Crozier in *The World of the Office Worker* (Chicago: Univ. of Chicago Press, 1971) examines the work and lifestyles of Parisian insurance company clerks. His incisive analysis of the importance of status stratification to white-collar workers points to an important basis of work legitimation among clerks. Two authors stand out in German sociology's long tradition in the study of white-collar workers. In *Occupation and Ideology of the Salaried Employee*, trans. Eva Abramovitch, Columbia

Univ., Dept. of Social Science (New York: Columbia Univ., 1938),which focuses on clerical workers, Carl Dreyfuss carefully dissects the sources of the salaried employee's ideology which "blinds him to his true situation." Especially important are Dreyfuss's emphases on the importance of the hierarchical ranking of corporate enterprises in affecting workers' consciousness and on strategies by employers to divide workers. Hans Paul Bardht in *Industrie-bürokratie: Versuch Einer Soziologie des Industrialisierten Bürobetriebes und Seiner Angestellten* (Stuttgart: Enke, 1958) examines how organizational structure itself, especially through its standardized definition of tasks, can dominate white-collar employees, especially clerks, and alienate them from work.Finally, Thomas P. Rohlen in *For Harmony and Strength: Japanese White-Collar Organization in Anthropological Perspective* (Berkeley: Univ. of California Press, 1974) provides rich ethnographic data on Japanese bank workers which indicate that these workers see the world very differently from their American counterparts and that cultural variables are critical in shaping people's experiences in bureaucratic structures.

8. Despite a fine general analysis of the mechanization and bureaucratization of white-collar work, C. Wright Mills treats clerical workers as such only briefly in *White Collar*. Those studies which do take clerks as their primary subjects often focus on only one aspect of clerical work. For instance, Ida Hoos in *Automation in the Office* (Washington, D.C.: Public Affairs Press, 1961) and Jon Shepard in *Automation and Alienation* (Cambridge, Mass.: MIT Press, 1971) have studied the impact of automation on clerks. George Homans in "Status Among Clerical Workers," *Human Organization*, 12 (Spring 1953), 5–10, analyzes status differences among groups of clerks, and Edward Gross in "Cliques in Office Organizations," *Readings on Economic Sociology*, edited by Neil Smelser (Englewood Cliffs, N.J.: Prentice-Hall, 1965) looks at the social divisions which emerge among office workers. Finally, Barbara Kirsch and Joseph Lengermann in "An Empirical Test of Robert Blauner's Ideas on Alienation in Work As Applied to Different Type Jobs in a White Collar Setting," *Sociology and Social Research*, 56 (January 1972), 180–194 apply Robert Blauner's differential analysis of alienation developed in *Alienation and Freedom* (Chicago: Univ. of Chicago Press, 1964) to bank workers, stressing the role of office machines in creating alienating work conditions. However, by focusing on the alienating quality of particular machines, Kirsch and Lengermann miss completely the deeper and far more critical passivity enforced on workers by market cycles and allocation of work using scientific management procedures. These are issues which are explored in chapter 3 of the present work.

However important these studies of specific aspects of clerks' experiences may be in themselves, they are too narrow to be more than partially useful for a comprehensive appraisal of work legitimations. However, some more general studies of clerks' "work values" such as those by Nancy Morse, *Satisfactions in the White Collar Job*, Univ. of Michigan, Survey Research Center (Ann Arbor: Univ. of Michigan, 1953) or by J. M. Pennings, "Work-Value Systems of White Collar Workers," *Administrative Science Quarterly*, 15 (December 1970), 397-405, are even less useful than more specific studies, although they have the requisite level of generality. Both Morse and Pennings employ a quantitative methodology which fails to capture the complexity and ambiguity of clerical work-worlds. As it happens, journalist Elinor Langer's participant-observer study of telephone company workers in "Inside the New York Telephone Company," *New York Review of Books*, March 12, 1970, pp. 16 f. and in "The Women of the Telephone Company," *Ibid.*, March 26, 1970, pp. 14 f. is a more richly textured picture of clerical workers and of their legitimations for work than many academic studies. The same praise, however, cannot be given to some other journalistic efforts; see, for instance, Mary Kathleen Benét, *The Secretarial Ghetto* (New York: McGraw Hill, 1972).

9. Chris Argyris, *Organization of a Bank* (New Haven: Labor and Management Center, Yale Univ., 1954).

10. This increase in the number of checks cleared, dramatic in itself, might be accelerating at a geometric rate if present predictions hold true. The following figures, drawn from several sources, indicate the historical and potential growth of checks cleared.

Year	Checks Cleared (billions)
1939	3.5
1950	6.5
1960	13.0
1965	17.0
1970	22.0
1980°	44.0

°approximation

See Boris Yavitz, *Automation in Commercial Banking* (New York: Free Press, 1967), p. 11; Mark J. Flannery and Dwight Jaffee, *The Economic Implications of an Electronic Money Transfer System* (Lexington, Mass.: D. C. Heath, 1973), pp. 41-42; and James Vaughan and Avner Porat, *Banking Computer Style* (Englewood Cliffs, N.J.: Prentice-Hall, 1969), p. 11.

11. Among the many descriptions of this phenomenon, see especially Robert Presthus, *The Organizational Society* (New York: Alfred Knopf, 1962), pp. 59-92.

12. The evidence about the impact of social factors on workers' attitudes towards work is somewhat unclear. Michael Crozier, for instance, found that social factors play little part in clerks' responses to their work; see *The World of the Office Worker*, pp. 101 f. However, in American studies, the social factors of age, sex, race, and education have some impact on work attitudes; see Harold Sheppard and Neal Herrick, *Where Have All the Robots Gone?* (New York: Free Press, 1972), pp. 5-10.

13. Jon Shepard, "Functional Specialization and Work Attitudes," *Industrial Relations*, 8 (May 1969), 185-194; also, "Functional Specialization, Alienation and Job Satisfaction," *Industrial and Labor Relations Review*, 23 (January 1970), 207–219.

2 Theoretical Perspectives: Meaning, Legitimations, and Power

Work and Meaning

First Bank of Columbia clerks feel fundamentally ambivalent about their work. Their simultaneous attraction to and repulsion from their work situations is rooted in conflicting experiences. These workers, for example, see their work as economically essential but also as routinized, tedious, and underpaid; as providing a secure, but sometimes overwhelming organizational structure; as a place where they can claim social honor or win approval from authorities, but also where they experience status inequity and fear of authority.

Such ambivalence is itself fashioned by the contradictory meanings workers assign to their work. Meaning structures experience and makes it intelligible to actors. People may not always act intentionally nor with a clear understanding of the personal significance of their actions. They are, however, capable of explaining why they act. They may, for example, direct their actions according to internalized self-images and to corresponding images of appropriate activities;[1] in such cases, they are able to describe both their self-images and their own rules for behavior. If people act without conscious recognition of such images, they can, at the very least, give an after-the-fact explanation of what they have done. In both instances, actors express meanings which interpret their actions; their statements are generally intelligible to other people, and, in most cases, are made publicly on the supposition that they are socially acceptable. Since meaning structures experience, contradictory meanings given to a specific situation produce ambivalence and consequent psychological ambiguity. A recurring theme in this book is the deep ambivalence and ambiguity of bank workers' experiences.

16

THE SOCIOLOGY OF LEGITIMATION

Despite such ambiguity, First Bank of Columbia clerical workers do come to live with their work. They do so by *legitimating* their work situations in various ways; their legitimations of work give direction to their actions and enable them, although frequently with difficulty, to accept their ambivalences. Legitimations are special types of meanings which people assign to their activities; in Weber's sense,[2] they are subjective attributions of validity to some established order. Legitimations may, at least for the purposes of this study, be considered primary among the meanings clerical workers give to their work because, in the act of attributing validity to their work, workers make their continued participation in that work possible; their participation in turn constantly recreates the established order of their particular work-world, here the bank.

Legitimations for work are intermeshed with other meanings, observations, and feelings that people assign to their work. It is only with detailed analysis of interviews that the subjective patterns of stability, which legitimations fashion, begin to emerge. Two sociological concepts are especially important analytical tools in discerning people's legitimations—the concept of motive and the concept of accounts. Each concept refers to a different type of legitimation.

In a sociological sense, as Weber has noted, a motive is a "complex of subjective meanings which seems to the actor himself or to the observer as an adequate ground for the conduct in question."[3] Considered in this way, motives are not, as in psychological usage, forces in human nature which impel behavior, but are internalized social guideposts which *steer* human action. Motives are simply words with which people explain their behavior to themselves and to others; they are social rationales which facilitate behavior. Through words, motives tie people securely to the judgments of others and, through those judgments, to the social structure. As long as the motives which people enunciate for an action seem valid to the actor, to the observer, or to both, motives legitimate behavior. Because an everyday activity like work is often taken for granted, motives for it are infrequently enunciated. Motives for such commonplace activities do exist, however, and it is, in fact, by exploring the underlying motives of people's everyday activities that one may understand their dominant concerns.

Motives for any activity are neither universally available in a society nor randomly selected when available. Even in a mass bureaucratic society like the United States, which is marked by high rates of social mobility and concomitant emulation of lifestyles, the availability of motives depends upon a person's economic class, occupation, education, and social status. The rationales of a patrician senator for his work, for example, are hardly suitable for an urban worker. The availability of motives, therefore, means the appropriateness of motives to a person's social position. Moreover, people do not randomly select motives from all those available to them, but are guided by what seems appropriate to themselves—that is, to their own self-images. Since self-images are socially fashioned, what people think other people think of them becomes a controlling force in their selection of motives. Generally, we may assume that people explain their activities by selecting motives which protect or enhance prized aspects of their own self-images.

Once selected from those rationales which are socially available and personally acceptable, motives coordinate people's behavior and ideas, affecting not only the individuals who express them but their social groups as well. When people verbalize motives for their actions, or, alternatively, impute motives for the same actions to others, they are not merely offering a description of the behavior in question. They are, rather, as C. Wright Mills points out, trying to influence others:[4] in verbalizing motives to explain their own actions, they are searching for the formula which will gain social approbation for those actions; in imputing motives to others, they are trying to explain the actions of others in terms intelligible to themselves and to their social group. Through this process, people affect themselves as individuals and their relationships to their group. In expressing their own interpretations of action, people reconcile their own and others' actions with their own internalized rationales; in doing so, they more deeply internalize those sets of reasons and make them stronger forces in future actions. At the same time, people are implicitly representing the views of their own group in society.

While motives are legitimations which people use to explain the thrust of their activities, accounts[5] are legitimations which reconcile threatened human relationships. Accounts excuse or justify actions which seem, for some reason, untoward. By repairing such personal tears in the social fabric, accounts legitimate social action by allowing it to continue. Accounts are an important tool by which ambivalent workers continue their work. Workers who feel ambivalent about their work often become uneasy and even anxious and tense when questioned about those experiences which they interpret negatively. Such distress is probably related to the admission of failure to find total personal happiness in a society which extols fulfillment.[6] The enunciation of motives helps override such ambivalence by establishing goals which explain the overall meaning of experiences, including discomforting ones. However, negative experiences are sometimes so strong that workers feel obliged to excuse or justify their continuance in alienating situations. In such cases, accounts, which are basically defensive, not only repair strains between workers and an interviewer whose probes have exposed anxiety, but also strains which workers feel within themselves. Accounts thus mitigate the social meaning of ambivalence by appealing to socially recognized and approved excuses and justifications for ambivalence-producing actions. In this way, accounts legitimate behavior and complement motives in making sense of the world.

Legitimacy and Social Order

Legitimations for work are important materials for sociological analysis because they exemplify the subjective mechanisms which help shape social order. Several theoretical issues need to be discussed here. The sociological stance adopted toward the problem of social order determines one's notion of the structure of human behavior, at least for the historical period in question, and fixes the direction and categories of any analysis. Functionalist sociology, for example, assumes the existence of social order as the natural state of society, not only for primitive and peasant peoples, but for modern societies as well. In such a conception, human behavior is essentially cooperative and harmonious, and the task of sociology is simply to elaborate the structure and the functioning of that harmony. Functionalism postulates a common value system which, once internalized through socialization, guides people's behavior towards the maintenance of a general equilibrium.[7] By assuming order, the functionalist approach makes disorder, or social conflict, difficult to explain.

Because conflict is more often the rule than the exception in human behavior (at least in the present historical epoch and especially in the urban workplaces of this study), it is appropriate here to assume that conflict rather than order is the basic state of society. For example, bank workers and their managers have little in common which would underpin any assumption of harmony between them; indeed, despite their everyday association and roughly similar economic backgrounds, these workers experience considerable antagonisms among themselves due to social, educational, or ethnic diversity. In such cases, conflict is a better starting point for analysis than harmony. But to be realistic, most social situations—including First Bank of Columbia workplaces—do hang together rather than fall apart. How is such observable order possible given the conflict which one assumes to permeate modern human relationships in general and First Bank of Columbia workplaces in particular? Within such a theoretical framework, the sociological task is both to describe the underlying structure of conflict and to analyze the mechanisms people employ to resolve that conflict and achieve at least the semblance of social order.

Both motives and accounts are key subjective mechanisms for the achievement of social order. To the extent that people legitimate their social experiences, they remove themselves from social conflict and, in conjunction with others who share or accept their legitimations, help fashion social order. Legitimations for work are especially important since work institutions are microcosms of many key aspects of modern social structure. Work situations both create and reflect prevailing social relations in our society—particularly many conflict-laden relations like those of authority, economic position, and social status. By fashioning or accepting legitimations for their work, workers negate, deflect, or at least alleviate the personal impact of the conflicts inherent in the social relations which their work expresses and creates. In thus legitimating work, workers bolster key social relations underpinning the industrial society in which they live. By contrast, when workers de-legitimate their work by calling into question the meanings which have previously explained or accounted for what they do, they threaten the fragile social order which their legitimations helped produce. When this occurs, social conflict reasserts itself.

THE PROBLEM OF POWER

People do not, however, assert legitimating meanings for any activity within a social void—least of all for their work in a capitalist society. The power relationships of work situations and of other social contexts related to work influence their motives and accounts.

Theoretically, a focus on power follows the assumption that conflict, rather than order, is the prevailing structure of society and of human action during a given historical period. It is social power, however based, which resolves conflict, either by the direct imposition of one person's or group's will on another or, less directly, by the creation of the framework within which or the terms by which negotiated agreements can emerge. To exert control, people in power always try to impose their definitions of reality upon those subordinate to them. By thus controlling the meanings by which subordinates understand their experiences, those in power consolidate and perpetuate their own power. They create the material out of which legitimations are fashioned, if not the legitimations themselves. Furthermore, as many social thinkers of quite different perspectives have noted, those in power are generally successful in upholding their own views of the world.[8] Consequently, workers' legitimations for their work can only be analyzed by taking into account the power contexts which help shape their attitudes towards their work. In this sense, any study of legitimations is implicitly a political analysis.

Since work is such a diffuse experience in people's lives, many power contexts shape their perspectives. However, the field data of this study point to two general contexts of special significance in shaping bank clerks' legitimations for work—the organizational environment of the bank itself and the chosen lifestyles of workers outside of work.

It is hardly surprising that the First Bank of Columbia is a key determinant of its workers' legitimations for work. The success of corporate apparatuses like the bank depends to a great extent, as indicated earlier, upon the efficient, productive, and commercially-oriented labor of its employees. The bank rationalizes its clerical work roles to reach its goals, and, in doing so, creates the basic framework with which workers must, in some way, come to terms. Further, the bank complements its work role structure with carefully articulated financial and social programs designed to integrate workers into its organization and with an elaborate organizational ideology, disseminated through both literature and local authority figures, which seeks to provide workers with an interpretation of their experiences. The bank's local authorities not only insure workers' adequate performance through the constant evaluation of their work, but they are also the bank's mediaries in interpreting its official view of reality to workers. Local authorities are also expected to prevent the emergence of any disruptive counterviews among workers, especially if they assume an organized form.

The bank is by no means always successful in its attempts to shape directly the meanings its workers give to their work; however, the genius of a giant bureaucracy rests in its ability to influence enough workers so that it can contain the antagonistic interpretations of others. This process is explored further in later chapters.

For many bank workers, aspects of life outside of work are themselves key legitimations for work. For the most part, these workers' lives are focused around family or friends, or the pursuit of consumption or leisure, or a combination of these. These facets of lifestyle, which work makes economically possible, are themselves power contexts in relation to the meaning of work. Institutional and personal influences outside of work are diffuse and, therefore, more difficult to analyze than the influences of definable bureaucratic structures. Still, bank workers themselves emphasize that their perspectives are crucially affected by cultural and familial pressures to be independent, social pressures to consume or to employ time judiciously, and the economic demands of spouse and children, particularly when jobs are scarce. Later chapters examine just how, for some workers, such aspects of life outside of work become key legitimations for work.

One set of legitimations is, on the whole, notably absent in the meanings bank workers give to their work, that is, motives based specifically on their actual work tasks. Before we can fully understand the rationales for work which workers do use, we must explore what I think is a crisis of legitimacy for these clerical workers.

References

1. George Herbert Mead, *Mind, Self, and Society* (Chicago: Univ. of Chicago Press, 1934); see also Hans Gerth and C. Wright Mills, *Character and Social Structure* (New York: Harcourt, Brace and World, 1953), pp. 80–111.

2. Max Weber, *The Theory of Social and Economic Organization*, trans. A. M. Henderson and Talcott Parsons (New York: Free Press, 1947), pp. 124 f.

3. *Ibid.*, pp. 98–99. See also, with some qualification, the treatment by Hans Gerth and C. Wright Mills, *Op. Cit.*, pp. 112–129. Gerth's and Mills's treatment, based largely on earlier work by Mills in "Situated Actions and Vocabularies of Motive," in *Power, Politics and People*, edited by Irving Louis Horowitz (New York: Oxford Univ. Press, 1967), pp. 439–452, fluctuates between providing a theory of *explanations*, which is the basic meaning of the notion of motives presented here, and a theory of *accounts*, which will be discussed later. Though related, the concepts are somewhat different and should be distinguished. The work of Alfred R. Lindesmith and Anselm L. Strauss in *Social Psychology* (New York: Dryden Press, 1949), pp. 312–317, is also relevant to an understanding of motives from a sociological perspective.

4. C. Wright Mills, *Power, Politics and People, Op. Cit.*, p. 447.

5. Stanford Lyman and Marvin Scott, "Accounts," *A Sociology of the Absurd* (New York: Appleton-Century-Crofts, 1970), pp. 111–143. In their analytical treatment of accounts, Lyman and Scott draw to some extent on C. Wright Mills's notion of "vocabularies of

motive," although they modify and expand that concept. Donald Cressy also uses the idea of accounts, calling them "vocabularies of justification," in *Other People's Money* (Glencoe, Illinois: Free Press, 1953), pp. 93–137.

6. There may indeed be, as Robert Blauner suggests, a "cultural bias towards contentment," particularly when one is questioned about work which is such an important part of life in our society that "to demean one's job is to question one's very competence as a person." See "Work Satisfaction and Industrial Trends in Modern Society," in *Class, Status and Power*, edited by Reinhard Bendix and Seymour M. Lipset, 2nd ed. (New York: Free Press, 1966), pp. 486–487.

7. For a systematic statement of the functionalist perspective, especially regarding a postulated common value system, see Talcott Parsons, *The Social System* (Glencoe, Illinois: Free Press, 1951). See especially pp. 11 f.

8. For instance, Marx and Engels make this point in a general fashion in *The German Ideology* (New York: International Publishers, 1947), p. 39. Their position, which is often noted, is that "the ideas of the ruling classes are in every epoch the ruling ideas." They attribute this dominance to ruling classes' hegemony over the means of mental as well as material production. Peter Berger and Thomas Luckmann in *The Social Construction of Reality* (New York: Doubleday-Anchor, 1967), p. 109, make much the same point. Proceeding from a sociological theory of how mental universes are constructed and maintained, they indicate that "He who has the bigger stick has the better chance of imposing his definitions of reality." Lyman and Scott in their treatment of "Game Frameworks" in *Op. Cit.*, p. 66, concur with Berger and Luckmann, indicating that power is the most important social condition for the establishment of the frameworks within which any social games occur. Finally, in a seminal article called "The Cultural Apparatus" in *Power, Politics and People*, pp. 405–422, C. Wright Mills examines, on national scales, how the very terms with which people interpret their experience are shaped by select societal institutions which control the production and distribution of symbols.

part two

THE CRISIS OF WORK LEGITIMACY

3 Accounting for Rationalized Work

There is a quiet crisis of legitimacy for work among First Bank of Columbia workers. It is an undramatic crisis with one central feature: in the performance of their everyday work tasks, bank workers do not, in general, find positive legitimating motives for continuing their work. On the contrary, workers' experiences of the tasks and social situations which constitute their work are such that they find they must defensively account for the continued performance of essential features of their jobs. Unravelling this crisis sets several tasks before the writer which are the themes of this and the following chapter.

The first task is to analyze the experiential basis of this crisis of legitimacy. To a great extent, the everyday work experiences of bank workers are negative or, at best, neutral. Moreover, these experiences are not random or idiosyncratic, but cluster around the central feature of the bank's organization of work—namely, its highly rationalized character.

The second task of these two chapters is to show how accounts for work are both a symptom and a partial resolution of the crisis of legitimacy. Accounts for negative experiences excuse or justify those experiences; they do so, however, defensively. But even though they are defensive, accounts enable workers to continue working and, thus, help create social order out of conflict.

Finally, apart from delineating the crisis of legitimacy, there is the task of presenting the diversity of workers' experiences of their actual job tasks. Clearly, not all bank workers dislike their tasks. The diversity of their experiences points out subtle flexibilities found in any workplace and the crucial importance of subjective definitions in shaping experience.

Market Cycles, Work Allocation, and the Pace of Branch Work

The issue of control over the pace of work is an appropriate starting point for any analysis of work experience. Sociologists of work stress the importance to workers of control over their work pace.[1] As Robert Blauner points out, such control is important to people because it sets them apart from technology and is therefore an assertion of human dignity.[2] Although Blauner focuses upon the way industrial technology paces work in factory situations, his concern about workers' experiences of work-pace control is relevant in many white-collar situations, and clearly so in branches of the First Bank of Columbia. Bank workers have little control over the pace of their work. Unlike the factory situations which Blauner analyzes, however, branch work is not paced by visible technological implements, although computerization underpins its entire structure. Rather, the primary determinants of work pace are market cycles and managerial decisions about the allotment of labor-power to meet those cycles. Market cycles consist of time cycles and interest rates. Of the two, time cycles have more immediate significance for workers.

Time cycles are patterns of business activity set in motion by the bank's commercial thrust to extend and consolidate its share of the market; these cycles are weekly, monthly, and seasonal. The weekly cycle begins on Monday, which is always a pressured day; workers must process all work received during the weekend as well as handle the always heavy flow of customers entering the branch. Monday's pressure is exceeded only by Friday's, when the customer flow is even greater and when the bank shifts workers' time schedules to avoid overtime payments while offering late banking hours. Midweek periods vary in workload depending upon their coincidence with other cycles. Intense activity occurs at the beginning, midpoint, and end of calendar months; all these periods bring payrolls due for business customers, as well as a flood of individual paycheck deposits. Midmonth is, in many branches, the peak period for processing such accounts as deposits for a union's benefit fund. Billing cycles for interest payments usually fall due at the end of the month. At the seasonal cycles of Thanksgiving, Christmas, and tax-time, among others, check writing, credit card use, and lending greatly increase. When peak monthly or seasonal cycles intersect with each other, or when either or both intersect with peak weekly periods, most workers find the pace of branch work chaotic.

Interest rates, the second kind of market cycle, determine the flow of loans. These rates cut across time cycles and affect the work pace of phases of branch work, principally on the platform where loans are made and in note departments where loans are documented. The bank adjusts its interest rates according to the state of national and international money markets. When it lowers its rates, loans increase, and so, naturally, does the amount of work necessary to process them. In contrast, during the period of this study in 1973, the bank raised its prime interest rate, which affects all other rates, 15 times in response to increasingly tighter money markets. As interest rates soared, loans dropped off, and work pace noticeably slowed in those divisions principally concerned with financing.

The bank tries to cope with these quasi-autonomous market cycles by obtaining the optimum efficiency from workers. Managerial efficiency programs, therefore, mediate market cycles to workers. As one aspect of a more general concern with work efficiency, the bank's management has time and motion experts carefully measure every task of every branch job to the thousandth of a second. Such work measurement is codified in a computerized, quantitative analysis called the *Time and Allowance Practices Manual* (TAP) which gives local authorities strict criteria to follow in adjusting branch workloads. Operations officers are, for example, to utilize at least 95 percent of all the minutes of their staff's workdays.

In one way or another, then, market cycles and the bank's efficiency programs to cope with them affect the work pace of all branch clerks. Some workers, however, are less able than others to exert any control over their work pace. The workers with the least amount of control are those whose jobs connect them directly to market forces which, as it were, initiate their work tasks. For example, the work of tellers depends almost completely upon the daily flow of customers into a branch; or, again, machine operators must process the branch's work the same day it is received. The great majority of workers are in exactly this structural situation—that is, dependent on outside forces for the flow of their work. Depending on market cycles, their work pace alternates between being extremely busy and very slow. The bank, for its part, is concerned only that work is completed efficiently, and it provides no structures to help workers gain control of their work. The immediate task then is to analyze workers' experiences of their lack of control during the two key phases of market cycles.

BUSY CYCLES AND THE FEELING OF PRESSURE

Bank workers who lack control over their work pace because of their direct exposure to market forces experience a feeling of pressure during busy periods. Since they have no control over the pace or flow of work, the volume of work itself seems engulfing. A machine operator describes this experience:

No, I have absolutely no control over the work. If it's a heavy day, we really get bogged down. *All*° the work done in the bank comes here. When the bank closes, we still have a lot more work. Work is always backed up. Then after we finish running it through the machine, we have to photograph it. Photographing is a drag. Everything is a drag.

Workers in such situations have no way of insulating themselves from the insistent demands of market cycles; no matter how hard they work, during busy periods they feel that they can never really catch up. This feeling of overwork is, however, only half of the problem of pressure; the other half is the perception which· workers have of social demands to work faster. These demands are perceived to come from customers and especially from managers. Customers often get impatient while waiting

°All italics within quotes from interviews represent the subject's own emphasis, as noted by the author.

for service, and workers, particularly tellers, consider customers' annoy-ance a demand to work more quickly. Also, workers generally feel that authorities want work processed quickly so that everything will continue to run smoothly; during busy periods, workers often interpret the very presence of authorities as a demand for efficiency. In the midst of a very rushed day, a note teller describes her reaction to both sets of perceived demands:

I really hate it like this. I really get irritable. First, it's the customers who get pushy and then some of the officers—like this one guy over there. I really hate him. They come up here and hang around the counter and give me looks and I can't stand it. It's always like this when there is a long line waiting for you.

Occasionally, workers gain direct knowledge of managerial demands for faster work; if anything, that knowledge heightens their sense of being overwhelmed by the amount of work they have to do within a limited time span. A union clerk who posts deposits for a union's benefit fund on midmonth cycles relates:

See, when I started on this desk doing the union accounts, there were *six* girls for two unions. Now there are *three* girls. They had an evaluation. Methods Research evaluated us with a stop watch and all. I guess we should have slowed down, but we couldn't even slow down because we were here until 7:00 P.M. every night during that peak period. They told us, "Find ways to process that work faster. That's all. Don't ask us for more people." But there should be at least *two* more people. For the past two months, it's been busy *every* day, not just during the peak period. There's got to be a quiet time. Nobody can keep up a steady hectic pace.

Social demands to work faster, particularly when known to come directly from persons in authority, make even more difficult work which is already burdensome in its amount and pace.[3]

The pressure workers feel during busy periods from overwork and social demands is experienced as tension. On a day when customer lines stretched around her branch and out onto the street, a teller says:

The pressure never lets off all day. It's like a screw turning all day—at least to me.

Many workers express this cumulative tension with verbal aggressive-ness:

Yes, I've had tension here at work. . . . Some people say there's no difference between days either, but for me Friday—no matter what—is always the worst. You're always busy; I'm nervous, tense. . . . If anybody gets in my way, then I'm going to run them over.

Sometimes the pressure spills over and workers experience overt physical reactions to it. A union clerk in a large office discusses her reaction to peak cycles:

When the work gets really heavy, like about two weeks ago, everybody gets pressured. We were all going home crying each night. We were all hyper. It would take me hours to unwind when I got home.

Such strong reactions to pressure often affect social relationships outside of work, particularly intimate relationships. A posting clerk describes this experience:

There's too much pressure. It makes me sick. I go home and cry. I was crying in bed last Friday night. You really use your head in this. The work makes me depressed; it gives me headaches. I get nasty and then I get annoyed with little things my husband does, then I apologize because it's not his fault, then I feel badly and feel guilty.

How do workers who lack control over their work pace legitimate resulting experiences of pressure? Clearly, the negative quality of this experience requires accounts for its continuance. The most common accounts cluster into two categories.

The first category may be called denials of prolonged acceptance. These are basically assertions that discomforting situations are temporary because one is able or determined to change them. Most workers who use this account point to their ability to leave the bank situation entirely. Immediately after recounting his experience of work pressure, a teller says:

This job is strictly a stopgap. As soon as I find something else, I'm leaving.

By defining his situation as temporary, this worker both makes his experience of pressure tolerable and legitimates his present acceptance of it. Similarly, some workers assert their determination to reshape their discomforting situations. For instance, a clerk in a unit regularly overwhelmed by work expresses a determination to gain control of her work pace:

The pressure starts building up and then the peak period overwhelms us. I don't know how long it will go on. The three of us will go on strike. We're going to work at our own pace and if the work doesn't get done, tough shit.

There is, of course, a sizable gap between such verbalizations and behavior: strikes do not occur at the First Bank of Columbia, and those very workers who assert a determination to leave the bank at the first opportunity often stay for quite a while. To focus on this gap, however, is to miss the main point. Such discrepancies do not seem to matter to the actors involved. Rather, accounts allow them to claim, at least for a time, their control over situations seemingly beyond their control.

Significantly, workers who use denials of prolonged acceptance often evidence in their interviews a greater understanding than most other workers of the structural underpinnings of their discomfort. Those workers with less apparent understanding typically employ other types of accounts to legitimate pressure. These latter accounts are versions of what Lyman and Scott call appeals to defeasibility;[4] that is, claims of a break between one's action and one's intent, where, it is suggested, the latter miscarries for some reason.

Most workers who use the appeal to defeasibility to excuse their acceptance of pressure do so by invoking confusion about the causes of pressure. Confusion mitigates responsibility for accepting that pressure. For example, a machine operator, whose work is always heavy and pressured, almost pinpoints the structural basis of her work pressure, but ultimately falls back onto the defense of confusion:

I do more work than other people. I *know* I do more work than other people. Like I do much more work than a teller does. The amount of work is not a matter of pride to me. Far from it. . . . You know, sometimes people go to the bathroom 10 times; I'm lucky if I get to go once when I really have to. Supposedly, because of these time and motion studies, every minute of our time is scheduled. If they've done this, how come I don't have any spare time? Other people are walking around. I never have any extra time. I can't understand it at all.

A less frequent appeal to defeasibility than a statement of confusion is the claim of ignorance. For example, a union clerk details her own experience quite graphically, but exhibits no sense of why it is happening to her:

. . . everything kept piling up; it was awful. . . . See you want to get as much work done as possible and you end up by cutting lunch and that's bad. It's too nerve-racking during that period. I dread it coming. I don't know why there's so much pressure.

In the end, her very lack of understanding becomes the excuse for continuing the experience.

These appeals to defeasibility must be understood within the power context of the bank. Clerical workers have no organization independent of the bank; therefore, they have no social basis from which to assert a critical interpretation of work pressure. Because of the absence of a countervailing force, the bank need not explain work pressure and, to my knowledge, never has. There is, therefore, a vacuum of meaning for most bank workers about the causes of the pressure they experience, and their appeals to defeasibility to excuse acceptance of that pressure reflect that vacuum.

Workers' experiences of pressure are by far the most common and important experiences related to their lack of control over work pace. Less frequent, but still important, are periods of boredom created by slow market cycles.

SLOW CYCLES AND BOREDOM

For those workers directly affected by market cycles, slow cycles bring periods when there is not enough work to keep them occupied. This seems somewhat paradoxical because of the bank's emphasis on the efficient utilization of time. However, since branch jobs are generally structured to process work the same day it is received, these occasional slow periods are unavoidable.

During such "dead periods" workers experience boredom. This type of boredom stems from workers' negative definitions of not having enough to do and differs from the type of boredom which is created by repetitious work. The boredom at issue here is an experience of being restless, fidgety, and aware of time passing slowly. Speaking on a very quiet afternoon, a utility clerk relates:

Today is really bad—really bad. I'm having a bad time today. When it's like this, it's really bad. It's so boring.

Many workers watch the clock constantly during such periods, and many voice a desire for a busier although not hectic work pace. For instance, a credit checker says:

When it gets slow, it bothers me. . . . It gets boring. When it's busy, it's a lot better.

As with all workers directly exposed to market cycles, however, she has no way to pace her work to her liking.

The boredom of slow cycles is accompanied by a discomfort workers feel at not having any work to do in a social situation where they perceive that authorities expect at least the appearance of busyness.[5] Fashioning an image of busyness when there is little constructive work to do can be difficult. An automobile-financing clerk describes this problem:

You know, it's just as hard to fake work as it is to work; a lot of people are good at that and, when the big bosses come in, you *have* to. You know, you have to shuffle papers and bend over your desk and all.

Maintaining such a busy appearance becomes, at least for some, work itself, but work with no evident purpose or content other than managing impressions to placate authority.

The alternative, however, is to be assigned make-work by authorities, an experience sufficiently common to confirm workers' perceptions that management expects an appearance of industriousness at all times. A clerical-grade note head describes her own experience upon failing to convey a busy image to a branch manager:

We get off at five o'clock and it was four o'clock. It had really been a quiet day— nothing had come in. I had finished everything I had to do that day and all the girls in my section had, too. Nobody else had anything to do because it was so quiet that day so there wasn't even anybody to give help to. So, I'm sitting at my desk which is all clear and I have my hands folded on top. [The manager] comes over and asks if I don't have anything to do. I say that I don't, which is the worst thing I could have said, and he goes into the storeroom and comes back with two big boxes of rubber bands and two boxes of paper clips. Then he dumps it all on my desk and mixes them up and tells me to sort it and says, "*That* ought to keep you busy." After that, I always make sure to keep something around to work on.

Most clerks come to live with their boredom during slow cycles, and, by presenting desired images of busyness, they at least avoid make-work and gain thereby a measure of control over work pace.

Few, if any, legitimations for acceptance of slow-cycle boredom are discernible in workers' interviews. A few workers suggest that at least boring situations are conducive to daydreaming, an important form of coping with work for many. However, they relate the opportunity for daydreaming principally to their acceptance of standardized work, which will be treated shortly, and only tangentially to an externally-determined slow work pace. The absence of legitimations—even of defensive accounts—for the boredom of a slow work pace is in itself sociologically significant. When a person is unable to excuse or justify the acceptance of a negative experience, he has no defenses against the experience and personal tolerance of that experience becomes attenuated. Whenever individual tolerance of a situation declines, the structure of conflict underlying human behavior is likely to assert itself. A partial confirmation of this hypothesis is that managers consider the boredom of slow-cycle periods a particularly demoralizing condition. Their demands for at least the appearances of busyness can be interpreted as an attempt to shore up declining tolerance with ritualistic forms.

INSULATION FROM MARKET CYCLES AND CONTROL OF WORK PACE

Not all bank workers lack control over their work pace. Some clerks are insulated in one way or another from the fluctuations of external market cycles, and that insulation creates opportunities, which are not enjoyed by others, for controlling work pace.

This independence from cycles has somewhat different sources depending on the job in question. The few analysis clerks in each large branch derive independence from the way their work is alloted. At the beginning of each month, analysis clerks are given a certain number of accounts which must be analyzed according to a set formula to determine the bank's profit ratio; these clerks have their entire month's work in advance and can work at their own pace to complete it. Audit clerks, who check the work of other clerks or of the computer, are independent from cycles because their work schedule is two or more days behind the branch's daily schedule and they are under no pressure to complete work the day it is received. Finally, although the checks which payroll clerks must prepare go out in monthly or semimonthly cycles, these clerks are largely free of pressure during cycles because they work steadily at their own pace preparing their payrolls in advance during off-cycle periods. In short, all of these workers can themselves *initiate* their work; they have an active stance towards their work where others are passive.

Further, precisely because workers in insulated positions are not tied to the cycles of branch work, they gain some freedom from bank management's insistent measurement and supervision of clerical work; authorities direct most of their attention to workers more exposed to market cycles. Among other benefits, this lack of scrutiny gives insulated workers the added advantage of greater physical mobility than other clerks, a highly prized attribute in branch work.

These advantages become key justifications for the acceptance of jobs which many workers in insulated positions find troublesome on other levels. Their problems are usually rooted in the standardization of their jobs, an area to be examined shortly, but their control of work pace allows them to tolerate such difficulties. Very often these workers legitimate their jobs by emphasizing their advantage of physical mobility, which becomes a symbol of their control of work pace and of their relative freedom from authority. A payroll clerk, citing the need to confer with computer personnel in another department, says:

[One] thing that helps me is that I can leave when I want. When things really start getting to me, I'll just get up and leave. I can't imagine a job like this when you couldn't leave. I wouldn't take it.

Often, too, legitimations based on control of work pace are offered within a context of *negative comparison* with other branch jobs or workers. Negative comparison is a very common reflective process among bank workers by which they contrast their own experiences with their perceptions of others' experiences, favorably defining aspects of their own experiences by negatively appraising those of others. For example, an audit clerk evidences a lack of enthusiasm for his work, but then emphasizes his control over his work pace by comparing himself to a teller:

What do I dislike about this job? I don't know. Nothing I dislike; nothing I really like. They give me something to do, show me what I'm supposed to do. I'm on my own; responsibility lies with me. It's a lot better than being a teller. . . . I come in, see how much work there is, set the time to do it in—don't work too fast or too slow. I can set the time. A teller can't do that.

Like accounts, negative comparison is a defensive process. However, no matter how defensive the framework within which control of work pace is asserted, it remains very important to workers. Although it does not provide positive motives for working in the bank, it does give workers one way of shaping a truce with otherwise troublesome work situations.

The Standardization of Work

The extent of workers' interest or engagement in the actual job tasks they perform is another crucial aspect of any analysis of work experience. Work perceived as engaging both motor and mental skills, that is, as engaging the whole person, can be an end in itself.[6] Certain types of craft work, for example, enable the worker to so unite himself to the product and processes of his work that the legitimating motive for what he is doing is the work itself.[7] By contrast, when workers find their work tasks uninteresting and unengaging, work becomes troublesome and requires accounts. Most First Bank of Columbia workers fall into this second category.

THE SEGMENTATION AND ROUTINIZATION OF WORK TASKS

The First Bank of Columbia standardizes branch work for the same reasons that it measures tasks to apportion workloads—to achieve higher worker efficiency and productivity. An important aspect of this standardization is the segmentation of work into small, functionally-related but discrete parts. By carefully differentiating the type and number of tasks each worker in each job is to perform, the bank sharply delimits responsibility for work at clerical levels and thereby increases workers' accountability to authorities who coordinate those tasks. Differentiation of labor is inescapable given the scale and complexity of modern organizations. However, as Peter Blau points out,[8] differentiation of labor can be the basis for two quite contrary results: the first is specialization, the hallmark of most professional work; the second, adopted by the bank, is routinization, characteristic of most clerical work. In choosing routinization, the bank defines and simplifies every aspect of every clerical job. Thus, the bank makes almost all of its clerical work repetitious, aiming for speed through constant practice. The merits of applying such scientific management[9] theory to work organizations are highly debatable, as evidenced by the experiences of industries employing contrasting organizational techniques.[10] However, judging from internal management communications,[11] bank managers consider highly rationalized methods of organizing work to be important for effective staff utilization, satisfactory customer relations, and consequent high bank profits.

Segmented and routinized work is the norm for clerks in every division of every bank branch. There are three main divisions in each branch: first, operations, which handles most cash transactions and processes all checks; second, the platform, where loans are made and new accounts opened; and third, notes, which documents and processes all loans sold and receives all loan payments. As noted earlier, some branches have interior offices which are usually extensions of one or another of these basic divisions. For our present purposes, an analysis of a specific job will be more instructive than a general catalogue of all the standardized tasks in a branch. The work tasks of the commercial teller's role fairly exemplify the segmented and routinized shape of branch clerical work.

The range of technical tasks for tellers is narrow. Basically, they receive and disburse cash, both currency and checks. Their first concern is to be accurate in every transaction. When currency is involved, accuracy means counting carefully. When, as in most cases, checks are involved, either for withdrawal or deposit, the teller ascertains the identity of the customer and then verifies the balance in his account through the computerized account-status report which details the status of all accounts in the branch as of the opening hour. Checks drawn on another branch or on a different bank are verified by phone before the teller completes the transaction. In all cases, the teller keeps precise receipts of every transaction and, at the end of the day, she must balance her day's work before she can leave. As with almost all other branch clerical workers, once the teller finishes her specific tasks, the work passes from her hands to be completed or further processed by other clerks in the branch.

Each of these technical tasks within the narrow range of the teller's job is thoroughly routinized. The specific way for tellers to perform their work is explained in a six volume, looseleaf publication called the *Standard Practices Manual* (SPM), which details accepted practice for every branch job. Circulars from the bank's central administration, based on new work-measurement studies, periodically update and refine these procedures. Training manuals and films simplify and reinforce the SPM. Operations officers assign training manuals to new tellers, as to all new branch workers, and then test their knowledge. From management's point of view, the necessity for strict control of funds and for their proper documentation, as well as for worker efficiency, require that each branch job be performed simply and uniformly.

What are workers' experiences of and legitimations for their highly standardized work tasks?

ROUTINIZED TASKS AND BOREDOM

Bank workers consider routinized work tasks repetitious. Repetitious work is equated first of all with boredom. An audit clerk points to this equation:

Lately, I've been getting awfully bored. Doing the same thing every day.... It's the routine. I do the same thing every day. Same every day.

A teller echoes her feeling:

Being a teller is a *worthless* job. Oh, it's not worthless, but it's *repetitious;* it's *boring.*

The boredom created by repetitious work is different than the edgy restlessness characteristic of boredom during slow cycles. The boredom of repetitious work is a feeling of dullness and, for many, of mental stagnation. A utility clerk, whose job contains more variety than do most branch jobs, says:

It's the repetitiousness that bothers people. They come to work and they don't have to think. It deteriorates your mind. . . . I used to look forward to coming to work, but now it's repetitious, even with utility.

In discussing their experiences of boredom, workers sometimes employ mechanical self-images which further suggest the lack of mental activity at work. For example, a credit checker in a notes division says:

What do I like about this job? Are you kidding? This is a very boring job. I feel like I am already a robot, a machine.

For those workers who see their work as repetitious and therefore as boring and stagnating, there can be little positive, sustaining interest in their actual work tasks. In fact, such experiences create further problems.

The key problem for most workers is the absence of challenge in their jobs. Branch work does not have much room for innovation or creativity. After the details of a particular job are learned, there is, for most, no room for personal growth within the job. For instance, a commercial teller contrasts branch work with images of other work:

I'm bored. Bored silly. There's nothing for me to do from 8:30 AM—5:00 PM. There's nothing for me to do at all. . . . In the restaurant business, you have to think up ideas; think up a gimmick which will sell. There's luck involved, there's a lot of imagination, there's risk. Here, there's no variance. Everything is done by the book. There are no decisions to make, they're cut and dried. There are set rules for *everything*. . . . I've done little or nothing that has challenged me so far. It's all standardized, it's all in the books.

The more education workers have, the more acute is this experience. Schooling fosters expectations of a greater use of mental abilities in work. A college-graduated union clerk points out the tension between those expectations and the limiting character of branch clerical work:

I want a job where I can use what I learned in school and where I would keep on learning. You know, where I would learn how to solve a complicated problem that would do some good—to make the bank better, to make it earn more money, or *anything*. But something difficult and challenging. I don't want to do clerical work all the time. Even computer programming might be the answer. I mean it's difficult; you have to *think*. But clerical stuff, it's just a matter of reflex—you're doing it over and over and you're not doing anything new. It's just like washing your car. You do it and then the next day, it's dirty all over again. I want a *challenging* job—I didn't go to college for four years to do clerical stuff and make decisions anybody else can do.

Uninteresting work, however, is a problem that will not go away. To keep their jobs, bank workers must perform their tasks not only regularly, but well. Legitimations for the continued performance of work defined as routine become critically important both for the person and, within our larger sociological framework, for an understanding of the way social order is achieved. To legitimate their acceptance of routine, workers employ a wide range of accounts.

An important justification is what we may call the claim of available diversions where workers point to modes of mental escape from their situations, principally through daydreaming and humor. Daydreaming is widespread among bank clerks, and workers often cite it as an escape which relieves at least some of the distress caused by routine work. A teller relates:

Being a teller is routine but I can think about what I want. . . . I daydream a lot. I always think about something completely different from work. I think about the future, about going to Europe, about other things.

Daydreaming allows people to assert control over their work time by escaping mentally from boring situations. However minimally, it justifies acceptance of routine. Interestingly, however, daydreaming itself is often felt to need justification. Workers will frequently follow a claim of available diversions with a legitimation of the diversion itself. A utility clerk explains:

You know, you have to escape through daydreams. I think it makes the time pass quicker. Yeah, I think you have to. Your mind has to be active.

One account can bolster another in fashioning personal tolerance and social order, a recurring pattern in the data.

Workers also claim humor as a basis for diversion from routine. For example, a machine operator whose interview record indicates that she feels overwhelmed by the routine character of her work explains this use of humor:

... I psych myself into thinking that it's not too bad. If somebody says something that is really funny, then I think, "See, it's not so bad." Like the other day, I couldn't get the photograph machine to work, so I said to Sue who wanted to use it, "If you slam the top down, sometimes it helps." That didn't work. A few minutes later, Anne came over and said, "If you slam the top down, it helps." And she began doing it real loud. It really cracked me up. "If I hadn't been here," I say to myself, "this stupid, ridiculous thing wouldn't have happened."

Similar examples appear throughout the interviews of this study. Incongruous details of every sort—from another worker's bewilderment at what a customer wants to customers' scribbled notations on checks—provide occasions for humor which sustain workers through their routine workday.

We should note a final claim of available diversions for legitimating continuance of work defined as routine, even though, within this study's sample, only a few workers employ it. This is when workers point to the possibility of making their work more complex in order to reduce their boredom; this becomes an account which mitigates their acceptance of routine. For example, a payroll clerk:

How do I cope with this job? Well, I've developed my own systems for things, even for things nobody was really interested in having systematized. I do this because I was so damn bored. I just keep adding variables until it gets terribly complicated. For instance, before I worked here, there were no records of individual invalid accounts—those for which the bank has no records—so I had a [computer] card made up for each one, had it punched, and now there's a complete record. Now I keep a list and when I fill a page, I take it down and have it punched. When I saw that nobody had ever done it, I found myself thinking, "Oh, boy—here's something I can work out a system for." It doesn't make it more interesting, but it does make it less boring.

The availability of this account seems dependent on both opportunity and on personal background. As we have seen, not all workers have jobs which afford the measure of independence available to this payroll clerk. Further, the data indicate that it is more educated workers who are most likely to make work more complicated, and the account is important because of this. The educational level among bank clerical workers is already high and promises to increase.[12] The future may bring a situation where the bank is the unwitting beneficiary of a work structure made more complex by increasingly educated workers trying to escape the boredom of routinized work.

Claims of available diversions, however, have their limits, and workers legitimate their continuance of situations which they find boring in other ways as well. Another important justification is what may be called the denial of qualitative difference. Here workers, particularly those with less formal education, justify their present boredom by denying that the quality of their experience would change in any other job. For example, a union clerk says:

It bothers me when you get bored. But not every job is exciting. Every job gets boring.

An analysis clerk levels all occupations even further:

You know, most jobs are the same. They're all routine and monotonous.

There is a fatalistic tone in the denial of qualitative difference. By making all jobs equally boring, workers who use this account essentially resign themselves to a career of boring work. However, the account may also reflect a realistic appraisal of the actual job chances to which their educational status ties them. In any case, this account, as with others, helps workers develop tolerance for their own situations, and, indeed, a certain toughness which carries them through their work. The same analysis clerk quoted above concludes her statement:

But you get used to it. I can put up with it.

The last major set of accounts which workers use to legitimate their acceptance of negatively defined routine is one encountered earlier in this chapter—the denial of prolonged acceptance. In this context, the account takes two forms. First, many workers who see themselves staying with the bank for a while mention possibilities of either vertical or horizontal mobility; the hope of future variety becomes a claim which partially legitimates their present boredom. For instance, a utility clerk in a notes department relates:

I would like operations work and I think that I will try to move into it. I'm getting tired already of this job. . . . I don't understand how people can stay at the same desk for several years. Sometimes seven or eight years. I would stay at a desk for no more than one year.

The credibility of this account depends upon the actual rate of mobility in an office which, in turn, is dependent upon other factors, particularly turnover and relationships with authority. Workers interpret these factors differently, but they do link their claims of possible mobility to such factors. For instance, a note teller says:

I would get bored with anything if I had to do the same thing every day. The maximum for me is six months in a job and I'm getting close to that here. But the real difference is knowing this feeling can be dealt with. That the person in charge can do something. That depends upon the individual supervisor.

In offices where there is real mobility, therefore, many workers approach their branch jobs as temporary way stations; their everyday work assumes a transient quality which makes the routine of that work endurable.

The denial of prolonged acceptance with regard to routine takes a second form identical to one of its uses analyzed earlier: workers justify their present experiences of boredom by claiming that they do not intend to stay with the bank very long. For example, a teller says:

I don't feel like I'm doing anything much. I don't consider it too fulfilling. . . . I go home and wonder what it is I'm doing. *I have an inner urge to find a new job.* . . .

Her very intention of leaving the bank justifies staying in a situation defined as uninteresting. However, perhaps because work experienced as empty and boring is particularly troubling, workers seem to feel that such a statement of intention does not adequately account for the continuation of their situation. They often follow a denial of prolonged acceptance with another justification, which mitigates their responsibility for not having fulfilled a stated intention to leave the bank. The teller quoted above concludes her statement with what we may call an appeal to difficult circumstances:[13]

. . . but I'm so sick of filling out forms and going to interviews.

This particular appeal is a common one, and people who want to leave the bank use it regularly to explain why they stay. A machine operator, who finds her work very burdensome and evinces a desire to leave, says:

I think I've gotten into a rut. I don't know. Besides, when you're here every day, it's difficult to get to interviews and all.

As noted before, accounts can legitimate not only actions but other accounts as well. Here an appeal to difficult circumstances legitimates a denial of prolonged acceptance which in turn legitimates acceptance of routine. The structure of people's consciousness in legitimating their work, and implicitly their lives, is, more often than not, very tangled.

VARIETY WITHIN STANDARDIZED STRUCTURES

Some bank workers, who do not define their work as repetitious, do not experience the serious problems of boredom encountered by the majority of workers. Their attitudes indicate both the importance of subjective factors in any analysis of work experiences and the subtle flexibilities within the bank's routinized structure. These workers fall into three categories.

First, some clerks claim variety for their work within a framework of negative comparison with more repetitious work in the branch; actual variety is important to their perception, but so is their definition that, in this regard, they are better off than others. A boarding clerk in a notes department, where work is usually more varied than that in operations, illustrates this claim of variety:

This job is interesting because there are so many things happening different every day. A teller is routine work. This desk has a set way of doing things, but everything can happen on this desk. It's not routine.

The routine work of others in one's immediate situation shapes one's own sense of variety. However, some workers express ambivalence even when making such claims. Their ambivalence seems rooted in a sense that there might be larger frames of reference to take into account. A payroll clerk relates:

I do think this is the most interesting desk in the office. It's fun because you're always out of the office running around, and because there is the balancing problem at the end of the month when I have . . . to figure out, out of hundreds of possibilities, why something won't balance. . . .But I don't think that any job here really keeps your mind going too much.

However, even when such ambivalence occurs, a perceived relative variety of tasks still gives workers the basis for greatly reducing if not eliminating boredom.

Second, some clerks do not define their work as repetitious because their job allows them to control their work pace, and that control vitiates potential consequences of routinized work. Just as control over work pace can become a key justification for some workers in tolerating boring work, it can virtually eliminate the problem of boredom for others. The remarks of an auditing clerk bear this out:

The routine doesn't bother me. Here, in this job, I'm doing it myself. I have a great deal of freedom. I do it *my* way. I know what's what. I like to do things and know they're done.

While such control of work is relatively rare in bank branches, where it does occur, it constitutes a powerful antidote to routine.

Finally, the previous personal experiences of some workers are such that branch work is, for them, not routine at all. The chief examples of such workers are middle-aged women whose previous major work experience was in the home and who have only recently returned to paid employment. Almost invariably, these workers talk about their job tasks by negatively comparing housework with them. Consider, for example, the remarks of an auditing clerk whose work consists of verifying the computer print-out sheets of items from a single large account:

There is no comparison between the office and housework. You can do housework all day, and you can have it spic-and-span, and before you know it, it's a wreck and you have to start in on the same thing. It's different at the office. There are different problems and mistakes.

Looking at branch work tasks through the filter of a negatively defined experience shapes one's view of those tasks; it enables workers who do so to experience variety where others can find only routine.

SEGMENTATION AND INCOMPLETENESS

Many bank workers also experience a sense of incompleteness in their work. This experience emerges from the segmentation of their work which is, of course, a precondition for the routinization of labor.

Workers' experience of incompleteness consists, first of all, in their feeling that, despite a desire to do so, they do not understand the interconnections of work in a branch. This feeling is a direct consequence of the segmented nature of branch work. Since each branch job has a codified agenda separate from all other jobs, it is possible to perform one job with no knowledge of any other; the interrelated nature of branch work is not inherently visible. Depending on the size of the branch, which is the crucial variable in analyzing segmentation, workers often find themselves with little understanding of other jobs, even those immediately related to their own. Extensive crosstraining of branch workers—that is, providing the opportunity for workers to learn different branch jobs—is confined to small-size and some medium-size branches where workers must know a variety of tasks so they can cover the jobs of co-workers who might be absent. In the larger branches, crosstraining occurs rarely and, according to this study's data, usually as a reward allocated by authorities. Most workers interviewed want a broader knowledge of the interconnections of their work, and the absence of such knowledge is troublesome to them because, in their view, it implies a personal inadequacy. For example, a general ledger clerk in a large interior office relates:

I don't understand the work of other departments. I also only know a few desks here in the office.... It bothers me. I have a friend who is an operations officer at a small branch, and we can't talk about anything except general ledger. If something comes in, and I don't know anything about it, it bothers me because I've been here for five years.

A note teller elaborates this link between inadequate knowledge and feelings of personal inadequacy:

I resent seeing only one part of a job or one part of the whole picture.... It bothers me because I'm here for a specific purpose and if I don't know everything that the job has to do with, I feel insufficient. The more you know, the less problems you have. The more you know about a whole operation, the more satisfaction you have, of course.

A sense of incompleteness is also evidenced in many workers' feelings of a lack of accomplishment in their branch jobs. This feeling also arises, although less directly, from the segmentation of branch work and emerges most often when workers contrast images of ideal work with their present jobs. For example, a general ledger clerk:

I've often thought about taking a course in interior decorating. I enjoy things that are constructive, and that seems more constructive than working in a bank. What's constructive? I guess it's something you can do and see a finished product after it's done. It gives me a feeling of accomplishment that I've done something worthwhile—something solid. Here the only proof I have at the end of a day that I've worked at all is that my desk is clean. That's not frustrating to me. But, [pause] it's kind of a nothing feeling; not happy, not sad, not anything. It's "Whew! I'm finished and now I get to go home."

This sense of a lack of accomplishment seems primarily related to workers' perceptions of their service jobs as insubstantial—that is, resulting in no concrete product. This, of course, is characteristic of much white-collar work,[14] and clearly branch work has sharp limitations in providing experiences of a completed product. However, I would argue that workers' feelings of a lack of accomplishment are not only related to the nature of their work but also to its structure. Several experiments have shown that an integrated, rather than segmented, work *process* can partially substitute for the absence of a finished product and can provide workers with a sense of accomplishment in their work.[15] But in the bank, no such potential remedy to the ephemeral quality of service work is available because of managerial decisions to segment work. Workers are left, therefore, only with their insubstantial work and with the sense of a lack of accomplishment which that seems to foster.

Those workers who experience a sense of incompleteness in their work most commonly justify their experiences with a denial of injury or cost to themselves.[16] They experience the incompleteness as bothersome; but, since they can neutralize it, it is not overwhelming and does not therefore harm them. These denials of injury are rooted in their compartmentalization of work from life, a phenomenon with broad implications which is considered in detail later. The key aspect of this psychological process which is relevant now is the definition of one's job as tangential to one's life. For instance, a note teller legitimates her feeling of incompleteness by denying that it is harmful to herself; she does so by asserting a noncareer orientation to branch work:

It bothers me when I don't know what is going on or when someone asks me a question I don't know the answer to. But then again, it doesn't bother me if I don't know what's going on because I'm not going to make a career out of banking.

Defining a job as peripheral to one's life enables a person to deny any injury to self even though the job does not provide a sense of purpose or wholeness to the person. Implicitly, the judgment is made that a lack of knowledge or direction would be harmful only in those areas of life defined as primary. Moreover, because work does not require prized energies like worry or thought, which are reserved for areas of life deemed important, acceptance of factors like a somewhat troubling sense of incompleteness does not cost workers anything, and such troubling experiences become essentially moot issues. A bookkeeper relates:

I wonder about the purpose of my work but it doesn't bother me very much, I guess. Not enough to do anything about it. . . . When I go home I never have to think about it like operations officers must.

The sense of incompleteness at work is not a problem for some branch workers. A few workers—almost invariably utility clerks who perform any number of specific jobs—claim with credibility that they experience a sense of purpose and integration in their work because their knowledge of a variety of jobs gives them an understanding of the interconnections of branch work. It is more difficult to explain why other bank workers do not have problems of purpose and direction in work. On one hand, their work is very segmented and they lack the integrated practical basis to which utility clerks can point to claim wholeness. On the other hand, they do not define their segmented situations negatively; often, in fact, they do not seem to have reflected upon the personal meaning of segmentation at all. Some of these workers offer an interpretation of purpose and direction in branch work which is a reiteration of a managerial perspective often stated at branch staff meetings. A union clerk describes this view:

Each thing here is connected to the next thing. No matter how minimal the work is, how easy or whatever, it's a vital part of the chain of work. The most complicated and hard job requires [depends on] my own.

By linking one's work to that of others, at least conceptually, this interpretation provides workers who use it with a functional perspective on their jobs which seems to substitute for an integrated perspective achieved through practice. At any rate, such a perspective neutralizes the emergence of a sense of incompleteness in their jobs. However, nothing in the data indicates that these workers experience any sense of wholeness in what they do. In fact, many express serious dissatisfaction with their jobs. This seems to indicate the importance of managerial interpretations of reality where workers' experiences are unclear to themselves.

On the whole, then, bank workers' experiences of their actual job tasks are very problematic. They experience pressure and boredom from their lack of work pace control, and they find their routinized tasks boring and unfulfilling. But, at the same time, they do come to terms with those experiences. By legitimating, however defensively, even those aspects of their work which are experienced as alienating, they fashion social order out of situations where one could expect to find open conflict. Before further discussing the theoretical significance of these ambivalent experiences, I want to examine another aspect of bank clerks' work situations— namely, their experiences of the social demands made on them at work.

References

1. Nancy C. Morse and Robert S. Weiss, "The Function and Meaning of Work and the Job," *American Sociological Review*, 20 (April 1955), 191–198; and Gladys Palmer, "Attitudes Toward Work in an Industrial Community," *American Journal of Sociology*, 63 (July 1957), 24.

2. Robert Blauner, *Alienation and Freedom* (Chicago: Univ. of Chicago Press, 1964), p. 21.

3. See Chris Argyris, *Organization of a Bank* (New Haven: Labor and Management Center, Yale Univ., 1954), p. 159 for some examples of experiences of work pressure almost identical to those cited here. In Argyris's study, however, these experiences were restricted to machine operators in one department; in the present work, they are much more generalized. This generalization of feelings of pressure is almost certainly due to the advent of retail banking in the years since Argyris's study was done and its constant drive for greater business volume.

4. Stanford Lyman and Marvin Scott, "Accounts," *A Sociology of the Absurd* (New York: Appleton-Century-Crofts, 1970), pp. 115–117.

5. Erving Goffman considers this problem typical in "walled-in institutions"; see "The Underlife of a Public Institution," *Asylums* (Garden City: Doubleday-Anchor, 1961), p. 176.

6. In an analysis of data from the University of Michigan's Survey Research Center's *Survey of Working Conditions*, Neal Q. Herrick and Robert P. Quinn indicate that, of several specific aspects of a job, "the aspect . . . contributing most to workers' overall satisfaction scores was the extent to which they felt their work was interesting, rewarding,

and self-developing." See "The Working Conditions Survey as a Source of Social Indicators," *Monthly Labor Review*, 94 (April 1971), 21. See also William Roche and Neil L. MacKinnon, "Motivating People With Meaningful Work," *Harvard Business Review*, (May-June 1970), pp. 97–110.

7. For a fine ideal-typical analysis of the nature of craft work, see C. Wright Mills, *White Collar* (New York: Oxford Univ. Press, 1951), pp. 220–224.

8. Peter Blau, "Presidential Address: Parameters of Social Structure," *American Sociological Review*, 39 (October 1974), 625–628.

9. The classic statement of scientific management theory is Frederick W. Taylor's *The Principles of Scientific Management* (New York: Harper and Bros., 1911). A more recent work by Harold W. Nance and Robert E. Nolan illustrates how the theory is still applied to office work. See *Office Work Measurement* (New York: McGraw Hill, 1971).

10. There is a rapidly growing body of literature which details various innovative experiments in work organization. On the whole, the results of these experiments, which are based on giving workers integrated, varied, and self-controlled work experiences, indicate no decline in productivity and, in fact, show a noticeable decrease in indices of job dissatisfaction like absenteeism. A catalogue of some of these experiments can be found in *Work in America: A Report to the Secretary of Health, Education and Welfare* (Washington, D.C.: Government Printing Office, 1973), Appendix, pp. 150–159.

11. For instance, in a letter to all branch managers and operations officers in the bank's branch network, an executive vice-president documents this view. The communication is a cover letter accompanying the distribution of a manual called *A Guide to Effective Staff Management*. The letter points out the importance bank management attributes to one key aspect of the bank's work measurement program—the minute measurement of each clerical task by time and motion studies which are gathered in the *Time and Allowance Practices Manual* (TAP). In part, the letter reads:

> Speed of Service depends in part upon the numerical size of your staff but is *even more dependent* upon how effectively staff is utilized. Quality of service hinges upon adequate training and good morale. Both speed and quality can be greatly influenced by planning.
>
> To plan effectively, it is essential that every employe know what is expected of him (or her). This requires a well-organized, documented "work schedule" based on a thorough understanding of our "Time and Allowance Practices Manual" (TAP). TAP can be an invaluable tool to assist you in your planning, training, organizing and supervising. In short, it will help you provide good service at minimum cost. . . . The final result will be better customer relations—together with an improvement in branch profitability.

12. At the moment, 7% of the bank's entire clerical staff has finished college; 26% has between one to four years of college without a degree; 65% has finished only high school; and only 2% has less than a high school diploma. The high percentage of clerical workers with some college reflects the general level of education in the California labor market. This level is the highest in the country and is expected to increase. See Crocker Bank, *Skills of the Labor Force in California* (San Francisco: Crocker Bank, One Montgomery Street, 1973).

13. This account closely resembles that called the "sad tale," treated in Erving Goffman, *Asylums* (Garden City: Doubleday-Anchor, 1961), pp. 150–151, and also Lyman and Scott, "Accounts," pp. 122–123. However, as Lyman and Scott point out, the sad tale often involves a selective and distorted arrangement of past facts to explain one's present state; the appeal to difficult circumstances points instead to real, present difficulties which, although they could be overcome, tie one to a situation.

14. See, C. Wright Mills, *White Collar*, pp. 227–228.

15. Some of these experiments are detailed in Robert Ford's *Motivation Through the Work Itself* (New York: American Management Association, 1969). See also United States Senate, Committee on Labor and Public Welfare, *Worker Alienation, 1972* (Washington, D.C.: Government Printing Office, 1972), pp. 219–234.

16. As presented here, this neutralizing technique is used with respect to actors themselves rather than towards other objects or persons. Seen in this light, the usage varies somewhat from the concept of the denial of injury presented by Lyman and Scott, "Accounts," p. 121. The denial of cost is an almost identical account and is presented here together with the denial of injury.

4 Living With Standardized Public Faces

Another important issue in workers' appraisals of their work experiences is the extent of their personal freedom in choosing their public faces at work. Sociologists have for some time been concerned with how the commercial and bureaucratic conditions of modern work shape workers' personalities or at least their patterns of external behavior. For instance, Karl Mannheim talks about self-rationalization, where the person streamlines his character in accordance with organizational guidelines;[1] C. Wright Mills discusses how the commercial thrust of modern business has made personality a crucial, saleable commodity in the workplace;[2] and Joseph Bensman and Bernard Rosenberg point out how bureaucracy demands "compulsive sociability" from workers as an interactional mode.[3] While all these perspectives are useful in conceptualizing the experiences of bank workers, the task of this chapter—continuing the effort to understand why workers do not use their everyday job experiences to legitimate their work lives positively—requires a different emphasis. For our purposes, the best starting point is Erving Goffman's suggestion that a person's sense of personal well-being is closely related to his ability to choose the style and content of his impression management.[4] Impressions here mean both external appearances and interaction behavior; together these constitute a person's public face. When an organization requires a public face to which a person is not accustomed or one which does not correspond with a person's self-image, the result can be quite troubling even though, as many sociologists have noted,[5] skill at manipulating public faces seems to be a prerequisite for survival in bureaucracies. Clearly, the First Bank of Columbia does not try to dictate all the details of its workers' public faces. However, the bank does delineate two key areas, important to its own interests, where it expects workers to conform to bank-established norms of appearance and interaction. The first area is that of workers' dealings with customers, crucial for the bank's commercial image; the second area is that of workers' relationships with co-workers and supervisors, important for smooth organizational functioning. Many bank workers experience pressure to conform to the standardized public faces expected of them in these areas. When they do conform, these workers experience a sense of self-artificiality in their work situations. Before we examine these experiences, it will be helpful to look at the structure of the bank's standardization of public faces in greater detail.

The Standardization of Public Faces

The bank's standardization of workers' public faces has different features and emphases which vary according to the two social contexts the standardization is meant to regulate. It is in the area of workers' dealings with customers that the more thorough standardization occurs. As mentioned earlier, large branch banking systems like the First Bank of Columbia consider their local branches to be retail financial stores[6] and branch personnel to be salespeople who are to project a public image of attractive, efficient, friendly, and courteous service. This image involves aspects of both external appearance and interaction behavior, and it is considered to be the key to holding present customers and attracting new ones, as well as to selling all customers an ever greater range of banking services.

To convey attractiveness, the bank dictates external appearances to its workers. Each branch, under the direction of a regional administration, establishes a dress code based on local mores. Therefore, dress standards vary somewhat between different areas. In the branches of this study, all in a metropolitan area, the bank encourages[7] conservative expressions of fashionable styles—for example, women may wear pantsuits, but not unmatched coats and pants, and miniskirts, but not microminis. Everywhere, suits are required for male officers, and all women must wear nylons and bras. Codes also generally prohibit unusual hair styles or idiosyncratic accessories. Within each branch, particularly in established business areas, close adherence to the code is enforced, usually even in interior offices hidden from public view. Failure to conform to the dress code can, and does, result in reprimands and poor evaluation reports.

Even more important for the bank's general public image than the external appearances of workers is the way workers interact with customers. To make sure workers convey friendliness, courtesy, and efficiency, the bank has rules governing dealings with the public both in person and by phone. In *The Teller's Notebook*, a training manual which exemplifies the literature directed at clerks, workers are drilled on the importance of the customer: he is "the purpose of our work," "a welcome guest," "someone who places his trust in us." Therefore, anyone who has contact with the public must be "friendly and enthusiastic . . . courteous and tactful . . . efficient and dependable . . . and attentive and empathetic." Workers are expected to call every customer by name and "to smile with sincerity" during all transactions. Clearly, however, some key aspects of branch work militate against a successful projection of this image, particularly against congeniality. The pace of branch work is, as shown earlier, often harried, and this affects workers and customers alike. Many customers are impatient while waiting for service. Similarly, according to workers' interviews, some technical functions which workers must perform—for example, checking people's identities or their bank balances—irritate customers and create frustration which they direct at clerks. To minimize such potential friction and to sustain the desired commercial image of congenial efficiency, the bank tries to regularize workers' relationships with customers. Ideally, this means stylizing interaction between workers and customers;[8] but practically, it means making respectful restraint towards customers, along with congeniality, an integral part of any branch job.

The bank also standardizes workers' dealings with their supervisors and co-workers. Standardization in this area takes different forms than it does in the area of customer relations and, judging from interviews with managers, serves different organizational purposes. Standardization here is almost entirely concerned with maintaining what the bank formally calls "harmonious relationships"[9] with co-workers and authority figures. On one hand, workers are to get along, at least externally, and avoid open conflict which could disrupt the work flow. On the other hand, workers are to display towards their supervisors an attitude which is cheerful, cooperative, and supportive of the bank and its programs. Such behavior helps authorities efficiently coordinate the many tasks in a branch. There are no codified criteria to judge workers' conformity to these standards of interaction; indeed, the standards themselves are vague. However, individual supervisors, themselves attuned to what the bank wants and evaluated by their own superiors, judge their subordinates' handling of intrabranch relationships in performance reports. The most common behavioral characteristics looked for are a pleasant attitude to everyone in the office, acceptance of direction from authorities, and active participation in bank programs, especially in the regular sales promotion programs.[10]

Workers' experiences of the bank's standardization of their public faces cluster, as already noted, into two areas: a sense of pressure to conform and a sense of self-artificiality. Most often these experiences mingle with each other. However, for analytical purposes, it will be useful to consider them separately. Further, both experiences cut across the structural features of the bank's standardization of public faces just treated, and in developing the dimensions of workers' experiences, I shall return to some aspects of those structural features more than once.

THE SENSE OF PRESSURE TO CONFORM

Many workers feel pressured to conform to expectations for certain public faces both towards customers and co-workers. This sense of pressure emerges when workers unfavorably evaluate perceived demands to conform and when they feel pushed, especially by authorities, into conforming to those demands.

Workers feel pressure from a variety of managerial sources to present a standardized public face to customers. Many workers perceive, for instance, a general emphasis on projecting a respectable image. These workers neither identify with the public they are to impress nor agree with the image they are to convey, but, nonetheless, they sense continual managerial demands for such representations. A machine operator relates:

The bank is trying to appeal to the middle class. They want you to look typical middle class, and yet you have to stay in your place. You are a servant of the public. They don't want people to think that the bank would hire somebody who would spout radical ideas or something. They want everybody brainwashed. From the time you are hired, they are constantly trying to do that.

Other workers feel pressured to be constantly cheerful towards customers and point to more specific managerial sources of the pressure, such as signs or buttons distributed to workers with the legend "Smile!" or, often, published literature. A teller comments:

You should take a look at the brochure for incoming employees—*This Could Be the Start of Something Grand.* You should read the way they describe things. They want to get everybody walking around with a smile plastered on their faces. Nobody walks around with a perpetual smile unless they're moronic. They try to make the magazine very hip too. It's that whole image thing. They're trying to get you to fit a mold, and the mold is what they want you to be.

Finally, a great many workers feel pressured to shape their external appearances to accepted standards for the benefit of customers. The principal source of this pressure is overt enforcement of branch dress codes. In some branches, authorities act alone in enforcing codes; in others, they establish committees of selected workers who aid enforcement. In both cases, but especially the latter, workers experience a strong pressure to conform, and they resent it. A payroll clerk describes her reaction:

I really resent having a chart telling me what to wear and what not to wear. . . . Once [the operations officer] sent me home to change. I was wearing grey pants and coordinated jacket, but they really got technical. They said my jacket was black, not grey, and they sent me home to change. My first day here they told me my dress was too short and that I had too much makeup on and so on. Also, the girls . . . tattle on one another. They really get picky. So one day, [the manager] came up here with all 12 people on the dress code committee. He made me and several others stand up and do a little pivot on the floor. Everybody was really pissed. All the girls with him had little comments to make. . . . It was so absolutely degrading.

Demands for a public face the bank deems proper never really abate. However, as in the case just noted, when managerial demands are joined by authoritatively-sanctioned peer expectations, the pressure to conform becomes especially discomforting.

Workers also experience more subtle pressures to conform which emerge from their perceptions of managerial expectations for a proper attitude within the workplace. In most workers' eyes, having the right attitude means conveying expected images to authorities. Workers generally understand that projection of the right image is important for career chances in the bank or simply to obtain regular salary raises.

Projecting the right attitude means, first of all, being cheerfully cooperative in the office, a key expectation of superiors. A utility clerk describes the subtle pressures this expectation conveys:

> In the performance report, we're graded on . . . your attitude. What's attitude? Say you're kind of busy on your desk and your supervisor says, "Hey, help out here." And you say, "Say, I'm really busy. Can't you see?" That's bad. It's being cheerful, helpful; it's not being grumpy, refusing to get involved. This is entirely the supervisor's judgment.

Since it facilitates their own work, superiors tend to favor workers who evidence cheerful cooperativeness. This quite natural favoritism often puts further pressure on other workers to demonstrate more clearly their own cheerful cooperativeness in order to gain equal approval from authorities. As a corollary to cheerful cooperativeness, workers feel pressure to refrain from criticizing the bank, at least around superiors, since they know that any such statements are likely to be construed as evidence of a bad attitude. A machine operator relates:

> I think of myself as being outspoken. . . . I always express what I think in situations. . . . Once I get here, though, I have to control myself. . . . An operations officer told me that if I wanted to go higher in the bank, I would have to change my attitude. He had heard me putting the bank down one day.

Workers feel confined by explicit parameters established by superiors indicating how they may behave and what they may say.

Projecting a proper attitude also means not only performing work assigned but, in the process, giving the appearance of readily accepting authoritative direction. Generally speaking, workers consider their external demeanor towards authority figures a crucial component of how they will be evaluated. Some workers feel that they are expected to obey superiors immediately and unconditionally. For example, a bookkeeper interprets the meaning of "harmonious relationships with superiors" as follows:

> I think that means that they want you to do everything that you are told to do. At the first jump.

Other workers stress the necessity of maintaining an appearance of obedient malleability. A credit checker:

> They [superiors] say that they want you to be open and honest, but *no way*. They want you to be the same way they want you. They—like my performance report is coming up, so I kiss up to them and, of course, that's the way they want you to be.

Both sets of perceptions create a pressure which is best characterized as an apprehensive attentiveness to the wishes of authorities. In time, such pressure can be enervating. However, most workers, like the credit checker, find a partial solution to the pressure—they conform externally while remaining detached internally. In short, they suspend belief in their own social performances, adopting a slightly cynical, removed view of them, and satisfy themselves with the knowledge that they have outmaneuvered their audience—here, their superiors. Over a period of time, of course, as Goffman notes,[11] detached cynicism can become transformed into a sincere belief in one's performance. Alternatively, as Theodore Caplow suggests,[12] cynicism can become a permanent style. It may even, in some cases, be accompanied by an elaborate counter-ideology which justifies a person's continuance in an organizational role while allowing him simultaneously to excoriate the organization and its conception of the role. Such responses are most likely to occur among managers or professionals in an organization; clerical workers are generally both more passive and more ambivalent. For instance, in this study, the principal consequence among workers of the conjunction of external conformity and internal detachment is a somewhat removed, pejorative self-image. A payroll clerk illustrates this feeling:

How do I see myself at work? Well, I wouldn't associate with me given the choice. Tie, suit, sports coat. Everything geared toward doing what somebody else wants.

People in subordinate positions in a bureaucracy adopt the same behavioral patterns evidenced by those who are in higher positions, in this case, internal detachment from external behavior. However, the lack of autonomy characteristic of their subordinate status seems to make the meaning of such experiences more negative, and, at the same time, limits workers' opportunities to transform that meaning.

THE NEGOTIABILITY OF CONFORMANCE AND THE VARIABILITY OF PRESSURE

The degree of workers' strict conformance and the extent of their experiences of pressure to conform are, however, somewhat variable in the bank; different structural conditions underpin such flexibilities in behavior and experience. Within limits, conformance is a negotiable behavioral pattern; its negotiability depends principally upon the type of authority in an office but also upon workers' participative status and the degree of their public visibility in the bank. When the negotiability of conformance increases, feelings of pressure to conform decrease. Further, depending upon the extent of correspondence between organizational wishes and individual predispositions to conform, whether on specific matters or in general, workers may experience pressure to conform only in certain areas or not at all.

The negotiability of workers' conformance depends, first and foremost, upon how authority is exercised in an office. In offices where the dominant style of supervision tends to be authoritarian—that is, harsh and demanding—there is little negotiability for most workers. Rather, workers conform because they are afraid of authoritative action against them. The interview material is replete with a whole range of workers' stated fears in authoritarian offices—from the fear of being watched and the fear of giving the wrong impressions to the fear of incurring the anger of authorities. Two fears seem especially prevalent and emerge when workers account for their acceptance of pressure to conform. The first is the fear of receiving a poor performance report unless one exhibits the right attitude in the workplace. The second is more deep-rooted and more commonly stated: the fear of losing one's job. A bookkeeper in an office with authoritarian supervision states, in regard to what she considered an arbitrary admonition:

I was terrified. I thought I was going to lose my job. Maybe I'm exaggerating a little, but I really don't want to lose my job.

More often the fear is stated indirectly and attributed to other people in the office; sociologically, however, such statements must be taken as evidence of the respondent's own state of mind. A clerk accounts for her own and others' conformity to a situation characterized by authoritarian supervision:

Sometimes I wonder: Why don't people rebel? I think it's fear of losing their job. That's probably it. You're under their thumbs. They have a lot of authority.

In such situations, conformity is imposed rather than negotiated and the feeling of pressure to behave properly is marked.

By contrast, in branches where the style of authority tends to be characterized either by a functional, workaday mentality or by a tone of enlightened management, workers' conformance is much more negotiated and feelings of pressure are lessened. For example, a clerk with a neatly trimmed mustache and dark glasses describes his negotiated settlement of requirements for uniform appearances:

There has been pressure to do things the way they want. Well, yes and no. There have been little instances. I enjoy being myself. . . . It was suggested to me that if I were to shave my mustache and beard—when I had a beard—and cut my hair and stop wearing dark glasses that I would get a better performance report. . . . After I had been here a while, it kind of got into a mutual back-scratching arrangement, so I look presentable and they don't say anything.

Given the right supervisors, conformity in other areas can also be negotiated. For instance, a credit checker in an office with low-key supervision participates, but only minimally, in one of the bank's sales promotion contests between workers. The fact that she participates at all relieves managerial pressure on her since her superiors can claim that she *did* participate. This exchange neutralizes, for her, the pressure to conform:

I don't think that we should promote bank services. . . . People have so many complaints already; why get them in more trouble? They have these contests, but even though they pushed it, I didn't feel much pressure. See, I opened up one savings account to get them off my back.

Negotiation softens the insistence of authorities, which is the key component of the pressure to conform; when people bargain with authority to determine the parameters of behavior, even required actions can seem to be voluntary. Indeed, in some cases, they cease to be required in any sense.

Another condition determining the negotiability of conformance and resultant feelings of pressure is workers' participative status in the organization. The extent of workers' employment in the bank is the most important aspect of this status. Full-time workers, especially those who are concerned with advancement, are full participants in the bank and are expected, depending upon the types of authority they encounter, to conform wholeheartedly to regulations. Part-time workers, however, have a special status in the bank; they are marginal workers, and their marginality enables them to pursue silent negotiated settlements with all types of authority. This ability differentiates them from full-time workers, who can negotiate only with flexible managers. The key premise of part-time workers' silent barter with authorities is the mutual recognition that they have no ambitions in the bank. In return for the adequate performance of actual job tasks, bank authorities accept these workers' minimal compliance with rules or nonparticipation in bank activities. A part-time general ledger clerk describes such a transaction:

Promote bank services? There's no way that I'm going to participate in something like that. Nobody has bothered me about that. It's just as well. I feel that if I wanted to get anywhere in the bank, I would have to. But I don't want to get anywhere, so it doesn't apply.

As this worker points out, there is a general recognition that, should ambitions change, the terms of any agreement to ignore bank demands would be subject to revision. In all likelihood, the pressure to conform would, at that point, become a problem.

The public visibility of workers also determines their ability to negotiate conformance, although only on the issue of external appearances. In general, the more workers must interact with or perform their work in front of the public, the greater the pressure to conform to external guidelines like branch dress codes. When workers are removed from public view and work in interior offices, this pressure to conform decreases to some extent, although the whims of different types of authority are also a factor here. When workers in interior offices must go into public areas, they are expected, of course, to conform to the norms applied to workers in those areas. For example, a young woman who is allowed to remove her pantsuit jacket at her interior desk receives a sharp reprimand for being improperly dressed when she forgets to replace her jacket before delivering materials to the main banking floor. While conformance is negotiable, negotiability is always situational.

Finally, when organizational wishes and individual predispositions correspond, conformance seems natural, needs no negotiation, and is devoid of pressure. Such correspondence usually occurs only around specific bank demands for conformity, and, in such cases, workers experience no pressure to conform with regard to those specific demands. Some workers, for instance, take the bank's demands for an attractive appearance very seriously. Dressing well at work becomes symbolic to them of the respectability of the work itself. A credit checker evaluates the dress code:

I think it's really proper to be dressed in a certain way. We should represent the image of the bank; that is the way I feel.

Others simply enjoy dressing well and, it seems, use work as a place to display finery. Whatever their individual motives in this regard, these workers feel no pressure to conform since the meanings they give to the dress code allow them to behave comfortably within the parameters established by the bank. In some offices, the ready conformity of some to a dress code places another pressure—this time a peer-group pressure—upon workers who dislike the bank's demands for attractive appearances. In a similar manner, and for equally diverse reasons, some workers, with no sense of being pressured, readily engage in activities which the bank uses as one gauge of their attitude—activities which other workers find odious. For instance, a teller comments upon her participation in a sales promotion program:

I don't feel any pressure to cross-sell. We really pushed them [sales] this time. I really got into it too.... We really liked doing it because of the Blue Chip stamps. I don't feel pressured at all by cross-selling.

Some workers, then, have no problems with specific aspects of the bank's demands for conformity. These same people, however, almost always counterpose these favorable experiences with expressions of the pressure to conform on other issues. In short, their experience of the bank's demands for a standardized public face is an ambivalent one. For the bank's part, the success of its managerial strategy in this regard depends upon how well it can establish regulative parameters and rewards for the proper presentation of self which foster that part of workers' ambivalence favorable to the bank's goals.

With only a very few workers does such correspondence between organizational wishes and individual predispositions go beyond specific demands for conformity; however, there are some workers who do assert that a *general* conformity is necessary for social comfort. Although open acceptance of conformity is marginal, probably because of the high premium placed upon individualism in American society, these workers' experiences have resonances in the interviews of other workers. One clerk states:

Of course I conform. I've been brought up to know how to respond in certain situations. If you want to work in a bank, you *know;* you *should know.* Like, if I came into work without a tie, they would let it go one day, but not two. They wouldn't need to tell you. You'd feel embarrassed. In the Midwest, if everybody wore cowboy outfits, you'd feel comfortable about wearing them too. I've never met a person who was able to feel comfortable who acted different from anybody else.

For workers like this, conformity to standards obviates or at least alleviates some social anxiety by removing external grounds of difference between themselves and other people. For them, the bank's standards are not pressures to conform but, rather, guidelines for feeling socially comfortable at work. Their experiences resonate with those of other workers precisely here, even with those who define the bank's standards as pressures. One senses in reading the interview materials that workers may often conform to the bank's demands for certain public impressions simply because it is easier to do so. Although they may resent pressures to conform, the discomfort of yielding to those pressures is less than the social discomfort they think they would experience if they refused to wear the public face the bank expects of them.

THE EXPERIENCE OF SELF-ARTIFICIALITY

When workers do not negotiate conformance, the resulting experience of pressure to conform is often accompanied by a feeling of self-artificiality. This feeling consists of a sense of distance from self, and it emerges principally from workers' definitions of certain requisite social aspects of their roles as unnatural or strained in some way. Again, the experience occurs both in workers' dealings with customers and in some of their dealings with co-workers and supervisors.

Self-artificiality is a common experience among those workers who must deal directly with the public. The bank's demand for a public face of constant congeniality towards customers conflicts with workers' perceptions of many customers as rude and, therefore, not deserving of the friendliness workers must project. A teller indicates the social tension her role involves:

They [the bank] want you to project an attitude—to always be nice, to smile, to be sweet, never to get angry, to be helpful, and so on. We got all that down at the teller school where I was trained. . . . Since you deal with the public, you have to be congenial constantly. That's not difficult to do if they [customers] were nice, but they're not. . . . Don't get me wrong. I like people, but when you are working with their money, they can really be something else.

Workers frequently feel a desire, when dealing with impolite customers, to drop their prescribed public faces and to respond in ways they define as normal. Again, a teller:

Often you have an almost uncontrollable urge to be yourself and take a person outside and give them a piece of your mind.

However, displaying anger towards a customer is cause for immediate dismissal from the bank, and workers realize that they must curb behavior which they consider normal. Another teller:

You know, it's difficult at the window. That's because you can never actually be your true self on the window. If you really get upset, you just have to go back and cry in the backroom. But you can't show it publicly.

Workers must, in fact, maintain their congeniality without support from bank authorities, whom they perceive as offering little help when they are confronted with a difficult customer. Indeed, workers feel that officers more often than not publicly take the customer's side in a dispute, frequently excusing bureaucratic errors by blaming workers' inexperience.

However, most workers do not direct resentment against the bank for placing them in work roles where they experience self-artificiality; rather, they direct their anger against customers who, in a sense, activate their role tensions. Workers blame customers rather than the bank not only when customers are impolite for no apparent reason, but also when workers perceive that it is contradictions within their own roles which provoke customers' annoyance. For example, a platform secretary describes how she displaces anger for her own feelings of awkward strain:

The bank wants us to project an image of being friendly, helpful, useful, and resourceful, and so on. At the same time, they want you to be thorough; so thorough that often the customer thinks you distrust him. He gets angry, and you're still trying to keep friendly and so on. . . . What bothers me most is that these people [customers] put you down as a person because you followed bank policy. It's the bank's fault, but this makes you feel resentment against the person.

Workers express this resentment among themselves and in private, developing vivid images to characterize the public; in the process, they displace their latent anger. For instance, a teller projects an image of customers which is by no means unusual:

It's incredible the types you deal with. One half are nice and the rest are *crazy*. I mean really locked-up type crazy.

Other interviews are peppered with adjectives describing customers as "cranky," "nasty," "suspicious," "bitchy," or "mean." When workers direct anger at customers, thereby effectively blaming them for their own work situations, the workers are implicitly legitimating their acceptance both of the basic tension in their work roles and of the self-artificiality such tension produces. Customers are identifiable and socially allowable objects of resentment as long as anger is not displayed to their faces. More to the point, customers, unlike the bank, are harmless and unthreatening objects of resentment. Workers' anger at customers deflects criticism which might be directed against the bank for putting them in ambiguous positions where their public faces require them to take abuse without being able to make culturally appropriate responses.

Workers also experience self-artificiality in their dealings with supervisors and co-workers. They are required to project within a context of social isolation and social friction, a sociability which they do not feel towards the people with whom they work.

Bank workers are, on the whole, socially isolated from one another.

This isolation has several components. First, the great diversity of people's backgrounds—their varied ethnic characteristics, their different age levels, their diverse educational and work experiences, and finally the subtle differences in their class and status levels—provide them with little initial experience in common. Second, their jobs are not conducive to shaping sustaining common meanings. Third, clerks, at least, do not as a rule see each other outside the workplace. Only a few workers make the opposite claim and in almost every one of these cases, people who claim to see each other outside of work live in the same neighborhoods. Some clerks do belong to the BankColumbiaClub, a social organization for bank employees which sponsors, among other events, parties, dances, cruises, and tours. Clerical participation in these clubs, however, despite pressure in some branches to join, is generally marginal.[13] The result of such isolation is that, apart from some informal work groups, occasional friendships, or small cliques of friends, bank workers' interaction with each other most nearly resembles that of strangers who happen to be in the same place every day. Their style of verbal and nonverbal interaction is one of polite friendliness which is generally formal rather than casual. The larger the branch, the more formalized interaction becomes. For instance, this formality on the nonverbal level shows itself in lunchroom behavior in large branches. In one branch, it is not at all unusual for four workers entering the employees' lunchroom at or near the same time to sit at the four separate tables in the room. Verbal interaction, even though the casual idioms of American dialect are used, is best characterized as guarded.[14]

As is common in bureaucratic work situations, the social isolation depicted here does not preclude social friction.[15] In fact, workers indicate that they often feel antagonistic towards their co-workers and supervisors. This friction is discussed in more appropriate contexts later and can only be mentioned here. Briefly, the friction between workers and authority figures generally emerges from their conflict of interests. Officers' careers depend to a great extent upon how well they obtain adequate performance from workers; for their part, workers experience marked difficulties with their work, as we have seen, and they often direct their resentment against supervisors. In addition, status antagonisms between workers arise from conflicting claims based on grade and salary differences, type of work, and contrasting lifestyles. Moreover, competition for scarce managerial attention and approval is a principal point of friction, as is strife generated by the cliques within large offices.

In the bank, as in other bureaucratic environments, workers feel that they cannot reveal the social tension they feel towards their co-workers or supervisors. They recognize that they are graded by supervisors for sustaining an image of cheerful cooperativeness, and, more importantly, that they must get along amicably with a group of people with whom they have little in common and with whom they have not chosen to associate but whom they must see every day.[16]

For many workers, projecting sociability within this context produces self-artificiality. The experience often emerges most clearly in those situations which are supposed to be relaxing, namely branch parties. A teller describes her uneasiness at a get-together:

The party was really weird. People just talk to a few people and then leave. The people who stay are those who like to drink. They stay to get tanked. Nobody really enjoys themselves. I'll be sitting there smiling and saying to myself, "This is ridiculous." When you're around certain people whom you haven't chosen to be around, it gets forced and artificial.

Most bank workers feel on guard when they are at work, even during convivial occasions. Just as important, they sense that others are also on guard, and masks of sociability become key vehicles for allowing any interaction at all.

Somewhat more complicated and perhaps more typical, however, are workers' experiences of self-artificiality while projecting sociability on a day-to-day basis. Workers see their projection of a superficial sociability as artificial but necessary to help them cope with the latent friction around them. An auditing clerk explains how behavior which she considers artificial becomes imperative in her office:

At first, I thought everybody was nice [in the office]. After a while, you get to the point where you have to tell everybody how you really feel or you have to put on a superficial niceness. If you do blow up, then it makes things so difficult. It's better to be phony and not get into a hassle. Also, there are groups of people who hang together. If you get mad at one person, then you have four people down on you. I'm the type of person who if I don't care for someone—I'll tell them what I think. But here I have no choice. If something irritates me and I let it out, I know I wouldn't let it stop there.

The justification implicit in the statement may be characterized as an appeal to social inevitability. "Phoniness" or artificiality is inescapable because of the social demands of the work environment. Other workers repeat the same justification in different ways. A credit checker:

Phoniness is a way of life in the office. You'd better believe it.

A boarding clerk:

They want me to be phony. I guess that's how I'll have to be. That's the way people in this world are.

Tension between people, like that produced by the isolation and friction of bureaucratic work situations, can be either ironed out or suppressed. In situations like the bank—and in this the bank especially exemplifies modern urban society—there are few mechanisms to resolve differences between people. Suppression of tension is the rule, accompanied by external congeniality. The rare occasions when a worker openly displays anger or annoyance point out, by contrast, how widespread are expectations for external sociability. A machine operator relates:

Once I got mad and people got shocked. They said that I was just having a bad day. When you put on a little act every day, people think you're acting normal.

It is only through the observance of external niceties—as in workers' projection of external sociability—that conflict is not an open feature of work life in the bank. One of the costs of such social harmony, however, is the sense of distance from self experienced by many people.

AUTHENTICITY IN BANK WORK

Not all bank workers experience self-artificiality in their jobs even when pressured to conform to social expectations. Structurally, this variation depends upon the extent to which workers' jobs require interaction with the public. Constant public exposure accentuates the problems and dilemmas of self-presentation. Those workers who do not experience self-artificiality usually work in interior offices. They do not have to maintain constant congeniality towards customers, but only project external sociability to co-workers and supervisors. Besides public exposure, this variation is contingent upon different perspectives among workers, shaped by forces outside the bank. A few younger clerks bring a direct, matter-of-fact approach to interpersonal relationships, a style of "up-frontness" valued among the young which undercuts social expectations for external sociability. For instance, a young secretary illustrates this approach:

Everybody has their bad days, and I have disagreements with quite a few people; but it's forgive and forget. They're not—people don't hate each other or anything. We can work together. I'm myself here. I never feel that if I'm in a bad mood in front of my supervisor, it's going to affect me—I mean hurt me. You can't always be nice.

These workers perceive the self-artificiality of others' behavior but they resist being drawn into it. Another young clerk explains:

I've found that as you get up in your prestigious jobs in the bank—they all have to start out low—a lot of departments have this really phony attitude. They'll say "good morning" and so on and all the while, behind your back, they'll be saying, "That creep." I don't know what it is. It's like a little world all their own. I don't want to have to act like something I'm not. I want to be me. They're not really being fair to me if they demand that I put on a little act. I just don't want to do it.

Such personal resistance to perceived stilted relationships in the bank is significant. As Goffman points out, people often find their identities in the interstices of bureaucratic structures.[17] The fact that some people in the bank can assert what they consider to be authentic images of self in the course of their everyday work demonstrates both the resiliency of people's selves as well as the existence of crevices in the bank bureaucracy where individuals can claim some control over their relationships to accepted social practices. As the clerk just quoted senses, however, as one rises in the bank's hierarchy, the pressures on self become greater and the crevices become harder to find.

There are other workers who do not experience self-artificiality; they are numerically marginal in this study, but their experiences may have larger significance. These few workers, largely from ethnic minority groups, adopt a quite complex view of their relationships to co-workers and supervisors. Their view of themselves is more guarded than that of other workers, and they see themselves presenting selected self-images to others as a matter of course rather than as an artificial experience. A Chinese-American clerk relates:

I've never been angry since I've been here. Oh, a few days ago, it was deadline date, and I asked [the supervisor] for help; but four people had phoned in absent, and there was no help available. I understood the situation; if I hadn't asked her and nobody came, then I would have felt angry. Now it's only human to feel that way—you know, spontaneous. But if a person wants to say something, he should hold back and restrain himself—this is up to the person. I complain all the time—but to myself. . . . You can build up an image, but commit one bad act and destroy the whole image. You lose your cool and things build up. Then you're always trying to hide something. . . . Life is compromising with people. You don't want to build up a confrontation with another person.

The ambiguities of their minority status seem to have made these workers especially sensitive to the nuances of interaction. More than others, they are attuned to the negotiated character of interaction and of social identity. For them, self-artificiality is not a problem in the workplace; rather, their problem is making sure that they present and maintain the right image at the right time. Their emphasis on the adroit manipulation of images and on coolness as a personal style may be increasingly prototypic of values in a society where all social situations seem filled with risk. Where most other workers experience self-artificiality, these workers can find a kind of authenticity and, in this, they may point out the future for other people.

The Crisis of Work Legitimacy

The crisis of work legitimacy is implicit in workers' complex experiences of work tasks and of social dealings at work, as discussed in the previous two chapters. As stressed earlier, the roots of this crisis are workers' generally troublesome experiences of their immediate work situations. Highly rationalized work tasks leave little room for personal creativity; instead, most workers experience lack of control over their work pace, boredom, and lack of fulfillment in the tasks they perform. In addition, their rationalized social environment provides only marginal space for authentic self-expression. Under certain conditions, within certain parameters, and on specific issues workers' conformance to organizational demands is negotiable; nonetheless, most workers most of the time find that the public faces they must project are not to their liking nor of their choosing. As a result, two of the most immediate features of people's work lives—their actual work tasks and the social environments where they work—do not provide bases for positively legitimating their work; it is precisely this conspicuous absence of *motives* for work in their everyday activities that makes for attenuated legitimacy.

The accounts which workers use both point out this crisis of legitimacy and partially resolve it. The psychological defensiveness of accounts is a signal of personal troubles, an indirect disclosure that something is wrong with an integral part of one's life. At the same time, however, accounts patch up uneasy relationships between people as well as ease the strain of inner conflicts. Accounts allow social action, even troublesome work which must be faced every day, to continue. In doing so, accounts help actors shape a truce with their problematic situations. The meaning of workers' experiences is thus essentially ambiguous and that very ambiguity, while often enervating, is also stabilizing. Accounts help routinize the crisis of work legitimacy.

The past two chapters have attempted an anatomy of individuals' legitimations for their work problems and have therefore concentrated on subjective perspectives. But, as stressed earlier, subjective meaning does not arise in a void, but rather within a context of power. How does the power context of the bank shape workers' meanings for work, particularly of the accounts they give for work problems?

Some general characteristics of the accounts which have been examined and of their contexts of meaning provide clues to the impact of the bank's power structure on the meaning of work for its workers. By and large, the data show that the dominant accounts for work difficulties point to perspectives with one or more of the following characteristics: they are highly individualistic, emphasizing personal rather than social explanations and solutions to problems; they are fragmented, evidencing a confused, limited, and often fearful image of self and of one's personal and organizational situation and problems; or, finally, they are fatalistic, conveying a quiet resignation towards work problems because of their complexity and seeming immutability. These perspectives reflect privatized and consequently passive attitudes among bank workers despite their widespread dissatisfaction with their work. Clearly, such attitudes are congruent with the bank's standardization of work and of relationships and with its centralization of authority. However, the bank's rationalized work conditions, while they may underpin the emergence of privatized and passive attitudes, are insufficient to explain such attitudes fully. In fact, according to some studies of rebellious workers, the same conditions are proximate causes not only for dissatisfaction but for active unrest.[18]

The key to understanding bank workers' perspectives is that they have no independent, organized social bases to aid them in articulating their experiences and in shaping coherent understandings of those experiences. The bank certainly provides no such forums for workers. In fact, the bank is intent on preventing the emergence of any worker organization which it does not control and, further, on channeling all dissent through its own carefully regulated structures. Its clearly stated opposition to unionization efforts[19] as well as its range of managerial programs to locate and defuse dissent[20] are evidence of such intentions. The result of these bank policies is an organizational monopoly which, by precluding alternate social bases, creates, at the least, further ambiguity among workers where it does not succeed in directly suggesting to workers the meaning of their experiences. The upshot of this situation is that, without an independent social basis, workers, even when they reject the bank's definitions of their situations, often cannot interpret their experiences except in an individualistic fashion; they often cannot grasp the links between their own problems, those of other workers, and organizational policies. Finally, they have no reason to think about their experiences in any way other than as a framework which must be accepted as given. Workers' perspectives, reflected in their accounts, are indeed privatized and passive, but this is largely a consequence of their social situations at work.

The crisis of work legitimacy, at least in the bank, is likely to continue. Since, like other major banks, the First Bank of Columbia is intent on further expansion,[21] its rationalization of work can only increase; further, the rising educational level of its workers promises even deeper experiential problems than those discussed here. Even if workers succeed in achieving an independent forum in the shape of a union[22] (a development which would unquestionably improve the material aspects of workers' situations), only a union committed to achieving a genuinely democratic workplace will help workers gain control of and alter their everyday work experiences. The history of American unionism, however, clearly indicates that most unions are more concerned about wages and benefits than about the quality of people's everyday work lives.[23] Indeed, many union bureaucracies themselves exacerbate workers' everyday troubles and help make problems of work legitimacy a permanent feature of modern work.

What then holds bank workers' work-worlds together? Accounts are crucial; they remain, however, essentially defensive tools which can only patch together the tears in the social fabric. What are the positive rationales which form the warp of that fabric? The following chapters explore bank workers' motives for work, the contexts of which are, as it happens, as fully ambiguous as the areas of work experience already explored. Motives, in fact, are rarely asserted in a context entirely free of accounts.

References

The material in this chapter was published in a somewhat different form in "The Control of Public Faces in a Commercial Bureaucratic Work Situation," *Urban Life* Vol. 6, No. 3 (October, 1977), pp. 277-302, and appears here by permission of the publisher, Sage Publications, Inc.

1. Karl Mannheim, *Man and Society in an Age of Reconstruction* (London: Kegan Paul, Trench and Trubner, 1940), pp. 51–56.

2. C. Wright Mills, *White Collar* (New York: Oxford Univ. Press, 1951), pp. 182–188.

3. Joseph Bensman and Bernard Rosenberg, "The Meaning of Work in Bureaucratic Society," in *Identity and Anxiety*, edited by Maurice Stein, Arthur J. Vidich, and David M. White (New York: Free Press, 1960), p. 182.

4. Erving Goffman, "The Moral Career of the Mental Patient," *Asylums* (New York: Doubleday-Anchor, 1961), pp. 148–149.

5. See, for example, Joseph Bensman and Arthur J. Vidich, *The New American Society* (Chicago: Quadrangle Books, 1971), pp. 50–51.

6. The very term "retail banking," used by bankers themselves, connotes the image presented here. For a discussion of some of the dimensions of retail banking, see "Retail Banking Enters New Phase," *Bankers Monthly*, 84 (August 15, 1967), 20 f.

7. Proper dress is also encouraged through some of the bank's publications directed at workers. For instance, *The BankColumbian*, a monthly journal delivered to every worker's home, has a regular feature called "The Image-Makers." This feature presents carefully chosen female workers whose coiffures and chic dress are lionized as ideal for, in the feature's words, "saying through personal appearance" what the bank is all about.

8. The bank does stylize worker-customer interaction, although somewhat indirectly. For example, the bank provides tellers with a plastic chart detailing prototypic conversations to have with customers during various transactions. Similarly, *The Teller's Notebook* details a typology of customers and prescribes for workers appropriate emotional responses for each type. Essentially, then, the bank is trying to provide ways for workers to, in William Foote Whyte's phrase, "get the jump on the customer." But workers do not perceive it that way. Instead, they generally resent the bank's imposition on them of yet another set of forms. However, sustained interaction with customers—mostly strangers—seems, after a period of time, to demand some standardized responses. Workers therefore develop their own typologies and emotive responses to cope with customers. The forms of interaction they develop are, curiously, often an amalgam of those prescribed by the bank and those created by themselves. The bank thus, indirectly, gains its goals; but in the process, by trying to impose controls on people, it stirs up antagonism against itself.

9. This is one of the main categories on each worker's performance report, a semi-annual or annual evaluation depending upon a person's rating within her grade. The relationship of this evaluative mechanism to salary is discussed in the Appendix.

10. These promotional programs are, in fact, sales contests between employees. Clerks are to concentrate on making individual cross-sales to customers—that is, selling other bank services, like the bank's credit card or a savings account, to a customer who already has, for instance, a checking account. To heighten the competition between workers, the regional administration office, which supervises a number of branches within a geographical area, prepares and distributes weekly newsletters to each employee and scoresheets for posting to each branch indicating the leading sellers in the area. Each sale nets the worker/salesperson a prescribed number of Blue Chip stamps with which she may obtain consumer goods from a special catalogue or, in special contests, a paid trip. The bank encourages everyone to sell outside of working hours and, to involve everyone in selling, it offers twice the number of stamps for each sale made by employees who do not meet the public in their work. The bank explicitly does not give cash awards. As the prize catalogue for a recent promotional program entitled "Let's All Get Together" states, "Cash can be spent with nothing to show for it. Travel and merchandise awards are tangibles and provide more lasting recognition." The bank seems to be striving to insure that employees link, through the medium of an object or experience, their own personal gain with the bank's profit.

11. Erving Goffman, *The Presentation of Self in Everyday Life* (Garden City: Doubleday-Anchor, 1959), pp. 17–21.

12. Theodore Caplow, *Principles of Organization* (New York: Harcourt, Brace and World, 1964), pp. 199–200.

13. This is not true for officers who explicitly recognize the importance of joining the clubs for the furtherance of their career chances in the bank.

14. Michael Crozier found the same general formality and absence of camaraderie in his study of insurance company clerks. See *The World of the Office Worker* (Chicago: Univ. of Chicago Press, 1971), p. 114.

15. For instance, this combination is evident throughout Bensman's and Rosenberg's analysis of bureaucratic work. See especially "The Meaning of Work in Bureaucratic Society," pp. 182, 185, and 187.

16. In Chris Argyris's study, exactly the same pattern of separation of feelings from action emerges, especially in worker-officer interaction. See *Organization of a Bank* (New

Haven: Labor and Management Center, Yale University, 1954), pp. 93–97. Argyris interprets such separation, though with some hesitation, as further evidence of the fact of workers' organizationally selected acquiescent personalities, a thesis which I mentioned earlier. But Argyris's own data here contradict his thesis unless "personality" is equated only with external behavior, with no reference to inner values and meanings. Sociologically, however, it is precisely such inner values and meanings which constitute experience which is, in turn, the basis of personality. Clearly, in this context, Argyris is working with an inadequate notion of personality. In fact, his subjects seem to be responding to the same situational exigencies which impel First Bank of Columbia workers to suppress their feelings.

17. Erving Goffman, "The Underlife of a Public Institution," *Asylums*, p. 320.

18. The classic case of this correlation occurs in incidents of "speed-up," where a company's drive toward more efficient production demands further effort from workers. See, for example, Barbara Garson, "Luddites in Lordstown," *Harper's*, June, 1972, pp. 68–73.

19. This is documented especially in an internal publication called *Managerial Guide to Union Activities* meant only for bank officers and supervisors. The following quote is

We will . . . strongly resist any effort to organize any of our employees. . . . Senior Management recognizes its responsibilities in the matter of unionization. We will continue to review all policies relating to personnel in order to assure that those policies effectively discourage unionization.

The pamphlet gives explicit directions to authorities on how to keep workers' morale up as a guard against organized dissent; how to be aware of and report suspicious activities among workers; and how to blunt incipient organizing efforts.

20. There are two managerial programs with this aim, both of which are part of the bank's "Upward Communications" program. The first of these is a program called "Let's Have a Talk" which encourages workers to discuss their work problems first with their immediate supervisors, and then, if they are not satisfied, with higher branch authorities or, as a final resort, with a special office at the bank's central administration. This program not only helps the bank control the expression of dissatisfaction but, when appeals are made, to pinpoint those supervisors who have difficulty containing problems. The second program is called "Hot Line," and it encourages all workers to write a central administration office about any problems or questions they have concerning bank policies. All letters are answered individually and some, with their answers, are published in the monthly employee magazine *The BankColumbian*. This program gives management another way of pinpointing problem areas. Each month the coordinators of the program analyze all questions received; they do this, in the words of a brochure describing the program for management,

. . . to report [to higher management] on employe complaints that are general enough to be used in a union organization attempt—so that the Bank can take action first.

21. The large commercial banks in the United States which have adopted retail banking as their orientation depend in that phase of their business operations, as does any retail business, on *volume* of business in order to make money. In addition to extending services to customers in already established areas, this means continually expanding the territorial range within which banking services are offered. See Paul Nadler, "The Territorial Hunger of Our Major Banks," *Harvard Business Review* (March-April, 1974), pp. 87-98.

22. Two overt attempts to unionize individual bank branches have failed in recent years. However, there is a small clandestine group of workers trying to lay the basis for organizing the bank's clerical workers. Thus far, because of a justifiable fear of reprisal, their efforts have been confined to anonymously producing and disseminating literature critical of bank policies. In addition, some major unions have targeted the banking industry as the locus of the next big unionizing drive and the First Bank of Columbia, because of its importance in the industry, will surely be one focus of such an effort. For an interesting and somewhat

fearful managerial appraisal of the possible unionization of banking, see William O'Connor and Charles J. Coleman, "Unionization: What's Ahead for Banks?," *Magazine of Bank Administration*, 49 (May 1973), pp. 15–19.

23. See, for example, Stanley Aronowitz, *False Promises* (New York: McGraw Hill, 1973), for a critical discussion of this issue.

part three

POSITIVE RATIONALES
FOR WORK

5 The Importance of Working and the Drift Into the Organization

If people's everyday activities at work are more problematic than rewarding, why do they work? Further, why do they choose to work, and then continue to work, in a large organization like the First Bank of Columbia? The complex answers to these questions are the subject of the rest of this book.

This presentation of people's motives for work is an analytic one. A sequential presentation, recounting workers' motives in the order of their assertion, would have one advantage over an analytic presentation: it would allow others to see, perhaps more clearly, the relative priority workers give to their motives for working. But a sequential presentation can also quickly become a catalogue of motives which does not illuminate the internal consistency, or lack of it, in people's thinking. An analytic presentation of motives, however, aims exactly at exploring the inner logic or contradictions of these rationales. It seeks to reconstruct people's experiences analytically, to make them intelligible to others, and to allow others to enter into the worlds of the men and women under consideration. The analytic framework used to present bank workers' motives for work is fairly straightforward: it examines those motives according to the bases chosen by workers for asserting them. Similar bases are then grouped together into analytic wholes. The following chapters discuss three major groups of bases for motives: those based on conceptions about the personal importance of working; those rooted in the world of the bureaucratic organization; and those based on chosen lifestyles.

I must immediately make an exception to this analytic framework and point out the sequential and actual primacy of one set of motives for work—namely, those based on financial necessity. Almost all the bank workers interviewed feel they must work for economic reasons. Moreover, a question probing their motives for work strikes them as strange at

66

first because the answer seems obvious: work is necessary because work means money, and money is a prerequisite for survival. In modern societies, perhaps in any society at all, the necessity of work makes it a taken-for-granted phenomenon which remains unquestioned in people's lives.[1] Two examples illustrate these two recurring themes. A union clerk:

> Why do I work? To make money. No other reason. . . . Without money, you can't eat, can't travel—and there is no other way to make money.

Again, a bookkeeper:

> Why do I work? We need the money. . . . Other people work for the same reasons. Even women—like those who are sole supporters—they work to support their families. I mean, why else do you work? Pleasure? [laugh]

People work, therefore, because they consider it financially necessary and often, at first, other reasons do not occur to them. However, financial necessity is a socially defined concept to which people assign many shades of meaning. The following chapters explore the main contours of workers' social definitions of that necessity, but the touchstone of the meaning of work is its equation with money. This is a theme which appears regularly in all the analytic groupings of motives presented, if not in all their subdivisions.

The primacy of the idea of work as money often poses methodological problems for the researcher in uncovering other important motives for work. Indeed, it frequently obscures other motives even from workers themselves. Workers do have, however, motives for work not immediately related to notions of financial necessity. Data on these other motives can be obtained in a variety of ways. Sometimes simply asking subjects for their reasons for work beyond financial necessity will suffice. Sometimes a more helpful technique is that originally used by Nancy Morse and Robert Weiss.[2] Workers are asked to assume financial independence and then asked if and why they would continue to work. Sometimes, too, a subject's casual mention of a motive for work—for instance, the importance of work in structuring her day—leads to a whole vein of relevant data which might otherwise have been missed in that interview. Also, one person's mention of a motive gives the interviewer hints on areas to explore with other subjects. Not only explorations of the social meanings of financial necessity, but also probes into other, somewhat less obvious, areas constitute the material of the next few chapters.

What emerges first in this material is the importance of working itself to bank workers. The very fact of working at all carries special significances for them. These meanings are quite separate from the experiences of their actual jobs, which they find problematic and which they try to compartmentalize from the rest of their lives. The meanings associated with the idea of working at all constitute important legitimations of work and indirectly of workers' specific jobs. In workers' minds, work, through its financial function, is a basis for personal independence. More important, working at a job—that is, going to a definite place, during definite times, and performing definite tasks—becomes a framework which shapes the very structure of their lives. Finally, workers' feelings about working at all, as well as other related data from the field material, provide clues about the personal reasons and structural significance of why workers end up at a large organization like the First Bank of Columbia.

Working and Personal Independence

For First Bank of Columbia workers, work is a basis for personal independence. This independence has two meanings and at the core of each is the income which working provides.

SELF-RELIANCE

The desire for personal independence and its relationship to working is expressed first of all as a striving for self-reliance. Bank workers rely on the knowledge that whatever problems they may have with their actual jobs, they are nonetheless bringing in income—and this means that they are *earning* their living. Providing for oneself by working is defined as a social necessity. For instance, a utility clerk:

Why do I work? Why, I want to earn my life. [considerable surprise] Everybody has to work.

Working is a taken-for-granted activity by which people merit a place in society. Without work, one's social existence is insecure. Each person must realize this; everybody must pull their own weight. A boarding clerk:

The meaning of work is—well—it's like a necessity. . . . It always has been. On really rushed days, I ask myself "What am I doing?" But then, if you can't go to work and bring home wages, you're not going to be able to pay your way. Nobody's going to do it for you besides yourself.

Only by being self-reliant through work can one secure personal survival as well as social existence.

The importance of the idea of self-reliance often emerges even more sharply when workers pose what they see as alternatives to it. One alternative is to be dependent upon one's parents or upon one's children. Younger and older workers particularly express a revulsion to such dependence on cross-generational ties. Single younger workers regularly emphasize that the only alternative to work is dependence on parents, which is repugnant to them. When their school years end, these workers consider it imperative to break their financial dependence on their parents and to go to work. A note teller typifies this pattern:

See, when I quit school—my parents—I didn't make money living at home when I was in school, and I hate to be so dependent upon my parents. . . . I had to get out. Away from home.

Again, a payroll clerk:

My strongest point is my *need* to be independent. I've always been *independent*. I didn't want my parents to hinder my own feelings and beliefs. The job was necessary to break that hold of my parents.

Self-reliance through working enables these workers to escape the dependence on their families of origin which exacerbates, at least for them, the normally-felt complex tensions of the nuclear family. The choice to work sometimes involves privations, but the independence that work provides compensates for them. A payroll clerk comments:

I've cut back on what I spend. I only eat meat once a week now. Also, I can't afford the clothes I want to buy. Well, I don't really want them. I guess if I did, I wouldn't have moved out of my parents' place in the first place. You have to make a choice. Right now my independence is more important to me.

Older workers voice the same sentiment, with roles reversed. They do not want to rely on their children, and work gives them a way of at least forestalling that possibility. An elderly, widowed credit checker says:

The meaning of work? Knowing that you can take care of yourself. . . . I wouldn't want to be dependent upon my children.

Other older workers also hint that self-sufficiency and self-reliance free them from the feeling of being a burden to their children.

The value of self-reliance and its particular expression among younger and older workers to be free of familial ties is so ingrained in American-born workers that they voice their feelings about it in casual, matter-of-fact ways. This American emphasis on self-reliance is most noticeable in the surprise it creates in foreign-born workers from more traditional cultures who see reciprocal human and especially familial relationships as superceding any notions of personal independence. An older worker from Asia comments on this:

The attitude of people at all levels here is to take terrific pride in being independent. Old people, for example, take pride in saying, "I'm not dependent upon my children." The children say, "I'm independent," or they move out as soon as they can. All of this is especially true with old people. In the average American family, you see the father, mother, and the children—never the grandparents. In Asia, it is different. We say, "A home that has an old person in it harbors a jewel." A man that has three or four children—every one of those children will try their best to have that old person to live in their home, and they will give the old one the best food, and the best room, and so on. And the old person will do it serially between his children, so it will not appear as if he is favoring one child because it is a great honor for the child. Even if an old person doesn't have immediate children, there are always 1001 families eager to entertain that old person.

In American society, the social reciprocity which this worker recounts is largely replaced by an intense individualism, one aspect of which is the emphasis on self-reliance. Clearly, there are many diverse social roots for the cultural trait of self-reliance.[3] Karl Polanyi, however, suggests an encompassing perspective which links cultural norms of behavior with the social structure as a whole. In Polanyi's view, a market economy demands a market society.[4] A full scale market economy, devoid of residual traditional influences such as exist in the paternalistic organizations in Japan,[5] requires and rewards individualistic competitiveness in its participants; even though required forms of public interaction may cloak competitiveness,[6] the trait itself is the antithesis of reciprocal dependence and shared social cooperation. The operation of the market, with its simplifying cash nexus, rationalizes family structures, as it does all social structures, and, over a period of time, produces attitudes where family ties are not the primary norms for steering behavior. Instead, the dominant market ethos and its values guide behavior even within the family unit and, in the process, at least at some stages of family life, make family ties fragile. It may even be that at certain stages in the life-cycle—and the data of this study point to this for younger and older workers—people sense that, within a market society, the only way to maintain family ties at all is to become self-reliant and financially independent of those ties.

Workers consider dependence on public assistance an even worse alternative to self-reliance than dependence on family. Workers in all age categories express this repugnance. Here working becomes a matter of social pride which emerges through negative comparison. Workers project a negative stereotype of assistance recipients—that they are lazy, irresponsible, and so on—in contrast to which they see themselves as virtuous simply for working. There are different levels of meaning here. On one hand, workers feel a resentment towards those who do not work and are on assistance; since they work, with all the problems that entails, they feel everyone else should work. On the other hand, this resentment does not imply a desire to trade places with assistance recipients; in fact, self-reliance through working is seen as a social necessity because it prevents workers from slipping to the social level of people who do not pay their way. A conversation between two workers illustrates this perspective:

M.   I work so that I can put the clothes that I want on my back there, so that I can put food in my mouth and have a roof over my head. I don't want to sit back and collect welfare. I'd have to be really down and out to do that. I'm not in need of any given financial help. I feel that many people abuse this. I feel that as long as I'm in physical shape, I can get a job. I feel that if you want a job bad enough, you can get one. You're not going to get a job—find a job—sitting at home. Unemployment compensation breeds stagnation in people. Why work if you can get the money? As far as I'm concerned, as long as I'm able to get up in the morning, I'll go to work. If I were hungry—

(At this point, L., whose desk is directly in front of M's, turns around and interjects her comments; she had apparently been listening to M's remarks.)

L.   M., I want to congratulate you on expressing those views; I feel exactly the same way. The people on unemployment are lazy people. All those people on welfare and unemployment. The restrictions need to be a lot tougher to *make* them work.

M.   Yes, a lot tougher. In Utah they have a theory. Everyone is able to do something—even if you have only garbage pickup. It's like a feeling of accomplishment. You pull their [sic] own weight. A lot of people who are on unemployment—they don't need the money, but they say, "What the hell should I work for? I'll stay in bed till noon!"

L.   That's right. When we came here from [Eastern Europe], we were happy to find any work. . . . You have to work to pay your own way here.

Such images of public assistance recipients are fairly conventional, even though persuasive evidence indicates that these stereotypes have little empirical foundation.[7] The point, however, is that many bank workers perceive their own work against the background of such stereotypes. This perception not only displaces onto a specific target what seems to be a generalized resentment about workers' own situations, but, more important, it enables working by itself to become the basis for a general status-claim. To work means that one is self-reliant, and self-reliance in a society with an established underclass is one basis for claiming respectability.

ALTERING TRADITIONAL SEX ROLES

The second meaning of independence through working is akin to workers' desire for self-reliance, but with a shift in emphasis. This is the view expressed by many female workers that working helps them shape and reorder sex roles in their personal lives. The income from working provides the means to help these workers shape their personal relationships with men and with their immediate marital families. The contemporary feminist movement in the United States has stressed the necessity for economic self-support if women expect to achieve any lasting liberation from traditional sex roles. While this view cannot be called widespread among bank workers, it has made sharp inroads among them. Some single women, for instance, see working as a basis for self-support which will forestall traditional female dependence on males when marriage occurs. A secretary:

I also work because of Women's Lib. Maybe I'm working at the wrong place for that! But I want to support myself. I don't want a man to support me. My boyfriend makes a lot of money, but I don't want that. After we get married, I intend to keep working.

Several young married women, in particular, stress the importance of earning their own money in reshaping their marital roles. A general ledger clerk:

Work makes me feel more independent. . . . I like earning my own money.

A bookkeeper elaborates:

This job has made me more independent. It's shifted responsibility at home. I'm contributing income which is a real *symbol* of something. Just those things have all sorts of ramifications. I'm feeling more single. . . . The job frees me from the house and the child. It makes me financially independent. If I want to take somebody to the movies, I can do it and not feel guilty.

For these workers, working becomes one means of achieving a more equal footing in their relationships and especially in their marriages; it gives them a greater voice in how money is spent and the requisite status to bargain for a reallocation of domestic chores.

This last point is especially important and applies to older as well as younger married workers. Women often find negotiation for changes in marital or familial role duties difficult when they do not work for money. Housework and childrearing, however onerous they may be, simply do not have the same status as salaried work. Women without their own sources of income often feel, therefore, that they cannot broach the issues of an equitable distribution of household and parental labor to a husband or other family member who does work for money. In short, not working for money furthers traditional role constraints. A young audit clerk recently returned to work describes why working is important to her:

I like to be able to say to other people that I work. That's related to supporting myself. It has a lot to do with—well, being a woman. When my husband was working full-time and I wasn't working, I felt in order to—I felt that I had to have dinner ready for him. I couldn't ask him to help with the cooking or with the child. It wasn't a bad situation, but I felt that my life was being controlled by this. I was getting into a situation where I was afraid of being stuck. I think I see that in other women's lives. I see it as a bad thing.

Women feel that working alters in a positive way others' images of them and their own images of themselves. Their improved status is then the basis for redistributing domestic duties and this, in turn, lessens feelings of role entrapment. An older, in-mail clerk who returned to work after 20 years in the home states:

Before I worked, I cooked and cleaned up afterwards, and everybody else sat down, and I guess they figured that it was my job to do all the housework, since they had been out all day. They weren't considering housework really *work*. Maybe it's because in housework, there's no schedule. . . . It could also be that it's not paid. . . . Now that I'm working, they all pitch in and help me with the cooking and cleaning.

Working as a Structure for Time and Life

Working is also important to bank workers because they see it as a key way of structuring their time and, consequently, their lives. Lyman and Scott note the crucial significance of conceptions of time—what they call "time tracks"—in ordering experience.[8] Time tracks are cultural products which divide life into different spheres of activity. Of course, men and women ascribe their own meanings to their activities within the spheres, but the conception of the spheres themselves is culturally given and, by and large, taken-for-granted.

One classic time-track cycle in Western society is the notion of life as divided into work and leisure. Work provides the wherewithal to make leisure possible, and leisure restores one's energies for work. However, the two spheres are not to be joined; it is believed to be both desirable and necessary to keep them separate. Nonetheless, the spheres of work and leisure are inextricably joined both in theory[9] and in people's experiences. The data of this study, for instance, indicate that work seriously affects workers' leisure despite their efforts to compartmentalize work from the rest of their lives. The reverse, however, is also true and this seems to be a less commonly asserted point; experiences or expectations of leisure, or more exactly of free time,[10] affect people's definitions of work. Free time here means, in workers' minds, time not spent in a paid occupation where one must follow a fixed schedule. Even time spent in performing other work, such as housework, is usually lumped with free time and is not considered work because it is unpaid and unscheduled. While they want the free time that they have and while they often resent the time they must spend at work, most First Bank of Columbia workers would, given the choice, work in a job rather than accept more free time. They counterpose work time with images of empty free time, and through such comparisons legitimate working as a means of structuring their lives. Images of empty free time seem rooted in actual experience and are, in themselves, often reasons enough for work since they portray a deadening picture of life without a job. Although the specific content of these images varies with workers' life experiences, the images themselves evidence basically similar themes and cut across age, sex, and marital status.

The key themes here center around the boredom, isolation, and lack of direction workers either anticipate or have actually experienced in free time. They indicate repeatedly that the only alternative to work is boring free time. A young union clerk states:

Yes, I would work even if I had money. You'd get bored to death without work time. You know, having all that free time.

Part of the boredom of free time is its isolation; only by being on a common time track with other people, as on a job, can many workers find a structure to relieve isolated boredom. A young teller:

Why do I work? . . . I don't like sitting at home because I would be bored. . . . Even if I had money, I would keep on working. . . . I like to be out with people. Otherwise, I'd just sit home and brood.

Even workers who have set activities like housework and childrearing find them, in most cases, no substitute for a job because they are even more repetitious than bank jobs and, worse, because they are isolated activities. Several workers say that these domestic activities cause a sense of slippage in intellectual and social abilities. An audit clerk with growing children describes her life before she went to work:

I got bored at home. I was up to my neck in diapers. . . . When I stayed home, I felt unfilled [sic]. You have to do the same thing every day. . . . I was home for two years with the kids before starting at the bank and I felt like a vegetable. I was not getting enough adult communication.

Sometimes childraising and domestic life have provided meaning and purpose for female workers. The crisis for many such women occurs when children leave the home, and they find their days not only empty and isolated, but aimless. A payroll clerk:

Well, my son is [overseas] now and my daughter is in college. . . . There used to be so much to do and, well, there's not much to do any more. All I did was stay at home and eat. There are only so many hours you can put in at housework; you can only put in so many hours looking at stores.

The unstructured character of free time is as great a problem as its boredom and isolation. This trackless quality is, in fact, especially anxiety-provoking and most workers—of both sexes and of all ages and experiences—do not claim the personal resources to cope with the anxiety. Their idea of free time in any greater measure than they already have is of a void where they experience a directionless waste of self. A utility clerk's statement represents other workers' anxiety-laden perceptions of free time:

Even if I had money, I still would work. I hate to sit at home and do nothing. When I was at home without work I wasn't happy doing nothing. I felt tired all the time. I went to bed late, got up late, and felt tired all the day. I felt that I was wasting my life.

WORK AS KEEPING BUSY

These images of empty and isolated free time are the backdrop for understanding a key meaning of working at all for bank workers. In American society, having a job is one of the crucial, culturally prescribed means by which people structure their lives. Working gives people a scheduled set of activities which keeps them busy, and they value the sense of being active.[11] Workers repeatedly cite this aspect of working. A payroll clerk:

Work keeps me busy. I don't like to do nothing like sit around the house.

A secretary:

Why do I work? For money; for something to do. . . . I would continue working even if I had all the money I need. Work is something to do with your time.

At this level, it seems not to matter to workers that they have problems with their actual jobs. Nor does it matter that working is considered an essentially unpleasant necessity, despite the sense of independence and of social self-righteousness it brings. The point here is that, in providing people with set activities, working *structures* time and self, and that, in itself, is important. For example, a loan-boarding clerk comments:

You have to set your mind on the fact that you're going to be working and just live with it. That's all. . . . I don't work because I enjoy it; but then, I can't really say, because I wouldn't want to stay at home. I'd have to think about it. I wouldn't know what to do without work. I mean, how to rearrange my life.

Working gives people a way of arranging their time so they experience some measure of balance in their worlds.

An important part of arranging time seems to be the subjective sense that one's own time track coincides with the time tracks of others. It is keeping busy within a social context that counts. A rejected-items clerk states:

... I also work to *structure* myself. When I was home, I never went out. I was bored and I didn't want to do anything, and I would want to go out when my husband came home. I think I'll keep working.... I'm keeping up with everyday life. You know, with what's happening.

Working provides the opportunity for people to mesh their lives with the lives of others within a central time track.[12] Even though the social life of the workplace is, more often than not, laden with conflict and tension, the sense of social participation which it provides is far preferable to the isolation and consequent de-synchronization which workers expect to experience were they not working. For some, the exercise of the most rudimentary social skills is contingent upon this feeling of participation. For example, a teller:

When I wasn't working, I never had anything to say. I felt out of it. Now people seem interested in what I have to say, and I *do* have things to say now.

In a society where the central time track for most people is work time, the only way for many to feel a part of everyday life and indeed, for some, to experience their social nature at all is through working.

WORK AS A MEASURE OF PROGRESS

Many workers who feel that working structures their lives by keeping them busy also claim a sense of personal progress through working, even though such claims are usually vague and ambiguous. For a few workers, this sense of progress is tied to a feeling of social contribution through work; by working they feel that they are contributing to their community and society, and this contribution means personal progress as well. However, for the most part, notions of progress through working are individualistic and much less definite. Most typically, workers emphasize that working brings a sense of motion which is undefined and vague, but identified nonetheless as important. For example, an audit clerk:

I think work plays an important part in the way I think about myself. If I was not working, I would be home watching TV, and not getting ahead.... By working here, I am learning; and by continuing to work, I'm getting ahead. I'm gaining instead of losing, and that's important to me.

This sense of motion seems unrelated to any idea of organizational mobility, an important motive for work which has its own, quite different, roots. Rather, progress here is again associated with people's felt need to accomplish something with their time. This need is asserted even when working is defined simply as a way of making time pass. A note utility clerk voices the deep ambiguity which most workers feel about the connections between work, time, and progress:

Why do I work? I have nothing to do at home. Work is to kill time.... But, if I work, I'm sure that I have done something so that I know I don't waste my time. If I put work in second place, then I would ask what I have achieved after all these days.

Working at a job becomes a way of disposing of time and thus defending oneself against unstructured free time; simultaneously, it gives assurance to the actor that this use of time is not wasteful. A stop payments clerk specifies how working at a job helps her feel constructive:

When I'm working here—here I'm on a *time schedule*. I know I've got to get something done *today*. In housework, you can always let things go.

At this level of meaning, the specific nature of one's tasks is secondary. The knowledge that each working day will bring the completion of specified tasks within a given time period is enough for many workers to feel some measure of personal accomplishment and progress.

The legitimating force of this meaning of work is greatly reduced when workers reflect on the extent to which their *particular* jobs in the bank have contributed to their personal progress. Here their ambivalence about what they actually do all day and its overall meaning in their lives often obscures general notions of personal progress through working. This subject receives more detailed treatment later. However, even when workers feel that their work is not helping them progress, the structure of the workday itself, with its temporal framework and its set activities, often gives people something, however marginal, to point to as a measure of self-development. When asked if his job has contributed to his personal growth and development, a utility clerk responds:

I never thought of it. That's a tough one to answer. You mean, has what I've been doing here helped me grow? I think it has matured me as a person, but then I could have matured as much picking rocks out of people's shoes. I think there are a lot of people at the bank who have contributed to making me a man. Whatever that means. . . . I think it's helped me a lot. Meeting deadlines, for instance. It makes me feel good when I do have these things ready. I feel like I *did something*.

When nothing else about a job is clearly definable as benefitting self, the rhythm and activity of working itself are important to people and enable them to legitimate what they do.

SIDETRACKS AND DIFFERENT PERSPECTIVES

Some First bank workers do not consider work a structure for their lives. Instead, they think about their futures in terms of a career, even though their notions of specific careers are most often vague. In light of their ideas of future work, their present work is a sidetrack.[13] It is a period of waiting on a siding whether they visualize a career, already begun, with the bank or a future in another field. The career aspirations and the problems of waiting for workers who want a bank career are considered in chapter 7 as an aspect of motives of organizational mobility. The focus here is on workers who voice interests in fields unrelated to banking. These workers do not see themselves as yet on a career time track; rather, they are on a sidetrack where they are sometimes standing still, sometimes moving parallel to the traffic on main tracks, but marking time in any case while either trying to find their own main track or, once it is chosen, looking for a signal to switch to it and move ahead.

These workers' specific images of the future affect the quality of their present waiting. Some young married or engaged women, for instance, see their own futures principally in terms of their mates' future careers; their perspective on their present work is marked by a sacrifice ethic.[14] They see their own work as a necessary sacrifice to insure the future careers of their mates, whose success will benefit themselves as well. For example, a machine operator:

I'm just working until my husband gets out of school and gets a job and we can live off his income. . . . I've got to keep this job. If I don't, I'm ruining my husband's chances of improving himself.

Sacrifice for a loved one, and implicitly for oneself, gives powerful meaning to present waiting: one of the costs of the future is present work. The validity of this motive for the person making the sacrifice is, however, contingent on other factors, the most important of which is proper appreciation for the sacrifice being made. Sacrifice for another places responsibility for one's own predicament upon the other to some extent; the other's acknowledgement of the sacrifice is necessary to validate that transfer of responsibility. The more difficult a worker who is sacrificing finds her work, the greater the possibility for resentment against her mate if he seems insensitive to what she is doing. The statement of a union clerk who took a job at the bank to finance her fiancé's education demonstrates the latent anger that sacrifice can contain:

I'll be here I guess for four years. A lot of how long I'm going to stay depends upon how [her fiancé] does in school. I may be here longer or less depending on that. Sometimes I feel resentful about him. Like this summer, we were both going to work in camp, but then I got this job and we decided not to. Then when he was there, I began getting these letters telling me how great it was and how much fun he was having with the kids. Here he was getting paid for doing what he wants to be doing, and I was stuck here. I don't think it was fair at all. In fact, I was angry.

In another example, workers sacrificing for their mates claim that a common cause of dispute is the failure of their mates to listen attentively to the problems of the office. Still, proper appreciation of sacrifice is a negotiable, restorable aspect of most relationships and, as long as it is maintained, motives of sacrifice are powerful stimuli to work. As it happens, motives of sacrifice, in the sense presented here, are most often accompanied by desires for traditional female roles—still important for some younger workers—help people to live *at* the future and to make present waiting at least tolerable and often meaningful.

Workers who desire their own future work in fields unrelated to banking have more trouble waiting than those who work with a sacrifice ethic. The former workers, mostly young men and women with some college education who are single and unattached, or young married women influenced by feminist ideas, have general images of the type of future work they want. They want the independence, creativity, and prestige which they associate with being lawyers, biochemists, writers, dancers, commercial artists, or musicians, all occupations which they consider desirable. These people work at their present jobs out of financial necessity or out of a need for independence. Given the bank's low salaries, however, very few workers are able to save money either for careers or for other purposes. Apart from some part-time workers whose explicit goal is to put themselves through school, these workers are essentially waiting, and working in the meantime to get by. People in this situation see no connection at all between their jobs and what they think they really want to do. For the most part, they do not even experience the present as a sacrifice for the future. As a result, their experience is one of *simply* waiting. For instance, a teller who, among other things, wants to be a musician:

When I see what I want to happen with my life, this job doesn't fit in at all. I'm just waiting for my break.

Again, an audit clerk who would like to be a writer:

There's no connection at all between my work and the rest of my life. I'm just doing this for the time being.

In short, these workers see themselves on sidetracks that lead nowhere, ones with no connecting tracks to their futures. They sense that simply waiting in their present jobs has an inner dynamic which affects them despite their efforts to relegate work to a merely economic function. Many, in fact, feel that their present work is eroding the basis of their futures. In a typical statement, a payroll clerk who would like to be a commercial artist describes this:

The job takes away a lot of time and a lot of energy that I would normally have; it cages you in all day. It's a lot of frustration. It tires you out so that often you can't do what you want. I've been on a dry spell with my art for a long time now, and I think that it's because of my work. I used to be inseparable from my sketch pad; now I don't do much at all.

As noted earlier, the everyday performance of any job always affects people. For these workers, work helps them get by while they wait for some signal to begin their futures, but they often fear that the enervating quality of their present work might keep them sidetracked altogether.

The Drift into the Organization

However bank workers define their work—whether as life-structure or as temporary sustenance—they fulfill their needs by turning to a large organization. Given the structure of the American labor market, this is hardly surprising. Even by midcentury, more than 85 percent of the workers in the United States were employees and, of that total, more than half worked in what can be called large organizations.[15] We live in an organizational society, and the structure and tempo of our world are rooted in the increasingly bureaucratized shape of every institutional order. The manpower needs of large organizations, both public and private, shape labor markets. More to the point here, the needs of these organizations create the basis for individuals' perceptions of the existence or lack of personal opportunities. Still, specifically how and why do workers come to an organization like the First Bank of Columbia? Clearly, the reasons why most workers join an organization differ in some respects from the reasons why they stay; sometimes, though, their reasons for joining and for staying with an organization mesh. Here the focus is on a dominant characteristic of bank workers relating to both aspects of their experience, even though the principal concern is to discern why workers come to an organization. This characteristic is the phenomenon of drift.

THE MEANING OF PERSONAL DRIFT

Drift is basically a state of mind marked by unsureness about future goals and a related uncertainty about one's own abilities. In people's work lives, drift often results in workers ending up in jobs without knowing why.

Drift is evident, first of all, in the generally directionless character of workers' images of their futures. A great majority of the workers interviewed either do not know what they want in the future or, if they do have some goals, seem not to know how to reach them. Younger workers right out of high school and older women who have returned to work are particularly directionless. Younger workers often have no idea of what they want for their futures, at least regarding work. Schooling provides no direction at all for them and their bank jobs are frequently their first full-time working experience. Their work at the bank does not provide any clear goals for the future, although frequently it helps them develop a sharper idea of what they do not want. Women returning to work want to earn money and to structure time; and, in the beginning, virtually any job will do. Their primary reference point is still the home, and they generally have no clear work-images for the future. Other workers—particularly many of those who presently feel sidetracked—have a better grasp of their futures, but emphasize more desirable *conditions* of work rather than specific careers. Even when they have a specific, desired career, they have only occasionally done anything to further their aspirations, and one senses in the interview material a deep unsureness about what they really want. Except for the few workers who specifically want bank careers—and their aspirations almost always develop after they come to the bank—this unsureness about the future is the first key to understanding drift. For example, a general ledger clerk, in commenting on the meaning of success, says:

I'd say that it [success] would be whatever any individual wanted to do themselves. Whatever they wanted to be themselves. For me, I don't have any major goals. For that matter, I don't have—I have very few minor goals. I would be successful if I could figure out a goal to work for.

Such ambiguity—especially about the future—is a central psychological fact of modern society, and there is little use in simply noting its existence among bank workers. The issue here is rather to point out the marked extent to which the workers under study have adapted to that ambiguity. The remarks of a union clerk illustrate this:

> My goals? I live from day to day. I'm optimistic but not idealistic. I don't see miracles happening, or I don't see any great breaks happening right away or overnight. It's sort of, "I don't know where I'm going but I'm on my way."

Such adaptation to ambiguity can be taken as a sign of mental health in an age which has shattered most traditional systems of meaning. Yet, people constantly strive to create meaning for their actions and to make sense of their worlds; data already presented indicate that this is true for the workers under study. However, when it comes to deciding their future work, bank workers adapt to ambiguity and substitute a sense of motion for a sense of direction. Lacking reasonably clear goals, they often have no criteria even to select the kind of motion—in this case, the kind of job—they want, and, as a result, they end up drifting.

A similarly widespread uncertainty about personal abilities complements uncertainty about the future. This is an especially important factor in precipitating workers' drift into highly rationalized organizations like the bank. At issue are workers' perceptions of what *saleable* skills they possess—that is, what they feel they can do to earn a living. In general, bank workers feel deeply unsure of their marketable abilities, although their experiences vary with age, past jobs, and education. Younger workers just out of high school and women coming to work after years in the home feel inexperienced and unskilled; they approach the labor market apprehensively. Those workers who do have previous work experience have, with few exceptions, been clerks. Their uncertainty about other kinds of work leads them back repeatedly to clerical work, and, for one reason or another, to the bank. Workers with some higher education seem on some levels more confident of themselves than other workers, but they still show deep unsureness about how to earn a living. Their education gives them a basis for claiming prestige, as well as some images of what they want for their futures. However, upon entering the job market, they often find that their schooling has little relevance to market needs. Knowledge and skills won by hard work in school—for example, a fluency in other languages or a detailed knowledge of Western philosophy or of modern dance—cannot, without further extensive training, produce a living wage.[16] By and large, then, workers are unsure not only of where they are going, but of how best to earn a living in the meantime.

It is within this psychological context that one should understand workers' drift into the First Bank of Columbia. People who are drifting are in an especially disadvantageous personal position when they enter the labor market. Uncertain of where they are going or of what they can do, they often feel that they must take what they can get. This feeling is linked with a fear of rejection in the job-hunting process. Even under the best occupational conditions—for example, in professional work—job-hunting can be a painful process precisely because it involves the fear of rejection. Professionals, however, can buttress themselves against rejection because they have a reasonably clear knowledge of their future direction and of their own skills. Moreover, while painful when it occurs, rejection can often be blamed on conditions beyond personal control, such as a glut of Ph.D.s in a particular field. Such accounts are not available to people who are drifting. For them, rejection while job-hunting, or indeed, the very fear of rejection, deepens their self-doubt. They are quite ready, therefore, to join a large organization like the First Bank of Columbia either specifically to assuage that doubt or, as in most cases, to take what is at hand when accident or coincidence throws a job their way.

Workers in the most vulnerable subjective situations—in this study, usually older women returning to work—often turn to the bank by explicit design when they decide to look for a job. Despite their explicit intentions, this turn to the bank is part of the pattern of drift because it is rooted in their self-doubt about their futures and about their skills. These workers perceive the First Bank of Columbia as a large organization which hires unskilled workers and where even they can get a job without fear of rejection. An older clerk exemplifies this attitude:

I knew that at my age I might have trouble coming to work, but that's why I came to the First Bank of Columbia since I knew that they hire anyone.

Here personal self-doubt teams with aspects of an organization's image and together they produce an impetus for persons to drift into the organization. The bank's high turnover rate among bank clerks,[17] which is well-known by workers even before they come to the bank, seems to be one factor promising continual hiring. Even more important is the commonplace notion that "the bank hires people right off the streets," an idea related to workers' perceptions of the unskilled character of the bank's rationalized work structure. While the bank actually has some defined criteria for hiring clerks,[18] most people feel that anyone can do the work and, for those worried about their lack of skills, this is often a reason for coming to the bank.

Most workers, however, drift into their bank jobs not by design but, according to their own explanations, by accident or coincidence. Both perspectives reflect the lack of direction and the uncertainty about one's abilities which make up the pattern of drift. The less typical explanation for taking a bank job is to attribute it to accident. In a striking example of this, a young college graduate describes how she became a secretary in one of the bank's downtown branches:

I had come into the city with my mother to do some shopping and to pick up some job application forms from the Civil Service Center down the street. Then I came into this branch to cash a check, and the teller saw me carrying the forms and asked if I wanted a job. I said I was looking, and he told me to talk to the

·operations officer, and I did; and the officer asked me if I had gone to college, and then she hired me in two minutes. I had never worked a day in my life.

When workers do not know what they want, what they are looking for, or what they can do, they will often take jobs that fortuitously present themselves, whatever they are, rather than look further. Similarly, but even more typically, are attributions of bank jobs to coincidence. The most common form of this explanation is when workers credit their jobs to their acquaintance with or relationship to someone who knows of a job opening. For instance, a utility clerk:

How did I get into the bank? Well, I was home between jobs and my sister was working here, and one day she came home and asked if I would be interested in a job in this office. So I came and took it thinking I would only have it as a temporary thing, but I stayed.

Probably, a great number of jobs in the nation's economy are allocated by just such informal connections. However, what is important here is workers' implicit stress on their passivity either in the job-hunting process or in the actual obtaining of the bank job or both. Through some connection in another sphere of their lives, the job happens to them or, in a common phrase, they "fall into" the job. A bookkeeper describes how she took what coincidence provided while she was looking for a job:

[A woman in the same department] lives in my neighborhood, and she knew I was looking for something; and then this desk came open and she talked to [the supervisor]. That's how I got the job.

Again, a secretary tells how a coincidence determined the pattern of most of her life:

How did I come to the First Bank of Columbia? Well, my sister [who was working at the bank] pulled me out of bed one morning and said, "Come on, you're going to work." Now I've been here for, let's see, 35 years.

Passivity in the market and the sense of personal drift which underpins it create psychological states where it is simply *easier* for workers, in the absence of self-defined alternatives, to take what comes along. Giant organizations like the First Bank of Columbia, because of their size and constant manpower needs, and, even more simply, because they are always there, are often the beneficiaries of such personal quandaries.

References

1. For a treatment of the taken-for-granted quality of everyday life, see Peter Berger and Thomas Luckmann, *The Social Construction of Reality* (Garden City, New York: Doubleday, 1967), pp. 19–28. Also, Alfred Schütz, "On Multiple Realities," *Collected Papers I: The Problem of Social Reality* (The Hague: Martin Nijhoff, 1962), pp. 208 and 229.

2. Nancy Morse and Robert Weiss, "The Function and Meaning of Work and the Job," *American Sociological Review*, 20 (April 1955), 191–198.

3. See Philip Slater, *The Pursuit of Loneliness* (Boston: Beacon Press, 1970) for a general discussion of American individualism.

4. Karl Polanyi, *The Great Transformation* (Boston: Beacon Press, 1944), especially pp. 68–76.

5. See, for example, the studies of Japanese workers and their relationship to their corporation by James C. Abegglen, *The Japanese Factory* (Glencoe, Illinois: Free Press,

1958) and especially Thomas P. Rohlen, *For Harmony and Strength: Japanese White-Collar Organization in Anthropological Perspective* (Berkeley: Univ. of California Press, 1974).

6. For an interesting treatment of this discrepancy in the higher reaches of bureaucratic organizations, see Joseph Bensman and Arthur J. Vidich, *The New American Society* (Chicago: Quadrangle, 1971), pp. 44–60.

7. See, for example, Leonard Goodwin, *Do the Poor Want to Work?* (Washington, D.C.: Brookings Institution, 1972). In his study, Goodwin shows that welfare recipients' attitudes toward work are basically the same as those of the middle class.

8. Stanford Lyman and Marvin Scott, "On the Time Track," *A Sociology of the Absurd* (New York: Appleton-Century-Crofts, 1970), pp. 189-212.

9. C. Wright Mills, "The Unity of Work and Leisure," in *Power, Politics and People*, edited by Irving L. Horowitz (New York: Oxford Univ. Press, 1967), pp. 347–352.

10. Sebastian DeGrazia, *Of Time, Work and Leisure* (Garden City, New York: Doubleday, 1964), pp. 9-130. The distinction which DeGrazia makes and richly develops between the leisure and free time is important. Briefly, free time is time away from work, while leisure is pursuit of an activity for its own sake. DeGrazia argues quite convincingly that, while people in modern society have considerable amounts of free time, they know little leisure.

11. For some comparative data on this point, see Eugene Friedmann and Robert J. Havighurst, *The Meaning of Work and Retirement* (Chicago: Univ. of Chicago Press, 1954), especially pp. 29 and 173. In this study, keeping busy was the most important meaning of work for steelworkers whom they studied, and a significant meaning for coal miners, skilled craftsmen, salespeople, and even physicians.

12. This is not true, of course, for the many industrial workers who do shift work or for those in occupations which require night work. One of the most difficult aspects of such work is precisely its de-synchronizing quality. For a wonderfully stated example of this experience see Tom Nairn, "The Nightwatchman," *Work: Twenty Personal Accounts*, edited by Ronald Fraser (Harmondsworth, England: Penguin, 1968), pp. 34–54.

13. Lyman and Scott, "On the Time Track," p. 201.

14. With a different emphasis, Richard Sennett and Jonathan Cobb use the notion of sacrifice to explain a good portion of their material on blue-collar workers in Boston. See *The Hidden Injuries of Class* (New York: Random House, 1973), pp. 119-150.

15. For a treatment of the development of the organizational shape of our labor market, see Robert Presthus, *The Organizational Society* (New York: A. Knopf, 1962), pp. 59–92.

16. As it happens, even those *with* further extensive training are now having serious problems finding work matching their skills. See Ivar Berg, *Education and Jobs: The Great Training Robbery* (New York: Praeger, 1970).

17. Although during 1973, the year field work for this study was done, clerical turnover dropped to 20% per annum because of the onset of the recession, the average for the few preceding years was 33%.

18. Based on observation, some discussions with management, and the few statistics that are available, the following picture of the bank's image of desired clerical workers can be constructed. The bank wants fairly skilled workers who are competent and friendly enough to provide the efficient customer services which are necessary for branch success. However, it also wants workers without too much work experience because people must fit into its standardized work structure. In metropolitan areas, the bank rejects about 40% of the applicants for branch clerical jobs because they lack requisite skills and about 50% because they are overqualified. The remaining 10% of the applicants, whom the bank hires, are increasingly likely to belong to at least one of three categories: female, foreign-born, or minority groups. Because of independent factors in the labor market, those hired are also likely to be fairly educated, that is, with at least a high school degree. The job opportunities open to most of those whom the bank hires are limited. If these workers were not at the bank, it is very likely that they would be employed at a similar level in another large bureaucratic organization. Their relative immobility in the labor market, although personally disadvantageous, is an organizational benefit because it gives the bank the basis for some stability in its workforce. As a final note, it would be incorrect to apply Argyris's model of organizational selection, as developed in *Organization of a Bank* (New Haven: Labor and Management Center, Yale Univ., 1954), especially pp. 70–80, to the hiring process in First Bank of Columbia branches. In Argyris's study, selection of workers was highly centralized in the hands of two individuals, both of whom had a well-developed image of the "right type" of worker they desired for their organization. In the First Bank of Columbia, hiring takes place at the individual branch level; this means that hundreds of managers are involved in hiring decisions. The only criteria for selection which seem to be in general use are those described earlier.

6 The Organizational Context: Security

Large bureaucratic organizations like the First Bank of Columbia offer people more than a place to earn a living or to contain personal drift. They also present people with a context of meaning in which their everyday job experiences can be linked to larger legitimating themes for work which are extant in the social structure as a whole. Large organizations both reflect and shape general socio-cultural frameworks of meanings regarding work. At the same time, they condition workers' legitimations for work either by directly shaping them or by providing the specific material out of which workers, themselves acting with knowledge of what is socially valued, can fashion their own motives for what they do.

One of the principal motives for work among First Bank of Columbia workers, and very likely among many workers in other large organizations, is security. An individual's emphasis on security can be rooted in any number of perceptions: images of a desired predictable future, counter-images of a shaky labor market, or images of desired comfort in one's everyday situations. Whatever the personal initiating reasons for a focus on security, in our society the organization most often becomes the locus where people feel security can be obtained.[1] One reason for this is that organizations—particularly banks—vie with each other in projecting both to the public and to their employees images of rock-like stability in a troubled world.[2] Even the predictable sameness of routinized work seems dependable to many people. Further, and most important, many organizations are thought to structure relationships with their workers to provide them with a sense of security. In short, individual desires for security, whatever their sources, mesh with perceptions of organizational dependability and make the ideas of security and organization almost synonymous.

This chapter examines both the meanings bank workers give to security and how these meanings are related to the bank's organizational structure. The root meaning of security here, as one would expect, is financial surety. There is, however, another level of meaning apparent in workers' interviews—namely, that workers come to feel comfortable with their work and with their work situations. Since this second aspect of security is, to some extent, bound up with the same psychological factors which underpin the phenomenon of drift treated in the last chapter, it is appropriate to begin the examination of security here.

The Security of Being Comfortable

Workers who drift into a large organization like the bank will often stay in their jobs for considerable periods despite the intrinsic problems they experience in them. A major reason for this, though this is largely an unintended consequence of bureaucratic standardization, is that organizations provide people with known, relatively predictable contexts for work. Many workers come to feel a kind of comfort in their situations and experience psychological inertia. Although the comfort workers feel is riven with ambivalence, it is nonetheless a stabilizing and legitimating motive for continuing in their particular jobs. Essentially, the feeling of comfort is based on workers' familiarity, first, with their jobs and, second, with their social environments at work.

A SENSE OF COMPETENCE AND EMOTIONAL SECURITY

Workers like to feel that they know what they are doing. A sense of competence in work, even in work defined by the workers as simple, is important to them. The ability to do a job and to do it right becomes a prized aspect of many workers' occupational self-images. A new accounts clerk says:

I know what I'm doing here. I know what's required and I know how to do it.

Competence brings many a sense of comfort. For instance, a general ledger clerk:

I know my desk, and I'm comfortable here.

However, workers usually assert their claims of competence and of concomitant comfort in very ambivalent contexts. To some extent, the security and comfort which a sense of competence affords mitigate negative aspects of work—chiefly boredom or the feeling that their work is not challenging. A boarding clerk:

My main gripes? Supervision and, you know, my job itself. I guess I like my work. I mean it's boring but there's nothing I can't handle. To me it's a breeze. Basically, all the jobs here are easy. Doesn't take much knowledge.

Knowledge of the ability to perform both accounts for the lack of enjoyment or stimulation in work and partially substitutes for these lacks. This seems particularly true when workers glean reinforcement of their sense of competence by being of service to others and when their

competence is publicly validated. Consider, for example, the remarks of
a teller:

I'm sick of being a teller. I don't know what else to do though. I'm *sick* of being a
teller. . . .

[much later in her interview:]

I think that I'm a good worker. I'm always busy. I'm a pretty good teller. . . .
People come up and ask me questions, and I counsel them on what to do. If I help
a person, I don't feel so dumb. I feel that I know something.

Recognition for competence in work can at least partially restore a
damaged sense of self. But this is probably true only in the short run. Over
a longer period of time, workers' reliance on motives of competence in
work which they dislike seems to erode, rather than continue to produce,
genuine emotional security. What emerges instead may be called a "false
security" of the known, a fearful, paralyzing inertia which prolongs, and
thereby intensifies, negative work experiences. An auditing clerk, who
finds her work very problematic, typifies this kind of entrapment:

Why do I continue? Maybe I'm afraid. I don't like what I'm doing, but I know how
to do it. I don't know if I would want to go into something else. In a way, I've
gotten into a rut—false security.

Knowledge of competence in work, even work which is disliked, often
ties people to that work. While such knowledge is, on one hand, an
antidote for self-doubt and fears about one's abilities and future, it can
also simultaneously bind workers to a less than satisfactory present.

BECOMING SOCIALLY COMFORTABLE

In a complementary fashion but to a somewhat lesser extent, knowledge
of the social environment of the workplace is also, for many workers, a
source of emotional security and a motive for continuing work in a given
organization. Workers' assertions of being socially comfortable are somewhat paradoxical, given the general experiences of isolation and of
concomitant friction that run through the data. However, knowledge of a
social situation, however difficult the relationships it contains, makes the
situation at least tolerable. A teller, whose interview record fully evidences the complex social tensions that are the rule in bank branches,
says:

But I don't want to transfer really. I'm comfortable here. I know everybody.

Knowledge of other people does not necessarily imply liking them. In
work situations, a simple knowledge of people, which helps to make them
somewhat predictable, seems sufficient for most workers. Moreover, it
takes time to achieve that knowledge. Social knowledge of and, even
more, social acceptance into a workplace are hard won results of a period
of socialization. The prospect of going through a similarly difficult
period somewhere else often deters people from leaving a situation. For
example, a secretary:

For a new person coming in [the bank], it's an easy, quick way of getting a job. What happens later—well, it's laziness. It's not beneficial for me to stay on one level, but. . . . You know, about this laziness thing or being comfortable. It's like— well, when you go to any job, there's about two months of not being recognized as an employee at the place. At least in [this large city]. I mean, you know, what are the chances of new employees staying in a town like this? We won't even recognize you until we know that you're going to stay for awhile. You go into a new job, and you don't know people. You don't *want* to know the people, and they don't know you. Lunches and breaks are awkward.

People entering metropolitan workplaces often feel the tensions of being total strangers. The urban rootlessness of people in our mobile society makes many workers erect defensive barriers against newcomers; while these are never entirely removed, they make the early days of employment particularly difficult. In addition, a new worker must prove herself to others through her work as one basis for acceptance. Gaining a personal sense of competence, important in itself as seen earlier, thus becomes linked with social evaluations of one's work. A new accounts clerk:

When you don't know your job, every day you wake up and there's this sickening feeling that you don't know what you're doing. . . . In a new job, you don't know how competent they think you are, and you have to prove yourself to a whole set —a new set of people. You feel like you're on probation. . . . I know I respond that way to people when they first come in.

Workers' knowledge that fellow workers accept them both as individuals and as workers is significant to them. The discomfort of achieving that acceptance is remembered and is negatively compared with present comfort. Together with their achieved understanding of the social complexities of the workplace, workers' very sense that they have become a part of that workplace offers them a stabilizing, if ambiguous, emotional security.

The bank's organizational apparatus plays only an indirect role in the emergence of workers' sense of comfort both in their tasks and in their social situations. As already suggested, the bank's standardization both of work and of social appearances, though done with different intents, creates a framework within which some clerks can clearly perceive both work and social expectations, and generally understand how to act upon them. The bank's major contribution to whatever sense of comfort workers have is its structure and consequent predictability. This is confirmed in a negative way by the general uneasiness clerks manifest when new rationalizing techniques are introduced into branches. While on one level this uneasiness points to an almost instinctive wariness people in large organizations seem to develop towards organizational innovations, it also indicates annoyance at disruption of routines.

In the social realm too, the bank's unwitting contribution to the development of workers' emotional security motives is in providing a framework of delineated rules where social expectations achieve a degree of stability. When the bank oversteps this rudimentary function and tries deliberately to encourage belongingness or a sense of community, it often meets with scorn and, in some areas, resistance. The latter response is most evident in many workers' refusal to participate, even under great pressure, in the BankColumbiaClub, the bank's social organization. From the bank's perspective, this club encourages increased socializing among employees outside of work and, through such social ties, aims at strengthening people's ties to the bank. Many workers, however, view the bank's efforts here as encroachment. A machine operator's comments illustrate this sentiment:

They have a BankColumbiaClub where they try to push the socializing. If you're forced to be with people for five days, why should you spend your weekend with them? At the other branch where I worked, they practically *forced* you to join. They want to control your entire life if you let them. I want this job just as a part of my life which I can forget after I leave here.

Some bureaucratic work organizations have, it seems, a nearly totalizing thrust in their relationships with their workers.[3] In the bank, this tendency depends to some extent on the attachment of local managers to the organization and their consequent zealousness. Paradoxically, while this tendency aims to strengthen individual ties to the organization and while it is successful in doing so with some workers, it seems on the whole to disrupt the patterns of stability and consequent motives of emotional security which workers develop out of even troublesome work situations.

The Meaning of Financial Security

Motives of financial security underpin workers' sense of comfort at work and are also, in their own right, primary legitimations for work. Any sense of competence or of social comfort which workers get from their jobs would have little meaning unless they felt sure that those jobs and their income were there to stay. The reliability of a job is a key factor in shaping workers' views of their work. Further, at least for some, the sense of building financial security for the future through some of the bank's employee benefit programs is an important aspect of feeling secure.

THE SECURITY OF A STEADY JOB

Bank workers consider their jobs steady ones, and this perception becomes an important basis for their legitimations of what they do.[4] A payroll clerk exemplifies this:

The only good thing the bank offers you is *security.* You know that you won't get laid off. I really feel the need for security in a job. It's important to have a job I know I can depend on.

The emphasis on the reliability of bank work is especially marked when unemployment is high or when workers' general financial situations are shaky, a fairly common occurrence among the married workers interviewed because many of their spouses are wage-earners in low-grade or middle-grade service or blue-collar occupations. For instance, an insurance clerk says:

I can't stand coming here. I used to like it. But I don't have much choice 'cause we need the money. My husband is a [gas] station attendant. He's more liable to get laid off than I am, especially with the gas shortage. . . . What do I like about my job? Well, you know that the bank is more or less a steady job. I like to know you're always going to get a salary—even if it's low.

A certainty of continued employment and income becomes, in some circumstances, a substitute for enjoyable work or, indeed, for an income that workers consider fair.

This last point is particularly interesting since the very reliability of workers' pay seems to create for many a psychological inertia similar to the paralysis that being comfortable at work can produce. Almost all bank workers resent the amount of their pay, a subject which receives detailed treatment later. But the reliability of income, however low, allows people to set parameters in their lives within which they can balance their expectations. A utility clerk, adopting the role of observer in discussing another worker, exemplifies this; his attribution of motives reflects both his own and a more widely held perspective:

You know H. who has been here for 16 years? How could she do that desk for all those years without going off the deep end? But the financial security is there. I guess it's because people know that they can live within their salaries. They know their job; it's secure, and, as long as they have it, they're happy.

Steady income becomes a basis for establishing stability; other expectations get trimmed to fit that stable framework. Even among younger single workers, the security of having a steady salary defined somehow as adequate is reason enough to avoid forays into insecure situations, even though those situations might eventually lead to more satisfactory work. A young teller, who dreams of becoming a commercial artist, says:

People say that if you want something badly enough you would go to any extent to get it. No matter how long or how hard. I don't think that. I think that depends on how strong a person is. . . . It could be a fear of failure which keeps me from going all out. It could be that I've never earned as much money as I am now, and I'm not willing to sacrifice that to pursue something which I really want to do.

As long as it meets defined needs, steady money creates inertia and even causes some to mortgage a desired future for a kind of present security. The strength of this particular security milieu and of its concomitant psychological inertia can perhaps best be understood from the example of a part-time worker whose general, stated world outlook is radically different from that of other workers. Precisely because his stated beliefs are antithetical to the situation in which he finds himself, his experience constitutes a paradigmatic instance of how a regular income can shape and alter people's perceptions of themselves and of their work:

I see myself as a Communist-Anarchist and I work for and with other people with part of my life. . . . But the meaning of my work here is money.
. . . I took the job because I needed work badly. I had been looking for five months and I could find nothing. Finally, somewhere in there, I decided that I would work for whoever would hire me and that I would put in a good day's work for the pay.

... There's a lot of fear here—a fear of change. ... In a way I can understand it. I try to watch myself while I'm working and the most frightening thing is the beginning of satisfaction. Imagine that? Here I am putting in six hours of my day doing something I don't believe in and I'm not having any revulsion about it. Mostly, it's money and the fact that there's not too much else I could be doing.

[Two weeks later. Question: I've noticed that you have been staying later regularly—have you started working seven hours a day?]

Yes, and [patting his pocket] I just got my first paycheck reflecting that work. I think I may keep it up.

Particularly during a tight labor market, job and income security become crucial to people. Moreover, a steady income not only encourages external compliance with standards of work performance, but it also subtly shapes and alters people's perceptions of what they do. Steady income is often the broker of compromise not only between oneself and one's future, but also between oneself and one's deeply-held personal values. When work brings in steady income, most people can find a way to perform that work readily, if not eagerly.

Workers' images of the reliability of their branch jobs sharply clash with the technological realities determining the bank's future direction. Computerization, introduced into branch banking in the late 1950's, tends towards complete automation of branch work processes[5] which are presently, as seen earlier, labor-intensive. The nation's large commercial banks are, in fact, already planning electronic monetary transfer systems which, if successfully implemented, will effectively eliminate the need for cash, either in currency or in checks.[6] Such a development will drastically reduce the number of branch workers needed to process materials, at least of unskilled workers without backgrounds in electronic technology. Some banks are already experimenting with fully automated tellers as an interim step between the present labor-intensive system and the future technology. An examination of technological developments already underway suggests that the future of work in branch banking will be precarious rather than secure.[7] At the First Bank of Columbia, no authorities openly discuss with workers the bank's technological direction. Few workers, despite a generally sharp awareness of the present importance of computers to the bank, examine the latent implications of technology as it relates to their future employment. In the resulting factual void, workers base their assertions of job reliability on tautological perceptions of the banking industry.

Essentially, workers consider their branch jobs secure because the banking industry itself is perceived to be secure. The very size of the First Bank of Columbia, a prime representative of the industry, is for many a source of comfort. Such a large organization will, it is felt, always be around and will always need people. Because of its size, the First Bank of Columbia seems to some workers to be functionally indispensable to the American economic system; this is a perspective shared, and indeed fostered, by many bank officers. If the bank were to collapse, its demise would signal an economic apocalypse, and the personal experience of unemployment would, at least, be eased by the erasure of all social distinctions. In sorting out a personal quandary, a utility clerk links personal security with all of these elements:

I don't even know why I'm working here. I just don't know why. I know I wasn't put here on earth to become a banker. . . . There's too much security here. You know that the bank is never going to fold and, if it does fold, everything else is going to fold too. So people put up with low pay because of the security. . . . I think the security thing is very important. [People] know that their job is secure and that the bank will never fold and, if it does fold, everyone will be out of a job and they'll all be pushing apples on the corner. Everyone will be the same.

In this view, individual and organizational fates are intertwined, although hardly in a reciprocal way. Personal security and, indeed, long-run social respectability become, at least subjectively, guaranteed by bureaucratic permanence and concomitant economic indispensability. Despite the problems and consequent ambivalence they experience, many people feel that, in an age marked by economic precariousness, there is no individual security outside the organization.

BENEFIT PROGRAMS AS A CONTEXT FOR SECURITY MOTIVES

While job reliability is the most important aspect of financial security for most workers, the key parts of the bank's employee benefit package are also significant in shaping many people's motives for work and particularly for continuing with the bank. The bank has two kinds of benefit programs, which may be differentiated as standard benefits and long-term benefits. Standard benefits, which are not principally at issue here, include programs like a Health Insurance Plan and a Sick Leave Plan. These benefits are generally indistinguishable from those found in most organizations and are considered necessary to attract and hold workers. In the bank, standard benefits are most notable, from workers' perspectives, for their leanness. Long-term benefits are another matter. A careful examination of all the bank's literature related to employee benefits and, more important, interviews with managers involved in the administration of these programs suggest that the bank's strategy in offering long-term benefits is to tie workers to the bank for long periods of time while spending as little money as possible. This is the strategy both for those programs geared to eliciting security motives and those directed towards stimulating consumption desires. The latter programs—which consist principally of giving workers special loan and credit card interest rates— are considered later when the relationships between workers' consumption desires and their work are analyzed. The focus here is on those long-term benefit programs which promise workers some kind of financial advantage in return for and in proportion to longevity of service. We may call these security benefits. Before exploring the meanings workers give to these benefits, it will be helpful to indicate the structure and purpose of these programs from the bank's perspective, since the bank's strategy here affects workers' experiences. The paradigm of the bank's approach to security benefits is the Estate Plan, a profit-sharing program.

The Estate Plan is explicitly designed to encourage workers to stay with the bank for long periods. Although the bank enrolls the worker in this plan after three complete years of full-time employment, she will not gain any benefits from it unless she stays with the bank for at least five full years. Even after fulfilling this service time requirement, the worker does not receive any of her earned returns from the plan before quitting or retiring. Rather, beginning with the worker's fourth year and for each subsequent year that she stays with the bank, she accumulates units—one unit for each completed year of service, and one unit for every $100 of regular annual salary. These individually earned units are multiplied by a measure of the Estate Plan called the annual unit-value to obtain the sum annually credited to each worker's individual account. The unit-value itself is a ratio: the total number of dollars allocated to the Estate Plan for the year divided by the total number of units earned by all employees for the year. The money allocated to the plan each year buys bank stocks for a trust fund and comes from three sources—an annual bank contribution of 4 percent of its consolidated net earnings; reversions to the fund from workers who failed to serve the prescribed number of years necessary to receive their full share; and any earnings or dividends on shares already held in the trust fund. From her fourth year of employment on, the worker is credited with funds, in the form of bank stocks, proportionate to her annual income and years of service and to the total amount available in the plan. These funds accumulate in her individual account until she leaves the bank. However, the bank structures a timetable which allots to workers only a fraction of their earned share unless they complete a full 15 years of service in the bank. Table 2 indicates the number of years a worker must complete to receive a given percentage of her earned share. Thus, for example, a worker leaving at the end of nine years of service gets only 45 percent of whatever is in her account; the remainder reverts to the trust fund. On the other hand, a worker remaining with the bank for 15 years gets her full earned share for all years of service, beginning with the fourth year. An employee staying beyond 15 years continues to accumulate money, and is assured of eventually receiving all of it.

The Estate Plan therefore tries to attract long-term service through the graduated sharing of available funds.[8] Yet, the plan's actual monetary value to the worker is not large, particularly for clerks whose base salaries are low. As a rule of thumb, the annual dollar value to the employee totals about 5 percent of her annual income. Thus, a clerk whose average annual salary for her fourth to fifteenth year is $6,600 would have about $330 per year set aside for her, or an accumulated total of $4,950 at the end of her fifteenth year. Even given compounding effects or splits in the bank's stock, both of which would raise this amount, the total is small and is taxable when withdrawn. Moreover, the actual value to each worker decreases steadily since the unit-value, the key multiplier in the plan, slips each year.[9]

The Estate Plan then combines all the elements which, from the bank's perspective, constitute a good benefit program which appeals to security

Table 2

Estate Plan - Years of Service and
Percentages of Earned Share Alloted

Calendar Years of Service	% of Earned Share Alloted
5	25
6	30
7	35
8	40
9	45
10	50
11	60
12	70
13	80
14	90
15	100

motives.[10] The program is designed to encourage people to stay with the bank. The longer people stay with an organization, the harder it becomes to leave, not least because, in the bank, it may mean sacrificing part of what one has already rightfully earned. In addition, the more time and labor people invest in any organization, the greater the likelihood that they will identify at least an aspect of their personal fate with that of the organization. By gearing workers' monetary rewards to the bank's profits, the Estate Plan tries to link individual and corporate well-being. Finally, the plan costs the bank very little, but—at least for some workers—conveys the illusion of much larger benefits than actually exist. The other security benefits offered by the bank incorporate one or another of these elements. For instance, the Retirement Plan requires an employee to have at least 10 consecutive years of full-time salaried service at the age of retirement to receive one-half of the average of her five highest consecutive annual salaries. There is a bonus of a few hundred dollars for service beyond 25 years. The Educational Benefits Fund pays for college courses related to banking upon approval by bank authorities, but pays only up to $500 per year which, with the rising cost of education, assures the bank of several years of service from anyone who seriously pursues a degree through this plan. A final example is a fully-paid life insurance policy for workers, issued by a wholly-owned subsidiary of the bank, which lasts as long as a worker stays with the bank. In a word, while keeping costs low, the bank's security benefits are structured to encourage people to predicate personal security on their tenure with the organization.

ADJUSTMENT TO THE ORGANIZATION AND BUILDING SECURITY

Workers' experiences of the bank's security benefits and their subsequent assertions of security motives vary with their ages and with the length of time they have spent with the bank.

Younger workers new to the bank, though very concerned with job security, pay little attention to the bank's security benefits. With the exception of a few programs like the Educational Benefits Fund, younger workers see no tangible payoff from security benefits since most require longevity of service before workers are even eligible for them. As a result, younger workers are more concerned with standard benefits which are immediately accessible to them, in particular, with sick leave and health benefits. However, their experiences of these programs are principally negative since, wherever longevity of service cannot be secured in return, the bank seems most concerned with keeping costs low. A young teller comments on the bank's Sick Leave Plan:

The way it works is that after you've been at the bank for six months, you're allowed one day a month sick leave each month—that's 12 days a year. But if you're out that much, you're in trouble. They're either going to give you a stiff talking to or you're out the door. They think six days a year is too much.

Again, a young auditing clerk discusses benefits in general and the bank's Health Care Program in particular:

Benefits? They're only good for somebody who is here for a long time. The medical benefits are that $100 deductible for both medical and dental care, and you pay half of the premiums anyway. But you know it doesn't cover pregnancy, and, when we had the baby, we had to cover *all* the cost—$2,000. I had a Caesarian operation and that's a pretty complicated operation, and the insurance policy is supposed to take care of complicated operations; but they said it didn't, and we had to pay the whole amount.

Younger workers new to the bank learn early that large corporations give only when they get something in return. Although these workers are aware of potential advantages of security benefits which accrue with longevity of service, they do not personally experience those advantages. Instead, they experience an organizational closeness when it comes to time and money that is scarcely conducive to underpinning security motives for work.

As workers stay with the bank, however, security motives, based on the growing advantages of security benefit programs, become increasingly important in legitimating work. There are different stages in the development of these motives. Following disillusionment about the inadequacy of programs accessible to them, many younger workers undergo a period of adjusting to the organizational environment. This adjustment is essentially a change of perspective which itself can result from any of several factors—for example, a feeling of ego-investment because of time spent or a simple redefinition of one's situation because of habituation. Although workers' job situations remain very problematic, they learn to live with them more easily. The important point is that security benefits mediate this process of adjustment by providing tangible rewards at given stages of a person's work career which facilitate this alteration of perspective. A secretary who has been with the bank for seven years comments:

Am I satisfied with my work? It's a job—just that. How many people do you know that are really *into* work? I mean, there just aren't that many jobs around that you can get really excited about. So, yes, I'm satisfied but—I don't make it into a big deal. Like when people try to make their corporation into the best in the world. They're all trying to make it special. Like people who have been here for 20 years. They have to believe it because they spend so much time with it. It's—well, people work longer and longer for the bank, and their attitudes change. When I first started, people would sit at lunch and really *cut down* the bank. But after three years, you have the stock purchase plan and it sort of eases the pain. And then there's something you get at five years—it's a retirement fund. It's called the Estate Plan. You get a certain part of it if you leave. This is a good plan, but to a new employee, it doesn't mean much. But after you've been here for awhile, it begins to look better and better.

The meaning of security benefits changes as workers gain a stake in the programs; in turn, these benefits bolster redefinitions of the work experience, making difficult situations at least more tolerable.

Workers undergoing such an adjustment of perspectives regularly voice a set of two accounts which bolsters their increasingly altered views. In the first account, workers appeal to potential loss to justify staying with a situation experienced as unsatisfactory: leaving the situation would mean the loss of everything already earned. The second account reinforces the first with a shift in emphasis: appealing to the fear of new beginnings in consideration of gains already made. A teller justifies continuing her job:

You know, I'm embarrassed to tell people how much I make at the bank. People in other jobs get $700 to $800 a month. I could get something like that [somewhere else]. But I just hate to lose all my benefits, my seniority. I've only got a year to go and I get three weeks vacation.... I've been here *four* years and I'm really high up in seniority. If I had to go someplace else, I'd have to start all over again.

The revulsion against losing what one has worked for and the fear of starting from scratch both account for and facilitate the reluctant integration of workers into the bank's organizational structure. The bank's Estate Plan is often the focus of workers' statement of the revulsion against loss. The fear of starting from scratch seems more related to workers' perceptions that, as long as they remain at the clerical level, even a change of jobs would not greatly improve their situations, neither regarding working conditions nor regarding benefits. Again, a worker with the bank for 11 years states:

You know, the big thing that keeps me here is that I hate the idea of losing my full share of the Estate Plan. If I left now, I'd only get 60 percent of what I've put into the thing, of what I've earned. But if I stay for four more years, I get my full share. Besides, until I finish school, there's no chance of getting a better job anyway and most places don't have any better programs than the bank. I'd lose what I have, and I'd have to start the same type of thing all over again.

In addition, then, to offering workers rewards which encourage their subjective adjustment to the organization, graduated security programs like the Estate Plan also stimulate anxiety, a revulsion against potential loss, which becomes an added reason for staying with the bank. The development of security motives for work based on benefit programs is thus often closely linked with feelings of insecurity, also partially shaped by the organization.

The final stage in workers' development of security motives based on benefits is a focus, particularly among older workers, on "building security" against images of uncertainty and even of jeopardy in old age. Workers' assertions of this motive are again most often laced with accounts. On one hand, working for security justifies experiences of unsettling self-appraisals emerging from work. On the other hand, desires for security are positively asserted as necessary concerns as one grows older. Although in some ways a special case because of his declassed status and because of his relatively short tenure at the bank for his age, a foreign-born clerk nonetheless typifies how the idea of building security accounts for deep uneasiness and simultaneously offers a positive rationale for work:

I'm not unhappy, but—the people are very good here—but I have a personal regret because the large experience and background which I've got is totally wasted. At home, in my business, I would travel to Japan and deal with all the big companies. I have travelled very widely. I can get along with any nationality or class of people at any level. And I feel that I could be doing a lot more meaningful work. Do you know what I mean? . . . I wouldn't change now though. At my age—51 years— four years service is something. Building up security. If I moved now, I'll only have four years service. In this country, a man can't live on social security. . . . The security is important; even though banks don't pay much, they offer you that.

Building security means erecting retaining walls around oneself in the present and fashioning a sure haven in an uncertain society for the future.

ALTERNATE PERSPECTIVES ON SECURITY BENEFITS

There are two worker perspectives about security benefits which vary from the general picture drawn in the foregoing sections. The first of these is really a matter of emphasis and tone; the second represents a quite different experience. In both cases, they are the views of older workers.

In discussing security benefits, a few older workers adopt a tone which is quite at variance with the generally moderate, if ambiguous, one already presented. This tone is a markedly zealous celebration of the bank's benefits; it springs from a general identification with the organization not necessarily restricted to older workers. In this view, the organization's benefit programs are unparalleled elsewhere. They become a crucial measure of the bank's generosity to its workers and a principal reason for remaining with the bank. This perspective predictably distorts important details of the benefit programs but, if anything, such alteration of facts heightens its motivating force. A middle-aged clerk, employed in a note department and with the bank for 10 years, illustrates this perspective:

You have terrific benefits at the bank. Just great. The stock sharing plan [Estate Plan] especially. I mean, you have it prorated after you've been with the bank for five years. If you stay for 15 years, you get the whole amount. It must be worth $15,000 to $20,000 by this time. You share *in the profits.* Maybe I'm a little high on that $10,000 to $15,000 estimate, but it's real good. It's prorated on the basis of your salary. If you stay on the teller line the whole time with the bank, then naturally it's going to be lower than somebody on the platform. . . . There are all sorts of other benefits too. The bank really does right by a person. . . . I really get riled up about the First Bank of Columbia benefits. You know, another thing is that these kids coming in can get *free* college courses which the bank pays for if they pass them. They can take whatever they want as long as it benefits them, and it will help the bank because they're more knowledgeable. I mean, what more could you want?

Workers who express such zealous views—and I suggest they can be found in every workplace—have an impact beyond their relatively small numbers because their views generally reflect both published and in-person managerial perspectives. With such tacit authoritative sanction, they are freer to express their ideas than are those workers who might be critical of the bank. It is difficult to ascertain with any exactness the specific effect these workers have on other workers' views of security benefits; however, their zealous enthusiasm and particularly their over-statement of the actual worth of benefits can, it seems, create false impressions among some other workers. Certainly, managers do not make any effort to correct such overstatements. On the whole, however, the net impact of such zealous views is probably most marked as an addition to the general confusion workers already experience in the absence of any independent communal forum where they could hammer out the unclarities of their work experiences.

There are other older workers who see the bank and its benefit programs very differently. Although they are few in number in this study, there are some indications from other research that they represent an important, if still hidden, proportion of older workers,[11] perhaps especial-ly in highly commercial, profit-oriented establishments like the bank. Briefly, their work and organizational experiences have left them bitter and angry. Job security is a central concern for these workers, as with most workers in the bank. However, their age makes them more suscep-tible than others to illness. Therefore, they often link their anxiety about job security to a perceived inadequacy in the bank's benefit programs, particularly those which cover workers' health. Essentially, they experi-ence a lack of organizational concern for their personal well-being. For instance, an auditing clerk with the bank for nearly 30 years and the sole support for an incapacitated husband feels organizational pressure on her rather than support for her during troubling periods of illness:

After all these years with the bank, the greatest and most terrible pressure which I feel is that pressure which they're putting on me because of illness. Last year I had four serious illnesses—one of them because of an accident here at work—and now, all the time, there are subtle innuendoes that I might be fired if I get sick again.

These workers' desire for security remains strong and, in addition to their concern about the felt lack of health benefits, the bank's security benefits are particular objects of their resentment. To a certain extent, these workers still legitimate their work on the basis of these benefits because they desire them. However, their legitimations in this regard are marked by the deepest ambivalence because they perceive the organization not as a munificent donor of security, but rather as an unfriendly, indeed potentially malign force which, given the opportunity, will take away what they feel is rightfully theirs. A 55-year-old analysis clerk, with the bank for 17 years, exemplifies this viewpoint:

Benefits? They're lousy. Like you can't accumulate sick days anymore. Which you can never take anyway. You're allowed one day a month, but if you take that day, you're put on probation. They don't want you to take those days. . . . Also, they want you to quit [your job] sooner so they don't have to pay you the Estate Plan. Everybody says that. Anyone here any length of time tells you this. . . . If I weren't here for so long—so many years—I sure wouldn't stay here. The older you get, the worse they treat you.

Where other people, both younger and the same age as themselves, find bases for security motives and even stimuli to adjust to the organization, these older workers find the security the organization promises largely illusory. Even after they have spent all the time and work necessary to gain that security, they experience in its stead, in the last stretch of their work years, a draining struggle against what they perceive to be an imposed insecurity.

References

1. See, for example, William H. Whyte, Jr., *The Organization Man* (Garden City, N.Y.: Doubleday-Anchor, 1956), pp. 69-85. The classic case where this attitude holds is, of course, in Japan. There, at least among white-collar workers, personal security is seen to be wholly contingent upon the permanent employment system which large organizations have adopted. In fact, the larger the organization, the greater the security and concomitant social status. See Ezra F. Vogel, *Japan's New Middle Class* (Berkeley: Univ. of California Press, 1971), pp. 15-19 and 32-39; also Thomas P. Rohlen, *For Harmony and Strength: Japanese White-Collar Organization in Anthropological Perspective* (Berkeley: University of California Press, 1974), pp. 91-92 and 209-211.

2. Consider, for instance, a typical public statement in a bank brochure urging people to choose the bank for any trust services they desire: "The Bank is never ill, never absent, and never dies. This assures you that your wishes will be carried out without interruption or delay." Again, a very common statement among managerial personnel is, "The bank will always be here."

3. A classic description of this enveloping organizational thrust can be found in Alan Harrington, *Life in the Crystal Palace* (New York: A. Knopf, 1958).

4. Several studies point out that the desire for steady work is characteristic of workers at every level of the labor force. See *Survey of Working Conditions* (Survey Research Center, Univ. of Michigan, 1970), pp. 56 and 58. In *Automobile Workers and the American Dream* (Boston: Beacon Press, 1965), pp. 124–125, Ely Chinoy points out that the workers he interviewed "value a steady job over one that is not steady, even if the latter pays higher wages."

5. See James Vaughan and Avner Porat, *Banking Computer Style* (Englewood Cliffs, N.J.: Prentice-Hall, 1969); and Boris Yavitz, *Automation in Commercial Banking* (New York: Free Press, 1967).

6. For an analysis of completely electronic banking, see Mark J. Flannery and Dwight Jaffee, *The Economic Implications of an Electronic Money Transfer System* (Lexington, Mass.: D. C. Heath, 1973); and William F. Baxter, Paul H. Cootner, and Kenneth E. Scott, *Retail Banking in the Electronic Age: The Law and Economics of Electronic Funds Transfer* (Montclair, N.J.: Allanheld, Osmun & Co., 1977).

7. The potentially precarious future of branch banking work seems to be a growing present reality in other sectors of the white-collar labor force although for different reasons. According to the Bureau of Labor Statistics, white-collar unemployment has jumped 28% between the recession years of 1957 and 1975, so that, as of January 1975, 4.6% of all white-collar workers were unemployed. The causes for this growth are somewhat unclear although it seems that automation, the biggest hazard for bank workers' futures, has thus far played only a minor role in displacing other white-collar workers. Rather, early forced retirements, cost-saving layoffs, and a growing occupational immobility which prevents new positions from opening up are the principal identifiable factors in this new trend. See Peter T. Kilborn, "White-Collar Unemployment: No Drop in Sight," *The New York Times*, February 23, 1975, Business and Finance Section, pp. 1 and 9.

8. When the Estate Plan was instituted in 1950, the bank had an even longer timetable of 25 years, but competitive pressure from similar programs in other banks forced it in 1967 to reduce the schedule to 15 years.

9. The following figures show the progressive slippage in the crucial unit-value of the Estate Plan:

Year	Unit-Value
1950	$13.87
1955	10.55
1960	6.72
1965	4.68
1970	4.60
1973	4.44

According to the bank, the number of staff and the total of salaries have outpaced profits, resulting in a proportionate decrease in the money alloted to the trust fund and a corresponding drop in unit-value. One must accept this explanation, however, with a measure of skepticism since, while the total number of bank branches have doubled since 1950, with a corresponding increase in personnel, the bank's total assets have increased six-fold and its annual rate of profit over the last several years has been a steady 16%, one of the nation's highest for nonindustrial corporations.

10. A great number of industries have similar programs with, it seems, similar purposes. See *1970 Study of Industrial Retirement Plans*, Bankers Trust Company, New York, for a survey of 201 companies involving 7,800,000 employees. The programs surveyed indicate basically the same structural features presented in the foregoing analysis of the bank's Estate Plan.

11. See Daniel J. Barum, *The Final Plateau* (Toronto: Burns and MacEachern, Ltd., 1974) for an interesting discussion of the impact on older workers of the growing lack of job security, inadequate pension plans, and forced retirement in Canada. For a similar discussion of the problems of older workers in the United States, see *Work in America: A Report to the Secretary of Health, Education and Welfare* (Washington, D.C.: Government Printing Office, 1973), pp. 54–61. Also, Zena Smith Blau, *Old Age in a Changing Society* (New York: New Viewpoints, 1973), pp. 134-146. It is interesting to note that even in Japan where the permanent employment system guarantees job security for white-collar workers, most older workers are forced into retirement at the early age of 55 years. As Thomas P. Rohlen's study shows, this results in great personal bitterness and anxiety since it means not only financial insecurity but the loss of one's social circle. See *For Harmony and Strength*, p. 77.

7 The Organizational Context: The Ambiguities of Status and Advancement

Work-related prestige and the opportunity to move higher within an organizational hierarchy are, where they occur, principal motives for work in our society.[1] White-collar workers in particular are concerned with work-derived status, both within and outside the workplace, and with advancement in their organizational worlds.[2] These workers are propertyless and still largely unorganized politically and are consequently dependent upon the large organizations where they make their livings. Such dependence makes these workers particularly susceptible to the status-consciousness and emphasis on advancement which are characteristic of elaborate bureaucratic hierarchies. This chapter examines the status worlds and mobility desires of bank workers, and explores how these influence their legitimations for work.

As with so many other areas of their work lives, bank workers have ambiguous experiences of status and of organizational mobility; the legitimations for work based on these experiences are also ambiguous and tangled. I want to suggest here some guides for understanding this complexity. The last two chapters examined relatively clear-cut motives for working. Following Alfred Schutz's distinction, those motives may be labeled either "in order to" motives or "because" motives.[3] "In order to" motives state a goal—like achieving financial independence, structuring time, or earning security—which is the reason for an action. Action, in this case working, gains purpose and meaning from its goal. "Because" motives do not state a future goal, but explain action by referring to past events in a person's life. Workers' explanations of accidental or coincidental drift into the bank are examples of "because" motives. With important exceptions, workers' motives for work relating to status and organizational mobility do not generally fall into either of these categories. Rather, the motives emerging from these two areas, as well as those

associated with workers' authority relationships, the subject of the following chapter, are best characterized as *supportive, situational,* and
latent reasons for action. This means that most bank workers do not work
primarily or even explicitly for reasons of status or advancement, although some clearly do; rather, claims of status or desires for advancement opportunities, though important, are subsidiary motives for work.
Often, in fact, such motives are implicit legitimations of status or advancement *structures* rather than openly asserted individual claims or
desires. In other words, most bank workers cannot be said to work for or
because of work status or advancement. Rather, they work for or because
of other reasons, but status and advancement, as they emerge from
people's work or work-related experiences, are important secondary,
often implicit, motives for work. These supporting situational motives
have a potential to assume greater significance; for some persons, these
subsidiary motives become primary reasons for working.

There is a paradox here. Why are bank workers' motives for work
based on status and mobility generally secondary when, as indicated
above, data on other white-collar workers suggest the primacy of these
motives? On the whole, the workers of this study are in low-status
positions both in and out of the bank; further, they are not in advantageous positions to achieve organizational mobility whatever their desires
in this regard. Their experiences in the areas of status and advancement
then are deeply problematic and are often framed in very negative terms.
Thus, the motives for work in these areas which workers do assert are,
even more than usual, interlaced with accounts and other stratagems
designed both to neutralize troublesome experiences and to make the
best of what they have.

Clerical Work and Status Outside the Workplace

Since the turn of the century, a traditional concern of social observers has
been the steadily worsening social status of many categories of white-
collar workers. Despite the numerical ascendance of white-collar people
in the labor force, several long-term trends have negatively shaped
the collective social position of most salaried employees, particularly vis-
a-vis the numerically declining class of manual workers. In most literature
on this subject,[4] several themes recur regularly: (1) There has been a
narrowing of the historical wage-gap between salaried workers and
wage-earners and, in many cases, wage-earners have outdistanced white-
collar workers. (2) The rationalization of the office has essentially eradi-
cated actual differences between the work of the majority of white-collar
workers and that of most blue-collar workers; at the lower echelons of the
white-collar world, work is thoroughly mechanized and routinized and
often requires less skill than much blue-collar work. (3) Although white-
collar people maintain the important distinction of wearing street clothes
at work, most blue-collar workers now wear street clothes at least on their
way to and from work, blurring a traditional aspect of social differentia-

tion. Perhaps even more to the point, the mass consumer society erected in capitalist countries since World War II has homogenized the external accoutrements of lifestyles, making, social distinctions outside of work less visible and consequently more ambiguous. (4) Because they are highly unionized, blue-collar workers have far outdistanced their white-collar contemporaries in terms of social power. In fact, the increasing realization by white-collar workers of their precarious social situations is one reason for recent successes in unionization of the office. (5) Finally, the feminization of the lower echelons of white-collar work, especially clerical work, has further reduced the prestige of much white-collar work because of women's lower social status as workers. As long-term histori-cal developments, these trends seem indisputably to have occurred. But, what is the relationship between such historical trends and the conscious experiences of present-day white-collar workers? As Michael Crozier has suggested,[5] these workers do not necessarily possess any consciousness of historical devaluation because they may not have experienced it. In fact, workers' conscious experiences may be quite the opposite of being "proletarianized." The researcher cannot assume the content of people's experiences of work-related prestige; rather, he must discover that content. In the case at issue, bank workers' experiences of work-related prestige outside the workplace vary considerably. There are two dis-cernible variables which shape their perspectives: to some extent, peo-ple's social classes of origin mold their present experiences of work-related social status; more generally, the narrowness or breadth of people's everyday social milieux,[6] shaped by their present class situations, is the key factor.

SOCIAL CLASS, DESIRABLE WORK, AND CLAIMS OF PRESTIGE

In light of their class backgrounds and their present social circles, which both stem from and reinforce those backgrounds, a few bank workers define their jobs as desirable work and consequently claim from them a kind of prestige. Without exception these workers are from the lower working class and are the first in their families to achieve a white-collar position. For them, the classic distinction between manual and non-manual labor is important. White-collar work is considered easy work and, when contrasted with physical labor, desirable work. A clerk who is deeply rooted in the lower working class recounts something of her origins and the girlhood desires which grew out of them:

My father and mother are both laborers. They work in the cane fields in Hawaii on a plantation. . . . Working hard is when you work with your hands. This kind of job that I have [now] is not hard work. It's not as hard as a pineapple cannery. I did that for three summers in Hawaii. I hated it but it was the only kind of work a schoolgirl could get. We worked 11½ to 12 hours a day on the assembly line. . . . I've always wanted to work in an office. . . . When I had business courses in high school, I didn't like it because of the teachers. But still, I had the idea of working in an office. . . . Now I don't think that I want to work here [in the bank] because the salary is low here. But I think that I will still be working in an office.

While not necessarily considered better than manual work, office work does represent an escape from labor that is demonstrably harder. Other workers with similar origins stress that working for a bank is a respectable occupation and one which assures a future of similarly respectable work. It is therefore a basis for authentic prestige claims which seem to be honored in their social circles. For example, a clerk whose parents are also both laborers:

If people ask, I tell them that I'm a new accounts typist and that the process of opening accounts goes through me. People think that it's a good job. They think that I can go somewhere with this job. Most of my friends would like to find out how to work for the First Bank of Columbia because after you work for the bank—there's no question about your references after you've worked for a bank.

Other workers derive prestige from their bank jobs not because of future guarantees of respectability but because they, and apparently their social circles, regard the bank as a celebrity institution from which they can claim and receive a measure of social honor. The daughter of a migrant farm worker and wife of a factory operative:

A lot of people think it's great to work in a bank. It seems—just to be in it—that you work in a *bank*. I mean, it's so famous—especially the First Bank of Columbia.

Depending upon one's class origin and present social situation, then, important organizations and famous names can exert a somewhat magical effect on people. Here, prestige borrowed even on marginal grounds becomes a basis to legitimate work. This seems to be not only an indication of the social forcefulness of institutional fame, but also an index of people's felt and shared sense of social obscurity. Still, whenever social honor can be successfully and authentically claimed—and in the data at hand, this is the case for the workers just treated—it is an important motive for work.

SOCIALLY INSULATED MILIEUX AND STATUS NEUTRALITY

In partial contrast to these workers, another small category of clerks make no claims to work-related honor, but also do not experience any direct work-related social deprivation. Rather, they experience status neutrality. Some of these workers are from the working class, but from somewhat higher strata within that class than the workers treated above, and some are from lower white-collar classes. In any case, their present jobs place them at a level comparable to that of their social origins. Consequently, their bank jobs are simply jobs. What is crucial for their present status experiences is the narrowness of their social milieux. This means that these workers are not called to account for their work's status in their everyday social worlds. For example, an in-mail clerk who is the daughter of a warehouseman and wife of a bottler:

If people ask me, I say that I'm a clerk. Then I tell them what I do. I never get the "just a clerk" routine. I've never experienced that.

Again, a teller who also does other tasks and who is the daughter of a low-level salesman and wife of a recreation worker:

When people ask, I tell them that I'm a teller part-time and that I do accounts receivable and that I post those accounts. Also, that I loan board and do all the First Bank of Columbia deposits and odds and ends. People usually say, "Isn't it confusing working in a bank?" "Sure it is," I say, "it's confusing for anybody." But no one has ever hassled me [about my job]—no, no one ever has.

These workers exhibit no apparent defensiveness about their work status; this probably means that their social milieux do not include people of a higher social station who might stimulate status anxiety. The very narrowness of their milieux, structured by their class situations, is a stabilizing factor in their lives and checks the emergence of possible work-status anxiety. This is not to say that these workers, as well as those treated in the previous section, are not aware of more general societal devaluations of clerical work. Their exposure to key cultural institutions—for example, the media or, especially through their children, the school system—has produced in them definite images of the types of work considered important in America, that is, mainly professional work.[7] They also perceive that their own work is not among those valued occupations. This general awareness is accompanied by resentment; however, the resentment is not transformed into specific anger about personal status precisely because these workers do not meet people who denigrate clerical work. A reconcilement clerk, daughter of a draftsman for a power company and wife of a gas station attendant, states:

Every job has its bad points and its good points. Every one will have its ups and downs. The society praises some jobs more than others because they don't know the jobs or their content. It's impossible. They don't know or care what happens here [in the bank]. Here all these schools say "Become a dentist" and so on. You don't know what that job has in store for you. How do you know they wouldn't like banking work more? There are different advantages to different jobs. I think it's just a bunch of shit.

Outside work, I've never gotten put down for what I do. I usually tell people that I work in reconcilement. I tell them that I do the bookkeeping for all the large companies that have accounts with the bank.

Given the centralized cultural apparatus and the importance of hierarchical rankings in a bureaucratized society, most people will unavoidably have a general awareness of the relative values placed on occupations. How they interpret such rankings and apply them to themselves seems, however, contingent upon their backgrounds and their primary contacts with other people. When immediate social milieux outside of work do not bring work status into question, work-related social prestige can remain a neutral issue.

FLUID SOCIAL MILIEUX, STATUS DEPRIVATION, AND STRATEGIES OF SELF-PROTECTION

The class situations of most bank workers, however, are such that their social milieux do not insulate them from people who negatively evaluate their work status; much less are they in social situations where they can authentically claim prestige for what they do. With the exceptions already noted, most bank workers' class situations are in flux because of such overlapping factors as youth; the experience of some college education; aspirations for higher social positions; or marriage or liaison with people either of higher job ranking or with aspirations for such ranking. Such unsettled class situations, coupled with living in a metropolitan area noted for its mobile character, make for very fluid social milieux in which bank workers regularly encounter people who claim higher social status rooted in occupation. As a consequence, most bank workers are in difficult and ambiguous status situations.[8] They regularly experience both subtle and overt status deprivation, and this experience poses a threat to their work-related self-images.

Status deprivation is basically the experience of social identity being tarnished. In the present case, it occurs when workers perceive other people detracting from or "putting down" their work, and implicitly the workers themselves for doing the work, because of its adjudged low status. This experience is always accompanied by a defensive resentment. Two examples illustrate such status "put-downs" and the consequent experiences of tarnished identity and of resentment. First, a utility clerk who, before marrying a lawyer, struggled for eight years on a marginal income to raise two children from a previous marriage:

One of my husband's young colleagues—a young, female lawyer—came over to the house with my husband, and it was the first time I met her. When she learned what I was doing, she said, "Oh," she said, "you haven't made the little blue book yet" [i.e., are not a bank officer]. It bothered me. She said it in such a way that it bothered me. But all through that long economic struggle, people who were familiar with my situation always had respect for the way I managed.

This worker now regularly finds herself in a social milieu where her previous, socially-reinforced definition of herself as a good provider no longer matters. Her social identity, at least as it relates to her work, is now in jeopardy. Further, the fluid social milieux characteristic of unsettled class situations and of metropolitan environments also bring many casual encounters where work status becomes a problem. A clerk typist:

When people ask me what I do, I say I'm a clerk typist. I do most of the typing for the department. Their reaction? Well, it depends on whether they think you should have a high ranking job. That's the same kind of people who think I should be a certain way—I mean, the way they are. So they say, "Oh, I see," or something like that, and it's clear that they think it's *stupid*. Usually I get mad or uptight.

Tarnished social identity related to work, in a society where work is a primary criterion for all social identification, involves and threatens the whole person. One's work and others' opinions about that work often become the measure of oneself as a person.[9] Workers react differently to such threats to themselves and adopt different coping strategies. There are three discernible patterns of such behavior in the data.

The first strategy which workers adopt cannot be called a successful one. Many workers who experience work-related status deprivation identify with their perceived detractors; these workers pass harsh judgment on clerical work and implicitly on themselves for being clerks. In doing so, they try to indicate to detractors that, while they may be clerks, they are perceptive enough to realize the low status of their jobs. With such a strategy, which is clearly fraught with danger, they try to blunt or forestall others' criticism of their work status and, in some measure, control the shaping of their social identities. Most commonly, the identification with detractors is anticipatory—these workers assume pejorative judgments when asked what they do, and they leap to attack their own status before it can be attacked by another. A teller exemplifies this approach:

When people ask me what I do, I tell them that I'm a teller. I tell them that it's shitty. I can feel the vibrations. It's hard to say but I know that they are judging me.

The stance of these workers towards others regarding their work status is always defensive. Often their anticipatory identification is laced with accounts by which they try to exculpate themselves for working in a situation which they view with the same disfavor they attribute to their perceived detractors. A bookkeeper tells how she responds to inquiries about her work:

I say, "Oh God, I work for the First Bank of Columbia. It's a terrible place, but I really like to work. You know, it gets me out of the house and all—it's really not that bad." And people generally accept that, although they look at me a little strangely.

Although such accounts, even when honored only with silence or polite approval, temporarily extricate workers from awkward situations, they experience a deeper social disapproval of their work. In many cases, the sense of disapproval leads to a low self-esteem which undercuts their strategy of self-protection. When a sense of low self-esteem does emerge, in fact, the painful awareness of their perceived low status is only heightened by their identification with their detractors. A note teller:

[When people ask] I say, "I work in the loan department of the First Bank of Columbia as a note teller, and I'm finding more and more that I think it's a menial type job. I really know that I'm getting dissatisfied. . . ." I hate to be classified as a *clerical worker*. But, that's what it is. . . . Nothing to be very proud of. . . . I hate it because for myself what I've always wanted is a career.

Sometimes the statement of low esteem is indirect as workers try to remain in the role of their detractors; the reality of their situations, however, catches up with them, and they express the contradictory tensions of being at the same time the condemnor and the condemned. A utility clerk:

I would imagine that clerical work would be—well, not a last resort—but a clerical worker is someone who hasn't taken the opportunity to get educated to get a better job. It's someone who—well, they haven't given up yet; but—it just seems a waste to me. Here I am talking about it, and I've been here for three years.

Complete detachment is impossible when one's own identity is at stake. The intrinsic limits of the strategy of identification with detractors are apparent here. While it may mitigate present discomfort, it can in the long run undermine self-respect. In extreme cases, the pejorative self-image forged by regular status deprivation and strategic identification with detractors becomes itself a justification for status "put downs." An auditing clerk:

If people outside of here ask me what I do, I tell them that I'm a clerk. Other people may criticize me. . . . Why? Because it's a low job, that's why. But it doesn't bother me because I know I'm not smart. I think I'm dumb. I always think I'm dumb. I *know* I am.

Identification with detractors, then, often ends in a stripping away of all defenses and the willingness to accept even demeaning judgments of oneself.

Another group of workers adopt a quite different and somewhat more successful strategy to cope with the threat to self posed by status deprivation. Essentially, they disidentify themselves from their jobs and thus attempt to neutralize the issue of work status altogether. Such disidentification is done in a context of accounts. There are two common patterns in the data. First, in a pattern observed in another context, some workers assert the temporality of their present positions. Most often such denials of prolonged continuance are accompanied by what may be called appeals to convenience. A rejected-items clerk uses both accounts:

If people ask, I tell them that I work in a commercial interior department and I tell them what I do. Most of my old friends can't believe it. Because the First Bank of Columbia has such a bad reputation. But I just tell them that it's only for a year. The only reason I took this is because it was the most readily available thing to me when I decided to work.

Accounts of temporality and convenience serve to separate oneself from a social role and so neutralize the impact of negative status judgments on the person. Those judgments are directed instead, either with or without workers' approval, at the social roles themselves. In either case, the worker's identity is protected, but only insofar as she disidentifies with her work role. Clearly, the strategy of disidentification becomes more hazardous when accounts like that of temporality cannot be asserted. In such circumstances, workers disidentify with their work roles by asserting that work roles are only one aspect of social identity. Typically, they do this by condemning those who condemn them.[10] By turning the tables on their detractors, these workers try to point out that the labeling intrinsic to status judgments is a two-edged sword that had best be used gingerly. A secretary:

Well, I remember one guy . . . said to me, "Oh, you work for the First Bank of Columbia; wow!" And he said it like I was some sort of creep for working here. So I said to him, "And who are you? A dirty hippie?" And he saw right away that he was trying to put me in a box that didn't necessarily fit. And he didn't want to be labeled a dirty hippie. So that's the way I handle it if it comes up.

The condition of disidentification in this context is a negotiated mutual recognition that at some level everyone is vulnerable. In this instance, if the worker is not allowed to disidentify with her work role as she desires, she will retaliate by pejoratively labeling her detractor. Even if the grounds for retaliation are extraneous, they nonetheless attack some aspect of social identity. Some workers go so far in disidentifying with their work roles as to assert that one's personhood is separate from any social evaluations of one's work. They scornfully attack others who place importance on work status. After describing an experience of status deprivation, a clerk typist says:

I ask them, "Well, what do *you* do?" And then they say that they do this and that and I ask them, "Is that *you?* Your title? Is that what makes you a person?"

In this view, personhood and identity are not socially derived and least of all from one's work status. Most workers who assert that work is unimportant for social identity actually feel ambivalent about their claim. On another level, they feel that work status is indeed important, despite their de-emphasis of it. Many admit somewhat ruefully that, were their job situations different, they would not disidentify with their work. In a complex statement which touches upon many of the areas discussed here, a boarding clerk describes her reasons for disidentifying with her job, her strategy of inverting questions about work status, and her final, uneasy self-appraisal regarding her work:

If [people] asked me who I *am*—see, I don't think that my job is so hot that I should run around talking about it. If someone asked me what I *did*, I'd say that I work at the First Bank of Columbia. But I don't think telling someone that I'm a boarding clerk is going to impress anybody. . . . If somebody [put me down], I would ask him what he did that was so hot. I think that's just an ego trip. I think it depends on how you feel. I don't think this is a bad job. . . . I mean, it's not degrading or anything like that, but if I had the motivation, you know, [I would like] to get into something that 25 years from now I could look back on or fall back on, like a profession.

One's views of work, status, and self are interconnected but relative and shifting. People in clerical work often disassociate themselves from their work because they see little value in staking their self-definitions on their particular jobs. But even when they so withdraw from work-status competition, they know that it matters how others view and evaluate what they do. Identity is as much a social as a personal production and, at least in American society, work status is a decisive prop in the social drama.

There is a final strategy which some bank workers use to blunt the threat to self created by status deprivation. This strategy, which is part of an information game,[11] is basically an alteration of status which may be called "status-puffing." Workers do not typically employ status-puffing after status deprivation has occurred, but use it to avoid that experience altogether. Moreover, status-puffing potentially has its own rewards in that it can gain one a measure of social honor. Indeed, this latter reason for its use often seems primary in workers' minds. Status-puffing always involves some manipulation of one's audience since a principal require-ment of successful puffing is to conceal crucial job-related information from one's audience. Thus, workers hide facts which are relevant for their social identification. For instance, a stop payments clerk who also acts as a part-time secretary to the supervisor of a large, crowded office de-scribes how she claims social honor by concealing status-relevant infor-mation:

> Outside of work, if people ask what I do, I tell them that I'm a secretary to a department head. . . . They don't believe it at first because I've always been a crazy girl—never staying at one job. They're proud of me. They think I'm higher than I am. When you say "secretary," it makes them think of a private office and all. They'd never picture a place like this.

Here, concealing important information enables this worker to parley her actual job into one which seems more prestigious to others. Presumably, as long as she can successfully hide her situation from her audience, she can continue to employ this strategy. Some workers develop the game further by directly falsifying important aspects of their jobs. Sometimes this falsification involves a simple overstatement. For example, a recon-cilement clerk whose basic work is the repetitious auditing of checks against computer readouts, but who does have a measure of autonomy over one large business account, says to inquirers who ask about her job:

> I tell them that there's a special way of handling special accounts and that I control it.

Other workers bend the truth more noticeably. Most commonly, this involves altering job titles, upgrading in the process one's own work by borrowing prestige from recognized and approved occupational cate-gories. A union clerk, whose work consists of opening checks received by mail from union members and depositing them in the union's account, provides a typical example of status-puffing through direct falsification:

> Well, if I want to impress people, I tell them that I manage some accounts for a union. Like a teller makes a little more money than me, but if a newsman asked two people, a teller and me, what we did and I said I manage some accounts for a union, he would think that I have a higher job than the teller—that I was doing more important work.

An altered title then often provides an appropriate mask for seeming to be what one is not. Such seeming is important to workers to avoid status deprivation and to gain at least some social honor. Adding an ingenious twist to his explanation, the same union clerk points out these common reasons for status-puffing:

Why do I say that I'm managing union accounts? Well, it's embarrassing if people ask what you do—I mean, it's embarrassing to *them*. So I use the title of managing union accounts. People expect more out of you, especially if you've been to college. And you try to get mileage out of what you've got.

At least for some workers, dissimulation about their work status becomes an integral part of their social interaction outside of work. They pretend to be other than they are because they want the social comfort and approval that their own jobs cannot bring.

This final issue is particularly important and points to a common feature that all the strategies treated here share, besides their intended purpose of self-protection. Identification with one's detractors, disidentification with one's job, and status-puffing all assume the low status of clerical work. At one level, such an assumption is a recognition of the obvious. At another level, however, even in their personal attempts to escape pejorative social evaluations of their work, these workers implicitly legitimate the status system which defines clerical work as menial.

Status Within the Organization

Status experiences within large organizational workplaces are, if anything, more immediate and more important for people than problems with work-related prestige outside of work. Bureaucratic workplaces are maelstroms of status rankings, work-based differentiations, and variegated social groupings. As a result, such workplaces constantly, rather than sporadically, place workers in situations where their positions relative to other people become an issue. Clerks in particular are in problematic status situations in bureaucracies. In organizations like the First Bank of Columbia which employ mostly white-collar workers, clerks are, as a group, at the bottom of the organizational status hierarchy, a position which fosters experiences of status inequity. Within their own ranks, particularly in large urban workplaces, clerks are differentiated from each other both by organizational criteria and by social distinctions imported into the workplace or manufactured outright by workers. Within these quite complex status frameworks, few clear-cut primary motives for work appear in the data, but the social nuances and distinctions of these status worlds are crucially important for workers' everyday lives.

OFFICERS, CLERKS, AND THE EXPERIENCE OF STATUS INEQUITY

The experience of status inequity is the recognition of hierarchical differences accompanied by an implicit or explicit judgment that the disadvantageous position of either one's self or of one's group is somehow unfair. For most bank workers, the immediate sources of this experience are their perceptions of the marked status discrepancies between themselves and bank officers.

Such discrepancies are rooted in hierarchical authority arrangements and a concomitant uneven distribution of privileges. Every branch has several officers and, although there is considerable scrambling for status among officers themselves, all officers are clearly in superior status positions with respect to clerks. Status discrepancies first become an issue, however, because workers feel that officers *assert* their bureaucratic superiority. Although workers perceive such assertions in different ways, their perceptions are invariably accompanied by anger. Sometimes workers simply sense that officers claim superiority. For instance, a teller states:

The officers here look down on us. They think they are above us. But without the tellers, things couldn't operate. It really annoys me. I really hate it.

Often clerks point to specific interactional behavior on the part of officers as manifestations of superiority claims. A utility clerk describes in some detail his own and others' reactions:

There's a bad feeling between the loan officers and us little people. Loan officers want nothing to do with you. All they want is the information from you which you have, which is necessary for their job. . . . Down here [referring to the clerks' section], this is the working class. The loan officers feel that if they're caught talking to an in-mail clerk—"Oh, God." I never had an animosity feeling, but now I do. I've heard other people talk about it. Like a bunch of us peons will be in a group, and the loan officers will refuse to say hello, and people will really get angry. You can feel it with people. . . . It's principally the loan officers. They have, on the average, this uppity type of feeling. Once I had to go and see a secretary on the platform about work and, God, the stares I got from the officers, that I would *dare* to walk around the platform and talk to one of *their* secretaries.

Officers are regarded as living in a world closed to the lower ranks. In this view, officers' status distance and snobbery are not only assertions of superiority but boundary-maintenance mechanisms[12] which establish and protect the perimeters of the official as opposed to the clerical world. Occasionally, workers get direct verbal evidence of such status boundaries, but the information simply confirms what they already know from their day-to-day social interaction. A boarding clerk discusses such a revelation:

See, the operations officers—well, they're *lifers*. I do worry when I have to go to supervisors. They keep themselves above you. They're *officers*. They're not like one of the gang. . . . I think they are told that they are *supposed* to keep above us. When I was at another branch, I had a friend who was an assistant operations officer, and she told me that she wasn't supposed to be friends with me. They [the bank] don't want them to mingle with their staff. They're *up* higher than you are. I don't think that's right.

In status hierarchies, occupants of lower positions are in disadvantageous situations. In particular, a recognized lower ranking makes interaction with superiors worrisome and awkward, and often this anxiety itself triggers a definition of such situations as unfair.

In two particular areas of workplace experience, workers find strong, almost tangible status barriers between themselves and officers. First, when officers maintain strict status distance from clerks, principally by defending and asserting their authority at every turn, status differences are constantly at issue, exacerbated by the complicated question of authority. A teller notes how some loan officers display their authority and how the platform, where these officers work, assumes a sacrosanct air which both symbolizes and reinforces status distance:

I talked to S., the [officer in training on the platform]. We are not supposed to know as much as they do. But she was giving an account to a bank employee and closing a previous account. It was lazy. She should have transferred the account. So when the person came over here [to complete the process], I told her that. S. came over and said, "What seems to be the problem here?" I sensed anger that she thought that I was putting her in her place, and you can't do that because technically I don't count. I don't count *because she's on that side* [i.e., on the platform]. There's a huge barrier. The barrier is that they're *God*. You kiss their ass. Anyone on that side thinks they're king-shit. That doesn't carry much weight with me. Take Mr. T.; when he comes, everyone sits up straight. [Just then, Mr. T. did come into the tellers' section, and the subject sat up straight.] They all think they're *top shit*.

Status barriers emerging from assertions of authority usually produce the requisite deferential behavior from subordinates, but this is usually a deference laden with resentment.

The second area of particularly strong status barriers is also interactional, but relates not so much to displays of authority as to clashes over definitions of work and of work obligations. Workers often feel that officers do not consider clerical work important; these clerks see their work being defined, principally through interaction with officers, as petty, detailed, and undesirable. For instance, a boarding clerk:

I see it mainly with the *work*. [The officers] often come up to me and drop stuff off and then walk away like it's beneath them. . . . Then I have to go after them and ask what they want done with the stuff.

Often, too, workers feel that officers will not take the time to do even the minimal amount of detailed work that requires their attention and that is essential for the progression of clerical work. A clerk typist:

I don't like authorizing checks—I mean getting them authorized. The officers are always busy and send me to somebody else. You get put off no matter what you do.

Such small slights experienced through interaction are occasionally highlighted by statements of officers which disparage one or another clerical job. For instance, a credit checker tells how her operations officer quiets talkative younger workers:

Another thing that D. doesn't realize is how she talks. Like she'll say to those girls over there, "If you don't keep quiet, I'll make you into a credit checker." She makes you feel so low.

Such attitudes on the part of authorities, however indirectly or unintentionally expressed, sharply illuminate for most clerks their disadvantageous organizational station. In addition, more obvious evidence is available to clerks to indicate status disparity, namely, the actual division of labor in branches.

Who is perceived as actually working and who is not is always a matter of concern to people in a workplace. Although first-line supervisors usually do a great deal of work themselves, higher-ranking officers—like loan or operations officers—do not engage in much visible work, at least of the clerical variety which, to hard-pressed clerks, is the kind that matters. In workers' eyes, this exemption from or refusal to work is another indication of the status disparities in branches. A new teller, upon entering the lunchroom on an extremely busy day, casually remarks:

Is J. the boss around here? [Informed that he is.] I thought so. He doesn't do anything but sit there, does he?

Again, somewhat more strongly, a rejected items clerk:

You know when I first started here, I thought, "Oh wow! The First Bank of Columbia!" But there's no prestige here—none at all. At least for me. I mean the bullshit around here. I mean, how many operations officers do they have around here? D. [the head operations officer] is always big shit. He doesn't really sit down and *do* anything. I think people should cooperate, but they don't. That's crap.

Visible idleness while others work is a privilege of bank officers. Loan officers are often seen chatting with one another, doing crossword puzzles, engaging in sexual byplay with platform secretaries, or evaluating the attractiveness of customers.[13] Operations officers spend an inordinate amount of time on the telephone, all of which is by no means business related, according to field observations. Actual work takes on a character of necessity while visible idleness becomes a mark of distinction, although one which, as with all claims and symbols of status, also causes resentment.

Significantly, workers' principal defense against feelings of status inequity involves the disparagement and rejection either of officers' idleness or of their actual work. This defense neutralizes explicit or implicit official status claims and reduces the impact of status inequity. While idleness is recognized as a symbol of official status, workers often speak of it scornfully and reject it as a positive value for themselves. A union clerk:

I would want a job where I could feel like I had *done* something—not just sitting there all day and maybe patting somebody on the head to solve some problem. . . . I don't want to sit around all day doing nothing like an operations officer.

Here the value of work as constructive activity is asserted against the status of being free in the workplace. Idleness is considered soporific and something to be avoided. Similarly, some workers disparage and reject the kind of work officers perform, sometimes by leveling managerial work and equating it with clerical work. Here the disparagement is a double one, since it also involves self-disparagement. An auditing clerk:

I just can't see myself in that *kind* of work. I mean managers and clerical workers are doing the same thing. Managers *are* clerical workers too. Have you noticed that?

Instead of blanket leveling, other workers adopt a more selective approach and focus on the standardization of official work which, in their eyes, is as thorough as that of clerical work. A secretary discusses the work of loan officers:

Some people ask me why don't I go into lending? Why do I bother to be a secretary? Now possibly they're putting down secretarial work in saying that. Or they're asking why I haven't become bored with it. But you know, I don't think that there's anything fantastic about being a loan officer. They don't use any of their own judgment. All their work is guided by strict guidelines. They even have these score-sheets for loans.* [In a sarcastic tone:] That takes a lot of brain power! So I deal with this simply by recognizing that their work is not so great.

The problem with this defense is that often workers who use it simultaneously undercut their felt aspirations for advancement.

At times, workers seem to lack any defenses against the feelings of status inequity which emerge from their relationships with organizational superiors. Along with their anger and distress about their status, and in spite of the defensive efforts already mentioned, most workers' ambivalence towards their superiors makes them susceptible to the prevailing status definitions in the workplace. I shall only briefly mention some key patterns here since chapter 8 treats in full the complex relationships between workers and authority figures. Workers desire the attention of authorities and some want their friendship. Such desires are principally expressed in wishes for ideal superiors who "care" about workers or in wishes for proximity to authorities. While these desires quite often coexist with deep-seated antagonisms towards authority figures, they seem, on the whole, to evoke a worker responsiveness to the way authorities define workplace realities, including definitions of status structures. Despite the status inequity and concomitant resentment which workers may feel, they come to live with their difficult status situations because they accept or want to accept the authorities over them and, in turn, be accepted by

---

*The reference is to the "Consumer Loan Score Sheet" used by all loan officers specializing in consumer loans. The officer asks the applicant a series of prescribed, closed-response questions dealing with incomes, prior loans, age, occupational tenure, and active First Bank of Columbia accounts. There is a set score for every possible answer to each question. If the applicant scores less than 25 points, the application is rejected. If the applicant scores at least 25 points, the officer sends the application to a credit checker who verifies the information. The application is then returned to the officer, with a revised score if warranted, and on the basis of the checked application, the loan is given or not. Officers have no latitude for independent judgment since the decision is made strictly according to score.

them. By legitimating authority, many workers legitimate, among other things, their own workplace status. However, such legitimations apply only to workers' relationships with officers and not with other clerks. As the following sections make clear, status competition among clerks is quite marked.

ORGANIZATIONAL BASES OF STATUS DIFFERENTIATION AMONG CLERKS

Like all bureaucratic organizations, the First Bank of Columbia has an intricate ranking system which hierarchically structures all jobs in the organization. The bank's key structures for ranking its employees are its grade and salary steps. Taken together, these are of great importance to workers because they are authoritative designations of the relative position and value of each bank job.

Every job in the bank has an assigned grade which, from the bank's point of view, designates its relative complexity, the skill it requires, and its general level of responsibility. Grades are, therefore, official labels of achievement and ranking. Almost everyone knows everyone else's grade. This is not difficult at the clerical level since the grade range is narrow. More than 90 percent of all branch clerks are graded either G3, G4, or G5.° The remaining 10 percent are graded up to G7, but these higher grades are given only to highly skilled secretary/stenographer positions in the very large urban branches. Even if the range were broader, however, it is likely that the same consciousness of grades would prevail among clerks. In socially fragmented situations, authoritatively sanctioned rankings are always significant. To people who are isolated from one another, grades are the major and sometimes the only guidelines available to signal appropriate modes of interaction, especially proper deference behavior.

Even more important for clerks, however, grades determine salary ranges, and salary is a cardinal point of status differentiation. Salary ranges within grades are complex and multileveled, and salary raises are tied to evaluations by authorities in semiannual or annual performance reports. It would be burdensome to present all the details of this system here; the Appendix explains it in full. What should be noted at this point is that the multileveled salary structure within each grade—each grade has at least nine salary levels and many more are possible—greatly increases the bases of differentiation among workers. In fact, subjective differentiation based on salary differences, despite authoritative admonitions that workers not discuss their salaries, is a major theme in the interviews. Thus, tellers who are ranked at G4 not only claim higher status over bookkeepers (G3) by virtue of position, but also, by virtue of salary, over those tellers who are ranked at G4 but who make less money than

---

°G3 is now the beginning of the grade hierarchy; there used to be a G2 ranking, but this was eliminated late in 1973 in an upward shift in grade and salary scales to their present level.

themselves. A great deal of status envy occurs among workers even within the same grade because of salary discrepancies, even over a-mounts as small as $5.00 a month. Clearly, money alone is not the issue here. Salary differences represent to workers the judgments of superiors about both the importance of their jobs and their performance, and join with grades in shaping the basic status framework of the workplace. While workers may alter their individual positions within the framework through grade or salary mobility, there is nothing they can do to change the framework itself.

This is, however, only a formal picture of workers' status situations in the workplace. The organizational framework of status is important both because it structures overall workplace status arrangements and because the principle of hierarchy which stems from it infuses workers' other status assertions to be examined shortly. Especially where status is concerned, however, involving as it does critical issues of people's self-definitions, there are always complicating dimensions.

WORK AND CLAIMS OF DISTINCTION

The first complicating dimension of status rankings among clerks is the widespread tendency of virtually all bank workers to try to heighten or protect their status by asserting the relative importance of their own work. On the face of it, this is somewhat paradoxical given the problems most workers have with their jobs. However, what is viewed as a personal liability in one context is often asserted as a basis for social honor in the status arena. Workers of both higher and lower clerical grades claim distinction for their work, though with different emphases. Typically, clerks with higher grades—G5 or above—echo organizational judgments and, despite personal ambivalence about their jobs, claim honor on the basis of an asserted relative complexity and challenge of their work. A G5 payroll clerk:

I think that it's the most difficult job here. It's not so much that I feel intellectual strain, but I wouldn't want any other job here. This is the most challenging job here.

Somewhat differently, clerks in lower positions often claim distinction on the basis of hard work. A G3 typist:

Well, this is a very heavy job. I think that out of all the jobs in the office, it's the heaviest—the one where the work is the heaviest—heavy on the mind, every-thing.

Other clerks, particularly those in the middle clerical rankings, stress that their work is more interesting and more demanding than some other branch jobs. A G4 auditing clerk:

I think that my job is more interesting and more important than some of the jobs here. Like over in auto financing—they credit rate. That's all. Anyone can do that.

Whatever the grounds of their claims, most workers, however disparag-ingly they themselves might describe their work in other contexts, always seek, at least in their own minds, to raise their positions in the workplace relative to others. Their immediate work activity is the obvious place to start simply because it is often the only common denominator among workers.

Assertions of the importance of one's work activity are often heightened by status borrowing, which occurs when workers claim prestige for their own work because of their association with persons or symbols generally recognized as prestigious. Thus, platform secretaries, who work in the same physical area as loan officers and branch managers, claim and receive honor because of their daily contact with these high-ranking personages. Even very low-ranking workers like credit checkers can, although only in smaller branches, claim and receive some honor because of their slight association with loan officers. Tellers in the richly-appointed downtown branches claim distinction because their clientele are upper middle-class businessmen. Another symbolic basis of status borrowing is, appropriately enough, proximity to big money. For one thing, working with big money enables workers to claim a high degree of responsibility in their work. A low-ranking reconcilement clerk when asked to compare her job with others in her office says:

It's just as important if not more important. These big companies pay for this service—these accounts. If it's not handled properly, we lose a lot of money. For example [holding up account receipts], this baby here, the State Benefits Fund, is over a $1 million account. The bank can't afford mistakes with money like this.

Often, however, such responsibility is not claimed but, rather, simple proximity to grand amounts of money is asserted. Working with large amounts of the most desirable commodity in our society is status claim enough. A casual encounter between two foreign-born workers, V., an insurance clerk who deals in small money, and P., a participation loan clerk, illustrates the status power of working with big money as well as the deference it brings:

[V. had gone to get his coat to go to lunch and returned briefly to the office to put it on. His phone had rung while he was out and P. had answered it for him. When V. re-entered the office, P. with some disgust gave him the message:]

P.—That was a branch calling about some item for $4.80. Peanuts.

V.—Oh, P., and here you deal in so much money.

P.—Yes, here I am working with millions of dollars and here's a call for $4.80. Chickenfeed.

Whatever its basis, status borrowing is an attempt to improve or bolster one's own position in a status hierarchy. In situations like the bank, where ranking is very important, a person's own status funds often seem insufficient and, to protect themselves or to compete in the status arena, people often feel the need to seek credit wherever they can obtain it.

Status borrowing aptly illustrates the components necessary to have status claims honored in the workplace. Workers are not only making their own status claims, but they are simultaneously aware of others' claims which are frequently counter to their own. Within this hail of conflicting claims, the assertions with the most chance of being honored are those which workers can support with appeals, explicit or implicit, to external, already legitimate bases of prestige. Claims that are coupled either with socially recognized values, such as proximity to authority or big money, or with organizational sanctions, such as higher grades and salaries, are likely to be honored by others, even if grudgingly.

INFORMAL GROUPINGS, PERSONAL ANTAGONISMS, AND IDENTIFICATION

Other complicating features in workers' status situations at work are informal social groupings and personal antagonisms between workers. Social scientists have long noted how informal relationships in large organizations, among other things, regulate work, create secondary channels of communication, cause organizational bottlenecks, or fashion informal but binding status hierarchies in the workplace.[14] The emphasis here, however, will be on another aspect of informal structures—how they provide workers with a means of self-identification in an otherwise impersonal, hierarchical context.[15] In the bank, such self-identifications and the manner in which they occur create the social tone of workplace ranking systems, if not the actual rankings, and, to some extent, mediate workers' experiences of workplace status structures. As it happens, the identifications which emerge from social groupings and parallel antagonisms among workers are largely negative rather than positive assertions of cohesiveness. This requires some detailed explanation.

The best place to begin a clarification is with the exceptions to the general rule. In every bank branch studied, there are pairings or groups of workers which provide positively-based identifications to their participants; such identifications not only reduce the sense of isolation and impersonality endemic to bureaucracies, but they mediate workplace status structures for workers. The pairings between workers are friendship pairs. While these friendships almost always occur between workers from the same neighborhood, and are thus rooted in outside settings, they are important within the workplace. Friends stick together, shape their own images of the organization and of other workers, "pull" for each other's progress, and filter organizational status rankings with sympathy, shared anger, or ridicule. Social cliques based on language seem to serve somewhat the same function. Two groups of workers in particular fit this second pattern—foreign-born Filipinos and Chinese, who speak Tagalog or Cantonese respectively. These workers stick to their ethnic groups at work, trying to arrange lunch and break times together and snatching odd moments during the workday for conversation in their own languages, when authorities do not prohibit it. Overlapping patterns of sororal familiarity also develop in these language groups, and younger workers go to older workers for advice, not always on work matters. Although the language group relationships do not carry over outside the workplace— no one questioned in any such group claims continuing association after work—they are nonetheless groups based on a common cultural tie clearly distinguishable from the English-speaking majority. As with friendship pairings, therefore, they are bases for positive self-identification, and as such help buffer the impact of bureaucratic structures or indeed of the social hostility of other workers.

Given these exceptions, however, most discernible aggregates in the workplace cannot be called groups in the classic sense of the word.[16] They are rather what may be called "groupings"—collectivities not firmly based on positive grounds, but emerging principally in opposition to an external, negatively-defined construct which may or may not be another social grouping. In short, groupings and the personal antagonisms which often accompany them emerge from the process of negative comparison.

In general, social groupings emerge around two areas—work tasks and lifestyles. Groupings formed around common work tasks are not widespread in the data but they do occur. Clusters of workers who perform similar tasks often form amorphous units which they use to gain a sort of self-identification. What is important in their statements is that their self-identifications, while they may point to or assume the common work they share with some others, actually emphasize how their work is distinguishable from that of other units. Groupings stress the negative aspects of others' work, rather than the positive aspects of shared work. Note tellers, for instance, often assert the superiority of their work as a group vis-a-vis that of commercial tellers by downgrading the latters' work:

We're not like regular [commercial] tellers. Their work is very dull and routine. They get the same type of customer day in and day out. We have some variety in our work.

Regular tellers reject this claim, asserting that note tellers' work is as fully standardized as their own. Similarly, in one office, machine operators compare tellers negatively with themselves, and in another, reconcilement clerks form a grouping by criticizing credit checkers. In regard to work, then, social groupings are patterns of clustering behavior of workers who in performing the same set of chores find an initial point of contact between themselves, but who, because their work does not provide a durable, positive, common bond, criticize other categories of workers and thus achieve a measure of identification. Moreover, in asserting such self-identifications, workers modify the formal status structure of the office, if only by infusing it with more personal meaning.

In a much more widespread way, workers shape social groupings in the workplace on the basis of lifestyles outside of work. Again, however, despite some initial elements in common, such groupings emerge basically by negative comparison. Two elements of lifestyle are particularly important here. Education, in a broadly defined sense, is the first of these. Workers who consider themselves educated vaguely identify with others whom they also consider educated, but their common identification emerges from shared criticism of still others who are judged uneducated.

In a related way, aesthetic cultural tastes or interests are asserted by some workers as a basis of identification, but the interests are always articulated against a defined background of others' lack of such tastes or interests. A bookkeeper in a section of an office which considers itself culturally superior to other sections says:

> There is a real difference in . . . intelligence, taste, and lifestyle [in this office]. For instance, the bank sponsored the [art] exhibit at the museum and *everybody* in my section went to the show and got the book which we could get at a discount. Nobody, not a single person that I've heard of from the other sections went to it.

Actually, only four out of 15 people in this worker's section went to the exhibit, but, in her construction of reality, she shapes a basis of identification for herself, shared by some others in her section, against a selectively defined negative background. A second aspect of lifestyle important here are variations in dress within the bank's dress code. Often, workers who dress well vaguely identify with one another and contrast themselves with those who, in the words of one teller, "dress like little hoboes." Alternatively, workers who negatively value the importance of clothes often form a vague grouping whose only basis of unity is an antipathy against those who dress well. Within groupings, as within any collectivity of people, social norms develop—here around the shared antipathy—and these norms govern behavior, enforcing as it were the negatively shaped bases of identification. A general ledger clerk describes the confinement even such vague groupings can create:

> I do think that lifestyles give me something in common with other people. . . . There is this one thing that is really divisive. People talk about it all the time. I mean how we dress differently than people [in another part of the office]. It really seems to be important to people. Once I found a really cheap store and I bought a lot of cheap clothes, and there were a lot of comments here about how I couldn't say anything about [the other section] anymore because now I was wearing new clothes and short skirts.

Just as with asserted work differences, then, various elements of lifestyle become simultaneously bases of identification and of differentiation. But the basis of identification is precisely some element of differentiation. The emphasis and consequently the prevailing social tone of bank workplaces, therefore, is negative. In a very unusual but perceptive statement, a payroll clerk comments:

> You know, people tend to look at life in terms of what they're not. Everybody here relates in terms of what people are not. It means—well, it paralyzes action. It makes it difficult to approach the question of what is. It's so much easier to approach it negatively. I'm trying to think of how I see myself as defined by the bank. Working here I have to negate or block off part of my life—as simple as the clothes or as simple as the politics. This negative way of looking at things is about all workers here have in common with each other. What we have in common is what we are not.

Workers in large bureaucratic organizations often have nothing in common with each other except the organizational rules which bind them together. But people seek bases of identification even in isolated, impersonal situations. Bank workers turn to whatever is at hand to link them to other workers. Most often that consists of negative evaluations, shared by some others, of aspects of the work or lives of still other workers. The informal social groupings which emerge from such shared negative comparison are structures which overlap and complement more formal status arrangements.

The negative social atmosphere which underpins the social groupings in the bank often results in personal antagonisms between workers; such antagonisms occur both between and within social groupings. Between different groupings, personal antagonisms are intensely felt reflections of more commonly held attitudes. For example, a union clerk discusses social divisions in her office and describes her personal feelings towards the workers who form the antithesis, and the defining point, of her own grouping:

There is division between us and [another group of workers]. . . . They go around with their noses in the air. . . . [They're] *female, very female*. Like when a male walks in the office, they're like a bunch of high school girls. They're always giggling. They're a bunch of phoneys. There's one who drives me crazy the way she walks. She is shaped like a seahorse and the way she walks is like she's saying, "I'm beautiful." They are snotty. I feel awful if I'm around any of them . . .

Such strong antagonism is rooted in perceptions held by social groupings and clearly reinforces any boundaries such groupings draw; in its intensity, however, this worker's antagonism goes beyond the usual judgments extant in a grouping. While antagonisms are strongest between groupings, they also develop between people within the same grouping. The negative comparison which produces groupings is a principle which infuses most personal relationships in the workplace. A bookkeeper describes how she views her co-workers:

Actually, in any office, you sit, you start paying a lot of attention to people around you as a diversion. And you do this in a critical way. . . . Sometimes people's actions are so absurd. . . . By doing that, I'm making them into bizarre creatures instead of finding common ground. Sometimes I'm amazed that we could be of the same species and be so different. . . . It's subtle. The tone of voice, the content of conversation. It's verbal garbage. It's so trivial. Why bother to open your mouth and let it out?

Just as social groupings assert their collective virtues by focusing on others' negatively-defined characteristics and thus achieve a kind of identification, so do individuals try to fashion other, more personal identifications by criticizing others, thus indirectly asserting their own individual worth and even superiority. In the bank, workplace identities, not only of groups but of persons, tend to be negative.[17]

Identifications which are negatively derived, whatever their intended purpose, tend to intensify rather than reduce the bureaucratically structured isolation which workers experience. When identification is based on negative comparison, each individual knows that she herself may become an object of criticism. This creates an enervating apprehensiveness of others' judgments. An analysis clerk, when asked if she was staying for a branch party, expresses a widely felt anxiety:

Yes, I'm staying for the party this afternoon. Oh, I don't care about the champagne so much. I'm just staying to be sociable. If I don't stay—I stay because if I don't, they'll talk about me.

Such guardedness is an expression of isolation and is simultaneously isolating. It hints that other people, even within one's own grouping, cannot be trusted and that one must look to one's own self-protection. A boarding clerk comments further on this quality:

The way things have gone, it's made people turn against one another. On one side, you get hassled by [the supervisor]. And then, on the other, people talk about you. Everybody is two-faced, and you have to watch out for yourself.

The negative social atmosphere produced by constant negative comparison does allow self-identifications to emerge, but they are definitions which ultimately are individualistic and solitary. However, whatever final results the pervasive use of negative comparison may have, the informal groupings and personal antagonisms which flow from it are important in fully understanding status experiences in the bank. Workers' social groupings and personal antagonisms are in themselves status claims because they are assertions of superiority by one group or individual over others. Even though these are claims which are not usually honored but met instead with counterclaims, they still help shape patterns of interaction, infusing them with meaning beyond that derived from formal status structures. At another level, groupings and antagonisms constitute people's responses to their highly differentiated status situations in their impersonal, bureaucratic work worlds; they provide people with points of social reference which are of their own making. Even though the identifications which emerge from such points of reference are negatively based and lead to social isolation, they nonetheless allow people to direct, even to a small extent, their *experiences* of social positioning. That is always important to people, especially in situations where status is always at issue.

The Significance of Organizational Advancement

Most American workers place a high premium on advancement; even workers who stress other aspects of work are concerned with getting ahead. Indeed, there are few worse judgments in the American work world than to say that a particular job is a dead-end. Workers are concerned with advancement because it means simultaneously improving one's work-related social prestige and, particularly, bettering one's organizational status. In addition to very diffuse cultural influences, bureaucratic structures foster among their employees a concern with advancement, even though such structures often cannot fulfill the aspirations they generate. Here the focus is on bank workers' concern with advancement within their bureaucratic context. Among these workers, advancement cannot be called a dominant motive for work, but it is nonetheless a pervasive and unsettling concern which at least indirectly legitimates their work lives.

THE ORGANIZATION'S EMPHASIS ON ADVANCEMENT

In most bureaucracies there is an emphasis on advancement—a competitive ethos which stresses individual attainment and stabilizes modern hierarchical organizations. Approved competition for higher positions legitimates organizational hierarchies and reinforces expectations for compliance with organizational rules as well as for at least external conformity to organizational beliefs. In the bank, managerial influences actively stimulate competition for promotion.

The anxious competitiveness which infuses status structures in the bank is crucial in shaping an atmosphere where managerial sanctions for mobility are important. As we have seen, the bank's formal status structures generate considerable feelings of status inequity among clerks in their relationships to officers and considerable strife between clerks themselves over grade and salary differences. In addition, the informal social arrangements in these workplaces are formed by a widespread negative comparison which shapes divisive social groupings and personal antagonisms.[18] Within this intrinsically competitive environment, workers become structurally isolated from one another and consequently very susceptible to managerial influences which directly emphasize the importance of mobility.

The most important influence upon workers is the performance report which provides a regular evaluation of people's work performances and workplace behavior. The principal purpose of the report is to achieve work efficiency and compliance with organizational regulations; this is done by making improvements in people's grades and salaries contingent upon satisfactory, superior, or outstanding ratings of their performances. While the emphasis on advancement is implicit, it is no less forceful because of its indirectness. Essentially, the bank assumes that a drive towards advancement motivates its workers to work. In this, the organization is correct to some extent, not only because of everyone's desire for more money, but because of cultural predispositions towards upward mobility. Some categories in the performance report explicitly advocate the desirability of advancement. Workers are expected, for instance, to want to advance and to take steps for self-development towards that goal. The desire for advancement, or at least its appearance projected to superiors, becomes a prerequisite for advancement itself.

A second influence in shaping an organizational emphasis on mobility is an advancement ideology held by many bank officers. The essential component of this ideology is a stress on the unlimited opportunities the First Bank of Columbia offers its workers. For example, an operations officer:

Banking is such a challenge, and if you work hard and have the capacity, there are so many things you can do internationally and nationally. Take a clerk that's G3; from here, she can go [to another part of the branch] and learn reconcilement, and interior notes, then be a teller, and then a note teller, and then note head, and then utility and from there to assistant operations officer and then to operations officer—a grade 17, and if you have a big branch, you are an assistant vice-president. From there you can move to credit programs and then to lending, and then to national—there's no stopping.

In reality, according to the data, such wide-ranging opportunities for advancement do not exist in the bank nor do workers accept such ideological statements at face value. However, such ideologies, widely extant among careerist officers and openly expressed by them, as well as by a steady flow of official literature to workers,[19] help to produce an atmosphere in which advancement is considered important and possible and where failure to advance is the fault of individuals.

The presence of mobility ideologies among careerist officers reflects their own concern with advancement. Indeed, in the officers' work world, advancement is all important. The bank affirms this value, among other ways, by sponsoring celebrations whenever a higher-ranking branch officer is promoted. A celebration usually consists of an early morning coffee for the branch staff accompanied by appropriate laudatory remarks; voluntary dinner celebrations at outside restaurants are also held. These ceremonies of advancement, as they may be called, both symbolize and summarize the emphasis on upward mobility. Such ceremonies stress the corporate role played by clerks in furthering an officer's career; it is always emphasized at these occasions that, without the clerks' help, their officers would not be receiving promotions. The ceremonies thereby encourage an experience of vicarious mobility among workers, who are drawn into the officer's career progression and who participate in the officer's acquisition of increased prestige. Even more important, ceremonies of advancement lionize the very idea of upward mobility. Advancement is celebrated as a cherished organizational value which is both the promise and the expected goal for everyone. At least from authorities' perspective, the possibility of mobility, as symbolized by the advancement of some, becomes a primary institutional legitimation for the hierarchical structure of the organization.

THE AMBIVALENCE OF WORKERS' ASPIRATIONS FOR ADVANCEMENT

The organizational emphasis on advancement, reinforcing as it does cultural predispositions towards mobility, affects workers. Most bank workers want to advance and some strongly express this desire. However, both personal and structural factors blur the impact of the organizational emphasis, and, as a general rule, workers' statements about advancement are ambiguous.

Many workers' ambivalence towards advancement develops from their defined noncareer orientations towards the bank. Some workers see their bank jobs as strictly temporary and adopt an instrumental definition of work and advancement. The only reason for advancement is increased salary; in their view, one might as well make whatever money one can while in the organization. For a larger number of workers, a noncareer definition of their bank jobs is an aspect of personal drift. These workers' unsureness about what they want undercuts their attraction to the idea of advancement. For example, a clerk-typist:

I still don't know where I want to go in the bank. I might not stay here. If I stay here, I think I would like to get into counseling. I've done some of that at summer camps and all. . . . I don't know what I'm going to do. I'm kind of like sitting here and I—[the subject began to get visibly upset at this point and did not wish to continue the interview].

Sometimes the self-doubt characteristic of drift is enervating and clouds the future altogether. A reconcilement clerk:

I don't know what I want anymore. I don't know where I'm going. . . . I don't really want to be utility. I don't know what I want.

Personal drift is inherently directionless; in such a psychological state, advancement may remain theoretically desirable but, at least as long as drift continues, it is seen as personally inapplicable.

Even when drift eases, however, or when assertions of a temporary relationship to the bank become less useable with time, most workers' attitudes towards advancement remain ambivalent. Most view a gradual mobility as a natural part of their organizational tenure but, generally, it is not something avidly sought in itself. In this sense, advancement is a supportive motive often asserted in the context of other motives for work, particularly security, and it is dwarfed by that motive. A general ledger clerk exemplifies this:

I see me working up very slowly and gradually—like I don't think they'll ever give me my own branch or anything. I would stay with the First Bank of Columbia. It's security. . . . I need some security somewhere. [Q.: Where do you see yourself in five or 10 years?] Five years. I may think about that, but 10 years—oh, wow! I don't even want to think about it. In five years I can't tell where I'll be, position-wise. I can see me working up maybe two grades, depending on what's open and who's in what department when. But beyond that, I don't know. . . . I can't see myself working here for the rest of my life. The only thing I really see going for me here is security.

What is important in such frameworks is the security the organization provides. Gradual progression is an integral part of images of the future, but expectations for advancement are ambivalent insofar as they are unenthusiastic and tempered by the awareness of the contingencies of organizational life, especially where advancement is concerned. This last point is particularly important and provides a clue to a key source of workers' ambivalence about advancement—namely, their perceptions of structural blocks to mobility. Perceived blocks to advancement frustrate workers and temper their aspirations. Two sets of perceptions are at issue here.

The first structural block perceived by workers is the narrow range of real opportunities available to them. Sexual discrimination against women is not the major stumbling block here, as it still is in other large corporations.[20] Under both legal and social pressures, the bank has opened its managerial ranks to women in recent years; as of August, 1977, 41.2 percent of the official personnel throughout the bank are female. At least half of these are in middle-management positions rather than lower-ranking supervisory jobs. In the branches, women are even better represented and constitute 51.8 percent of the managerial staff. It is not, then, because most clerks are women that their mobility opportunities are restricted in the bank. Rather, it is because workers are clerks and the bank now rarely recruits its higher-ranking officers from its clerical staff. For the most part, the only career path even theoretically open to branch clerks is to become an operations officer.[21] Within the last five years, however, the bank has turned increasingly to college and especially graduate school majors in business administration to fill its officer positions. As in many other fields, educational credentials have superseded in importance all other criteria for hiring. As a result, the range of higher positions realistically accessible to clerks is narrow; at the most, they can hope to become lower level supervisors who, although they are officers, are accorded few of the perquisites and little of the prestige which come with higher rank. Thus, even when workers want to make a career in the bank, most perceive limits to how far they can go.

The second structural block to advancement perceived by workers is related to the process of advancement. Favoritism on the part of superiors, who selectively choose certain workers for special consideration, is seen as a common part of bank worklife. It is probable that favoritism of one sort or another exists in any bureaucratic structure. As Max Weber pointed out, the only way for bureaucratic personnel to maximize their own freedom within the organizational hierarchy is to minimize the freedom of their subordinates. The subjective application of impersonal bureaucratic rules is one way for authorities to claim control over their own work situations. In practical terms, and from workers' perspective, favoritism means that the people who establish the best personal relationships with superiors are the most likely to benefit from superiors' subjective application of rules. The most common and important form of favoritism in bank branches is not outright promotion, although that does occur, but rather superiors' selective granting of opportunities to learn different jobs in the branch; such knowledge is often the key to promotion at the clerical level. A general ledger clerk explains how this works:

. . . what I'm saying is that it's favoritism when someone is taken off one desk and put on another; because then the person can learn more and maybe be ready to become utility or supervisor when the position opens. This irritates me because this desk—I'm the only one who knows it, and so I never get the opportunity to go anywhere to learn anything. The way it works is someone will get in good with the supervisor—by going on breaks with them or whatever—and then those people begin to move around from desk to desk and get experience that you need to move up.

Such favoritism is usually accompanied by official promises of similar opportunities for all. However, for both structural and personal reasons, officers usually procrastinate in fulfilling those promises. A safe-deposit clerk describes her experience with a promotion which never comes:

I've been asking for years to learn something else. I've learned a lot of things half-way, but I wanted to expand. There was a secretary job that was opening but I didn't get that; they said because I hadn't been a teller. Then the new accounts job was open, and they didn't give me that either. I don't learn anything at this safe-deposit window because it's too busy. I wouldn't mind being a teller. But [the operations officer] said, "You wouldn't want to be an ordinary teller; I'll put you in the notes section." Then a job came up there, and it went to somebody else.... For me, there's always an excuse attached to things.

The only practical way to overcome such procrastination, other than becoming a favorite of supervisors, is to become aggressively loud and demanding. An auditing clerk, whose nonfavorite status and quietness has relegated her to immobility for some time, comments:

Around here, you don't get anywhere unless you yell. If I had yelled that I wanted to be this far or to go to notes or something—they have a tendency to forget about your request, unless you keep yelling.

In fact, however, most workers are quiet and unwilling to engage in what they regard as pushy behavior despite structural inducements to do so. At the same time, most are unable to establish the special rapport with superiors that would bring them advancement.

Workers' perceptions of favoritism do not diminish advancement desires but they do undercut expectations for fulfillment of such desires. The perceived unfairness of favoritism often produces a deflating disappointment which deepens the ambiguity of people's feelings about advancement. A clerk-typist comments:

It really makes me mad. Nobody can get an *outstanding* [performance] report around here. They say nobody's perfect. But I know some people get outstanding reports, and she's not a good worker. She's a friend of [the assistant operations officer]. That means she's getting a raise. That's not *fair*.... I work harder than they do, and still I got only a superior ranking.... I feel really disappointed. They keep telling me to wait. . . . It's not fair. Everything should be equal. Work and promotion.... I don't think that I can go further here.

The disappointed worker wants advancement but no longer expects to gain it in the bank; her disappointment often comes to replace her aspirations entirely. Disappointment is often accompanied by a sense of victimization, which underlines for workers their essentially passive role in gaining advancement. In this view, workers feel that it is authorities who decide whom they will befriend and on what grounds; the only measure of control left to the worker is to simulate characteristics which superiors are known to favor, but many are unwilling or unable to do this. As a result, they experience promotion as something which is out of their hands. A credit checker:

I was promised a promotion a year ago but no luck yet. . . . I want a change because I have been in this job a long time. . . . There is favoritism here; that is what I feel. "Whoever is near the kitchen doesn't go hungry!" I am a victim of sorts. I want them to like me for what I am rather than what they want me to be. If you have a weak relationship with superiors, you are hampered. Other people have had better relationships [than I have], and it has helped them.

However, despite such feelings of lack of control over their organizational future, most workers continue to want what they sense they will not achieve.

THE CONTINUING IMPORTANCE OF ADVANCEMENT

Workers' continuing desires for advancement, despite the uncertainty that their desires will be fulfilled, implicitly help legitimate their work situations. Two interrelated themes recur in workers' persistent emphases on advancement. First, the very idea of advancement—of moving forward rather than standing still—is important. The sense of forward motion which advancement promises and which, it seems, even the hope of advancement can bring, sustains people at work. Scattered throughout the data, even amid people's experienced ambivalence about mobility, this drive is often expressed quite strongly. A rejected items clerk:

I hate the bank and I think it's a terribly oppressive institution. . . . But I want to keep moving up in the bank while I'm here. I'm pending a promotion now. . . . I'll probably become a teller. . . . I want to keep moving even though I'll only be here a while. . . . I do want to do well here.

Doing well means advancing and that, in turn, brings a sense of personal motion which helps legitimate one's presence in a very difficult situation. A few workers express the desire for a sense of forward motion with greater intensity. For example, a clerk-typist:

I want to move—move! I don't want to sit in the bank for three to five years like a lot of people do. . . . What do people look for in a job? First, they look for promotion, and then they look for whether they're going to like it or not.

The organizational career which the bank offers or seems to offer can become a substitute for rewarding work. Indeed, a sense of forward motion in an organizational hierarchy, and even the desire for such motion, can become a reason for being in the hierarchy at all.

Related to this is a second theme which underlines the continuing importance of advancement—namely, workers' fear of going backwards. This fear may be stronger than workers' desire for advancement, though the two are clearly linked. Invariably, workers mention fear of retrogression with repugnance. For example, a teller asserts:

But I don't want to go down in grade and take a drop in grade. That's the last thing I want. That's for sure.

Going backwards represents a drop in status, a retreat to tasks already done, and, consequently, a stunting of growth even when growth is only vaguely defined. Even the idea of going backwards threatens the escape from workplace realities offered by organizational advancement. A boarding clerk, when asked if she would return to being a teller (which is a lower grade), says:

A drop in grade? I sure don't want that. Why? Well, I would be going right back to what I wanted to get away from. I would be losing rather than gaining.

Further, the personal necessity of forward motion becomes linked to an anxiety about skidding downwards. A credit checker:

You have to better yourself—even one step. You can't go backwards.

Even the absence of forward motion implies retrogression. The idea of advancement becomes an internalized moral imperative to avoid failure. Like the desire for more prestige, it lingers at the edge of people's consciousness and bolsters their other reasons for working.

References

1. *Work in America: Report of a Special Task Force to the Secretary of Health, Education and Welfare* (Washington, D.C.: Government Printing Office, 1973), pp. 76–77, summarizes the importance of these and other factors to workers; for a more thorough treatment of the importance of mobility see pp. 99–122. Another review of the literature can be found in Robert Kahn, "The Meaning of Work: Interpretations and Proposals for Measurement," in *The Human Meaning of Social Change*, edited by Angus Campbell and Philip E. Converse (New York: Russell Sage Foundation, 1972), pp. 159–203.

2. See C. Wright Mills, "The Status Panic," in *White Collar* (New York: Oxford Univ. Press, 1951), pp. 239–258; Michael Crozier, "Social Status," in *The World of the Office Worker* (Chicago: Univ. of Chicago Press, 1971), pp. 165–186; and Albert A. Blum, "The Office Employee," in *White-Collar Workers*, edited by Albert Blum, *et al.* (New York: Random House, 1971), pp. 3–45.

3. Alfred Schutz, "Acting and Planning," in *On Phenomenology and Social Relations: Selected Writings*, edited by Helmut R. Wagner (Chicago: Univ. of Chicago Press, 1970), pp. 126–127.

4. Emil Lederer, *The Problem of the Modern Salaried Employee: Its Theoretical and Statistical Basis*, translated by E. E. Warburg (New York: Columbia Univ., 1937); Erich Engelhard, *The Salaried Employee*, translated by E. E. Warburg (New York: Columbia Univ., 1939); Carl Dreyfuss, *Occupation and Ideology of the Salaried Employee*, 2 vols., translated by Eva Abramovitch (New York: Columbia Univ., Dept. of Social Science, 1938); C. W. Mills, *White Collar;* David Lockwood, *The Black-Coated Worker* (London: George Allen and Unwin, Ltd., 1958); Adolf Sturmthal, ed., *White Collar Unionism in Seven Countries* (Chicago: Univ. of Illinois Press, 1967); and Harry Braverman, *Labor and Monopoly Capital: The Degradation of Work in the Twentieth Century* (New York: Monthly Review Press, 1974), especially pp. 293–358. Michael Crozier, *The World of the Office Worker*, pp. 21–40, gives a nice summary of the literature on this subject.

5. Crozier, p. 19.

6. The concept of social milieu belongs to C. Wright Mills who defined it as "the social setting that is directly open to [the individual's] personal experience and to some extent his willful activity," in *The Sociological Imagination* (New York: Oxford Univ. Press, 1959), p.

8. In the sense used here, I am emphasizing the social relationships that a person normally encounters in the course of his everyday routine.

7. For evidence of the widespread and longitudinally durable positive status evaluations of professional work in America, see Robert W. Hodge, Paul M. Siegel, and Peter H. Rossi, "Occupational Prestige in the United States: 1925–1963," in *Class Status and Power*, edited by Reinhard Bendix and S. M. Lipset, 2nd ed. (New York: Free Press, 1966), pp. 322–334.

8. This phenomenon is commonly referred to as "status inconsistency" or "status incongruency." Of the vast sociological literature on this subject, see in particular Andrzej Malewski, "The Degree of Status Incongruence and its Effects," in *Class, Status and Power*, edited by Bendix and Lipset, pp. 303–308. Malewski's work is particularly applicable to bank workers' experiences because he stresses the interactional and situational character of status inconsistency, that is, its dependence on people's varying social milieux.

9. For an interesting discussion of aspects of this point, see Everett C. Hughes, "Work and Self," in *The Sociological Eye, Book II: Selected Papers on Work, Self, and the Study of Society* (Chicago: Aldine-Atherton, 1971), pp. 338–347.

10. See Stanford M. Lyman and Marvin B. Scott, "Accounts," in *A Sociology of the Absurd* (New York: Appleton-Century-Crofts, 1970), p. 122.

11. A thorough treatment of information games can be found in Lyman and Scott, "Game Frameworks," in *A Sociology of the Absurd*, pp. 58–66. The present analysis emphasizes only the strategies of the person concealing or falsifying information, not the probes of information seekers.

12. For a theoretical development of the notion of boundaries, although with a different application, see Kai Erickson, "Notes on the Sociology of Deviance," in *The Other Side*, edited by Howard S. Becker (New York: Free Press, 1964), pp. 9–21.

13. All of these statements are based on observations made during field work and on conversations with workers whose physical proximity to officers' desks gives them such knowledge. The last example given—namely, "girl-watching" by officers—is almost certainly a common pattern of male behavior in many work situations. The point here, however, is the leisurely attitude with which the activity is undertaken by bank officers. For instance, a platform secretary describes how the manager of a medium-sized branch has institutionalized a leisurely sexual distraction into each work day:

> Every day a certain woman comes into the bank—she's attractive but she projects an air of snobbishness and hardness. Anyway, whenever she comes, I have to go to Mr. S. [the manager]—this what he told me to do when I first took over this job—I go to him and I say, "Mr. S., she's here." That's all I say. And then no matter what he's doing, he leans back in his chair and watches her the whole time she's in the bank. Or else, he'll go and stand by the platform railing to get a better look and just stand there until she leaves.

Sexual fantasy is an experience available to everybody, and there are hints in the data that many workers use fantasy for distraction. Ostentatious fantasy in a workplace, however, is a privilege reserved for a few.

14. I shall mention only a few studies here. See Donald F. Roy, " 'Banana Time': Job Satisfaction and Informal Interaction," *Human Organization*, 18 (Winter 1959–60), 158–168; E. E. Ghiselli and C. W. Brown, *Personnel and Industrial Psychology* (New York: McGraw Hill, 1955); and William F. Whyte, *Human Relations in the Restaurant Industry* (New York: McGraw Hill, 1948).

15. Joseph Bensman and Bernard Rosenberg, "The Meaning of Work in Bureaucratic Society," in *Identity and Anxiety*, edited by Maurice Stein, Arthur J. Vidich, and David M. White (New York: Free Press, 1960), pp. 181–197.

16. David Ketch, Richard Crutchfield, and Egerton Ballachey, in *Individual in Society* (New York: McGraw Hill, 1962), p. 383, adequately express the classic definition of a group, taking members' subjective perspectives into account. They say:

> A psychological group may be defined as two or more persons who meet the following conditions:
>   1) the relations among the members are *interdependent*—each member's behavior influences the behavior of each of the others:
>   2) the members *share an ideology*—a set of beliefs, values and norms which regulate their mutual conduct.

The social groupings in the bank, while they approach these conditions on a number of points, never really fulfill them.

17. The exception is the case of the few workers who become organizational zealots. These workers, who positively identify with the organization, are aptly described by fellow workers as "very bank."

18. Michael Crozier's data on Parisian insurance company clerks point in a different direction. Essentially, he found that status structures in the companies he studied seemed to provide parameters of expectations within which a kind of interactional security rather than competitiveness emerged. See *The World of the Office Worker*.

19. Although the emphasis on promotional opportunities appears in all employee literature, it is most marked in orientation literature for new workers. Consider, for example, these excerpts from *This Could Be The Start of Something Grand*, a brochure for incoming workers:

Opportunites for Advancement:

One of the nice things about working for the First Bank of Columbia is that you can dream big and make the dream come true. The Bank want you to. . . .

The Bank has a policy of promotion from within. Look around. There are people with young faces, older faces, and in-between faces at the top or getting there. All these people have one thing in common. They wanted to make the climb and began with a first step. . . .

The Bank will do everything possible to help you on your way. . . . Look at it this way. The Bank can't grow and get ahead if you don't.

The role of such literature is not emphasized here because it is difficult to gauge its impact. I suspect that it is important but, in any case, it is secondary to the personal influence exerted by individual authorities.

20. See Rosabeth Moss Kanter, "Women and the Structure of Organizations: Explorations in Theory and Behavior," in *Another Voice*, edited by Marcia Millman and Rosabeth Moss Kanter (Garden City: Doubleday, 1975), pp. 34–74.

21. There is a dual career path in bank branches for officers. Operations officers pursue careers which limit them to moving from smaller to larger branches; the work which they do is basically the same in all branches although, depending on size, some branches have more of it than others. Their grades and salaries depend upon branch size. Loan officers can specialize in different types of lending; and, as the volume of money they handle increases, their grades and salaries also increase. Loan officers have higher status in the bank than operations officers; they consider operations work menial and a dead-end.

8 The Organizational Context: Authority and Ambivalence

Authority is the lynchpin of bureaucratic structures and of the worlds of meaning shaped within those structures. Positions of authority guarantee the complex web of hierarchically arranged, segmented roles which constitute at least the formal aspects of an organization; even informal structures, in their development and continued existence, must take the sanctions of authority into account. Most of the interaction, both formal and informal, which occurs in bureaucratic settings is thus coordinated, mediated, or tolerated by authority. Consequently, bureaucratic authority shapes, or at least conditions, people's definitions of their work experiences if only by providing frameworks within which people hammer out meanings. In short, within a bureaucratic context, all meanings for work—including the legitimating meanings which are the principal focus here—are conditioned by the power contexts shaped by authority; any analysis of legitimations for such work is incomplete without a treatment of people's perspectives and legitimations of authority itself. As with bank workers' feelings about status and mobility, their legitimations for authority cannot be called primary motives for work. However, in coming to terms with authority, the pivot of the entire institutional framework within which they find themselves, these workers fashion supportive rationales which bolster their other reasons for working.

Previous chapters have said a great deal about workplace authority. Up to this point, most of that attention has been directed to the power contexts shaped by organizational authority, that is, the institutional forces, unseen by workers, which make bank policy, establish work structures and disciplinary frameworks, devise security programs, and determine wage levels, formal hierarchies, and promotional criteria. Workers' experiences of such organizational authority are impersonal: most have not met and never expect to meet people from the upper echelons of power in the bank. What happens in those higher circles, though it deeply affects workers' lives, remains remote to them. Except perhaps for the bank's president, the organization's top officials are an unnamed "they" or simply "the bank." Not surprisingly, workers' legitimations of authority do not center on such remote figures. Rather, their principal experiences of and rationales for authority are derived from their everyday encounters with first-line supervisors, operations officers and their assistants, loan officers, and branch managers. These local officials both symbolize and mediate organizational authority to workers. These figures personally implement policy, enforce regulations, and evaluate performance; from them workers learn the ethos of authority and the styles of its implementation as practiced in the bank. It is at the local level then that workers must deal psychologically with authority because it is there that they experience immediate and visible control over their lives. This chapter focuses therefore, more specifically than previous sections, on the concrete local contexts where authority is meaningful to bank workers. As might be expected, their experiences with local authority are extremely complex and problematic. Their distinctly subordinate positions create negative experiences which demand accounts; simultaneously, they positively sanction their own subordination. To understand these experiences, the structural context in which they take place must be examined first; here this means an analysis of the several modes of exercising authority evident in the bank.

Styles of Authority and Varieties of Subordination

Authority is rarely exercised uniformly in any given bureaucratic organization; rather, depending upon a range of personal and structural factors, it is usually exercised with marked stylistic variations.[1] In the First Bank of Columbia, as mentioned in chapter 1, there are among local officials three distinct styles of management which may be called "authoritarian," "functional," and "enlightened."* These various styles exist despite the persistent efforts of the bank's centralized administrative apparatus to develop standardized managerial techniques which local managers are expected to implement. The variations in style among bank officers are important in shaping the tone of individual bank workplaces and therefore the tone of clerks' everyday work experiences. The task here is first to examine in an analytic fashion the types of authority observed in field research and derived from interviews with both managers and workers; and second to look at workers' dominant experiences with each managerial type and to examine the accounts they offer for those experiences. Since the job of local authorities is everywhere the same—namely, to

---

*These terms emphasize observable styles of management and apply to officers' performance of their managerial duties only. Since, in the text, it is cumbersome to reiterate phrases like "officers with an authoritarian style" and so on, abbreviations such as "authoritarian officers" or "enlightened managers" are used. No judgment is thereby extended to the total personalities of the officers in question.

assure continuing organizational control of workers and thus to coordinate them into the bank's standardized work structure—the following analysis will focus on the various managerial styles used to implement patterns of control.[2] As the data permit, I shall try to suggest the roots of these different styles.

AUTHORITARIAN MANAGEMENT AND WORKERS' EXPERIENCE OF FEAR

"Authoritarian management" is an appropriate label to describe officers whose treatment of workers is often harsh and domineering. This type of management, which is quite common in the bank, is, on the basis of interviews with officers, closely correlated with an aggressive career-mindedness. The bank's strict hierarchy, particularly in its branch system, and its paucity of well-rewarded positions elicits from many managers rigid patterns of control of workers, the successful coordination of whom is essential to managerial success. Rigid control patterns—"running a tight shop" in managerial parlance—are sanctioned ways to increase workers' productivity and thus to further one's own career in the bank. These patterns are particularly evident in the most pressured bank workplaces—operations divisions in large, downtown branches.[3] I will examine here only those control patterns which are most typical of authoritarian management and which distinguish this style of supervision from other styles, showing in the process how such patterns contribute to an atmosphere which for workers is predominantly one of fear.

First of all, officers with an authoritarian style strictly enforce disciplinary and other external rules for workers. All disciplinary rules of the bank's making, such as those relating to promptness, appearance, or language, are rigidly enforced by these officers. For example, they check workers' time sheets daily and reprimand anyone who is late; they carefully time clerks during coffee breaks; they pay close attention to dress code observance, passing out supplementary sheets detailing dress regulations. One officer measures skirt lengths against a set of lines drawn on a back room wall. Another fines workers who forget to wear their First Bank of Columbia name tags. As a rule, such officers insist that foreign-born workers speak only English to each other, rather than their native tongues. Moreover, these officers create their own personal rules which they enforce just as strictly as bank regulations. One officer, for instance, regularly goes to an interior office under his control and, with a string held by workers, lines up all desks in an exact row. Another insists that workers clear off everything from their desks except the one item on which they are working. Still another, through a subordinate officer, reprimands workers for not smiling at him and asks why they are not happy in their jobs. Clearly, officers exhibiting an authoritarian style of management are preoccupied with enforcing observance of external rules. Only scant primary evidence suggests why this is so, but external rules seemingly represent to such officials a framework of order which secures authority relationships and fosters an environment where, by doing things "by the book," productivity is maintained. From all indications, productivity *is* maintained in such situations although the reasons for this are unclear;[4] in any case, success in reaching bank-formulated productivity goals tends to reinforce the use of rigid disciplinary patterns. Despite their productivity in such situations, workers find rigid rule enforcement petty and annoying.[5] It also creates among them an atmosphere of uneasy anxiety and resentment in which external discipline is seen to take precedence over people's feelings.

In addition to their preoccupation with external discipline, authoritarian officers exert other stringent and more interactional patterns of control on their workers. A common pattern is an occasional display of controlled anger, directed at no one worker in particular, and often followed by silence. Both the anger and its silent aftermath are catalysts in an office, tightening up discipline and creating disincentives against any slackening of work efforts. These measured outbursts also create an anxiety in workers which stems from uncertainty about the direction of managerial ire and the fear that it might be directed at oneself. For instance, a general ledger clerk interprets the silence after a managerial storm:

. . . then she [an operations officer] would get really silent and you wouldn't know whether she was really moody or mad. I wouldn't ask for fear it was me. I think that [she] used that silence and restrained anger as a means of control. People were usually a lot quieter during those periods.

This worker sees such managerial anger as,deliberately staged. Although there are no materials in managers' interviews to support this view directly, field observations of the controlled judiciousness of such occasions as well as their universal use among authoritarian managers lend credence to this perspective. Clearly, the display of generalized anger is sanctioned only for authorities in the workplace,[6] although its use must be judicious to be effective.[7]

Another stringent interactional pattern of control is the harsh reprimand. Officers using an authoritarian style often correct workers for mistakes in their work or chide them for rule infractions in an abrasive way. Although such reprimands usually produce redoubled external efforts for accuracy or conformity, their principal psychological effect on workers is an exacerbation of the fear endemic in authoritarian situations. Workers interpret authoritative motives in issuing harsh reprimands very negatively, often attributing such behavior to power-seeking or dictatorial propensities. For example, a machine operator:

Here I'm always afraid that someone is going to call me up to the desk. Just yesterday [the operations officer] called me up to her desk and said, "What do you think this is, a speed contest or something?" [She] loves to use her authority to the fullest. . . . You're supposed to beg forgiveness when you make a mistake. . . . You can maintain control without being like a dictator. . . . Nobody wants to go and ask her for work—that's fear right there.

Quite often officers in such situations choose to rebuke workers publicly, pointing out their work errors to the whole office. Such "broadcasting of mistakes," in one worker's words, almost always accelerates the staff's industriousness; however, the resultant social discomfort which workers experience, or fear to experience, heightens their anxiety.

A final stringent interactional pattern of control recurrent in offices with authoritarian management is a process which may be named "calling into conference." This occurs when several authorities together confront a worker, who is alone, regarding a dispute or some transgression. Typically, in such conferences, workers, because they are without any social supports and are in the presence of multiple authority figures, become unsure of themselves and yield to managerial suggestions. Disputes, for example, often emerge over who will take responsibility for a monetary loss and, in authoritarian offices, calling workers into conference is a common pattern of resolution. Whenever money is lost, officers either must obtain a signed statement from a worker accepting responsibility for the loss or they must accept the responsibility themselves. Losses, however, count against career opportunities, and career-minded officers make every effort to divest themselves of responsibility for such occurrences. Even when systemic bureaucratic mishaps are responsible for a loss, workers are usually asked to take the blame. They often refuse to do so and, in authoritarian offices, are called into conference. In a case where $300 was lost because of an unusual discrepancy in accounting systems and the procrastination of an immediate supervisor in retrieving the funds, a teller was called into conference to accept responsibility for the loss. Her best friend in the office, who had been through the same experience, describes what happened in the teller's case and gives a good general description of the process itself:

So she [the teller] gets down there, and they ganged up on her. You know, they get three officers, and they all put on their officer suits and they put on their officer voice and say—official-like—"We *think* the bank would want you to do this"— talking about taking responsibility for the loss—"We *think* that it's *your responsibility* to do this." And if you don't know or if you aren't sure—and they all try to make you feel like you don't—then you give in. And she did; she signed it. Even though she felt that she shouldn't. I did it once too, and I didn't think that I should have, and neither did she.

Here, steady insistence by authority figures brings acquiescence even while, and perhaps because, it heightens anxious uncertainty. Officers also call workers into conference over extraordinary transgressions such as open rebellion against authority. In such situations, the steady insistence of authorities is traded for much blunter language; job security is threatened and other disciplinary punishments are often administered. What seems to be at stake here are workers' attitudes towards authority; under authoritarian management, displays of anger against authority are interpreted as general insubordination which might, unless checked, have further ramifications in an office. Authoritarian management itself generates workers' anger and then adopts patterns of control which overlay that anger with anxiety and fear.

The fear and anxiety produced by authoritarian control patterns deserve some further comment. These experiences can be outright destructive ones for workers, as is often the case for clerks who are called into conference or publicly reprimanded, particularly when poor performance reports or loss of jobs may occur. For the majority of workers in authoritarian situations, however, anxiety and fear are experienced more subtly as a general apprehensiveness which comes from constant attentiveness to the wishes of authority, a guarded wariness in the presence of authority, or a fear that one's work, behavior, appearance, or responses will not meet authoritative standards. For most workers, the anxiety and fear derived from experiences with authoritarian managers are enervating more than anything else; over a period of time, they are experiences which wear people down and sap work of any meaning at all.

Still, workers continue to work, and indeed work hard, even when their managers use authoritarian patterns of control. How do workers account for their acceptance of this kind of authority, given the anxiety and fear they experience? Apart from denials of prolonged acceptance—because workers either claim a temporary stay in the bank or hope that their troublesome superior will be promoted—there are two major types of accounts which mitigate workers' situations. The first of these is an excuse used in situations where the authority figures are women and may be called an appeal to biological/social inevitability. In this account, female workers excuse authoritarian behavior and their own acceptance of it as well by claiming that serious conflict will always emerge whenever women work together; female authoritarian management is considered a manifestation of this more general conflict. This social mythology is invoked even when workers have experienced behavior as bad or worse from male managers. More widespread, and used in all circumstances, is an excuse which may be called an appeal to personality; authoritarian patterns of control are regarded as personal quirks and idiosyncracies which must be accepted. A boarding clerk puzzles about her operations officer:

. . . you shouldn't put fear into people. . . . I don't know. . . . I think it's all personality. . . . It's all based on that.

A teller explains why one operations officer who has an authoritarian style is disliked by workers:

People have hassles, but it's largely personality differences. Some people don't get along with [the operations officer], but it's just personal differences.

The appeal to personality mitigates responsibility for acceptance of the anxiety and fear engendered by authoritarian supervision; no one is thought to be able to influence another person's inner make-up, and therefore there is nothing workers can do. This account reflects the pervasive American reliance on psychological interpretations of social reality. Clearly, authority figures do respond in different ways to the social structure of their work-worlds. However, these different responses are rooted not only in irreducible individual differences but also in the very social structures which elicit and sanction authoritarian, as well as other patterns, of control. The appeal to personality, like the appeal to biological/social inevitability, allows action to continue, and consequently social order to emerge from conflict, precisely by blurring constituent parts of social reality.

FUNCTIONAL MANAGEMENT AND TEMPERED FRUSTRATION

"Functional management" is a term which describes officers who have a stolid workaday orientation to their work and whose treatment of workers is a tempered reflection of bank policy. In the main, these officers staff the lower managerial levels in the bank; they are the clerical supervisors, note heads, and, to some extent, assistant operations officers—in short, the mainstays of the bank's everyday organizational operation. Often, these are employees who rise from the clerical ranks, and they develop, through organizational socialization, somewhat the same expectant attitudes towards bureaucratic careers and gradual progression which mark all of the bank's managerial strata. However, most of the 30 percent of bank officers with only high school education are in these lower-level branch positions. In light of the bank's increasing emphasis on educated officers, the deficiency in schooling gives these employees little real chance to compete for the already scarce higher managerial positions. The best that most can hope for is to make a respectable career in the lower levels of the bank, accumulating salary raises and waiting for the opportunity to move up, which for most will never come. Nonetheless, these officers work hard, adhere to procedures, and generally conform to organizational desires.

Managers with a functional style feel ambivalent about the bank. They frequently express gratitude to the bank, an attitude which, it seems, the bank itself tries to induce by promoting to lower managerial positions people who need help in some way or by using such positions as rewards for long service. Thus, an assistant operations officer is thankful that the bank gave her a supervisory job with a small pay increase when she was newly divorced with a child; a note head, for several years a clerk in the bank, is happy with her more respectable position. Occasionally, such gratitude is the basis for organizational zealotry. More often, however, it is intermingled with other sentiments. One senses, for instance, in the words of one lower-level officer whom the bank groomed for her job, both resentful gratitude and dependent resignation:

The bank sent me to a personal development program. I had a chip on my shoulder all the time. I was 19 years old, going to junior college, and working 30 hours a week. I was really illiterate. The program [selected us] and showed us how to dress, how to talk, how to act—they want to mold you into a characterization of what the bank used to be. They used to say, "You *have* to dress like this" and so on. I used to cry every day. I finally said, "I can't do what you want me to do. I'm just going to do my best." . . . In retrospect, I think I needed it. But I think it could have been a lot more gentle. They actually sent you out of class to scrub fingernails. But I would have been trapped in my neighborhood all my life otherwise. . . . I'll do my best [here]. But I really would like to get into something else.

The bank has shaped this woman's life, and although she guardedly appreciates the socialization the bank deemed necessary, she chafes against organizational envelopment. Ultimately, she accepts her lot in the bank, even though she wishes she had other options. However, most officers who exhibit a functional mentality have few other options since their only real skill is their knowledge of bureaucratic techniques. If they were not with the bank, it is very likely that they would be in similar positions with some other large organization. The ambivalence which runs through their interviews, then, can be seen as an emotional escape from the inevitable. In the meantime, they pursue the tasks at hand with thoroughness, if not with zest.

These officers' ambivalence towards the bank carries over to their treatment of workers. On the one hand, their supervisory roles require them to implement bank policies, many of which workers experience as onerous. On the other hand, these officers, perhaps because they themselves are in subordinate positions in the branches, recognize the onerous quality of the policies. The patterns of control which they adopt reflect their ambivalence: these officers exhibit a straightforward enforcement of policy but one regularly marked either with appeals for workers' understanding or, in the absence of that, with delaying tactics. They also quietly accept negotiated settlements with their subordinates. In return for work and requisite public appearances, they grant measures of autonomy to workers. The best place to begin an analysis of functional managers' ambivalent supervision is with an examination of how and with what results they act as a conduit for some typical bank policies.

The issues of workload and promotion, examined in detail in earlier chapters, illustrate functional management's situation and workers' responses to it. Officers' implementation of the bank's ever increasing workloads and restrictive promotional policies makes workers angry and resentful, and they often direct that frustration at their supervisors. But functional managers, who are, as already noted, generally in lower-ranking positions, can claim with some justification that they are only doing their jobs and that there is nothing they can do about bank policy.[8] Generally, such appeals to difficult circumstances are accepted by workers. In honoring such accounts, workers implicitly legitimate their own acceptance of functional management's authority. In their statements, workers often echo this classic excuse of functional management. For instance, though in different phrasing, a general ledger clerk in discussing the slow rate of mobility in her office says:

There's not really anything authorities can do.

A returned-items clerk excuses her functional managers for increasing workload in her office:

Our workload is always increasing. . . . The supervisors seem relatively powerless; maybe they're unwilling to do it [i.e., change the situation]. I don't think anyone here has the authority to do anything.

A few workers have an even more developed image of the structural bind which lower and, in fact, middle management experience. For instance, a worker, who had herself been an assistant operations officer, both describes and legitimates the classic impotence of the middle person in a bureaucracy. While the description applies to all branch authorities who, within the context of the bank as a whole, are all middle-level, it is particularly applicable to the lower-level management in branches since these positions lack even the semblance of autonomy available to branch managers and operations officers.

There is this paralysis at the middle levels of the organization. If you want anything done, you have to go to the top. You can't get anything from the middle because they're all scared stiff.... I was an officer from 1963 to 1967. I finally had to drop it because it really got to my health. It was always being caught in the middle and not being able to do a good job. That's why bankers drink a lot. They don't like their job, and they use alcohol to relax. Like when they have officers' dinners—they all get drunk. They are caught in the middle of the ladder. On one hand, they have the employees who are unhappy because of their salaries or their working conditions—you feel when you get out of here that you've been in a salt mine. On the top—they . . . are always putting pressure on you from the top.

While this perspective is much more detailed than most, workers' recognition of such organizational pressures is widespread and that recognition legitimates functional management at least in a negative way. The very problems of bureaucratic structures often create the material basis for subjective acceptance of those problems.

Sometimes officers with a functional managerial style must implement policies which workers define as so onerous that even organizational exigency seems inadequate as an excuse. Typically, in such situations, functional officers procrastinate. This involves postponing bad news to workers and, if necessary, judiciously concealing the truth of a situation. Thus, in the field data there are cases of officers not telling workers right away that they did not receive an expected raise or that an anticipated promotion went to someone else. Sometimes officers procrastinate until workers have no choice but to accept the situation. There are other instances of officers not telling workers that, instead of receiving extra help as expected, their work units will actually be cut due to recommendations from time and motion studies. Such procrastination seems to stem from the ambivalence which is so characteristic of functional management. Here the ambivalence takes on a new dimension: these managers must do their job, but they do not want workers to think ill of them. Bearers of bad tidings do not generally fare well, and procrastination is a temporary expedient to avoid and perhaps defuse workers' potential anger. For their part, workers are most often puzzled by procrastination, though it annoys and frustrates them considerably. When they try to account for their superior's behavior at all, and therefore implicitly their own acceptance of that behavior, they point precisely to their puzzlement, using an appeal to defeasability. By claiming that they do not know why their superiors act in a certain way, workers mitigate their own responsibility for accepting those actions. When the intentions of others' actions remain unclear, adjudged harm from those actions is somehow more tolerable.

We should note a final pattern of control characteristic of functional management: officers with this style are usually willing to accept negotiated settlements with workers. Typically, under this style of management, the initiation for negotiation comes from workers, usually around external matters such as observance of dress codes, talking while working, or some other disciplinary issue. In return, workers tacitly keep up appearances when higher management is around and accept authoritative excuses of organizational exigency when policy must be implemented. Negotiated agreements, even in situations where power is inequitably distributed, are self-legitimating. They temper many of the frustrations which emerge from functional management's implementation of bureaucratic policy. Essentially, workers and functional managers enter a silent agreement where each gives the other room—on one side, a greater flexibility in the workplace which makes frustration more tolerable and, on the other, an honoring of the middle person's ambivalent position.

ENLIGHTENED MANAGEMENT AND AMBIVALENT CONFUSION

"Enlightened management" describes a relatively new but increasingly important breed of managers in the bank whose approach to workers de-emphasizes their authoritative positions. As representatives of the human relations managerial tradition,[9] which has always been counterposed to the more authoritarian stance of scientific management, enlightened managers eschew overt authoritarian control as counterproductive and, in their interviews, emphasize the importance of maintaining good working conditions and harmony in the workplace. They want to make the bank a better place to work by treating workers as persons. By keeping workers happy and satisfied, they feel that they can achieve their own career goals and simultaneously make their own managerial tasks pleasant. Despite this public stance, however, managers with an enlightened style have complex and ambiguous relationships both to the bank and to workers. The patterns of control which they exhibit reflect that ambiguity.

These managers, who, in this study, all have college degrees, know that their education puts them in advantageous positions to advance in the bank's managerial ranks, and they want to move up. Some, in fact, have already been given their own branches as operations officers; more typically, they are high-ranking assistant operations officers. However, the classic path to real managerial success in the bank—the hard-driving managerial style described earlier as authoritarian—is alien and personally distasteful to enlightened managers. In fact, they privately ridicule managers with authoritarian styles. Nonetheless, to further their own careers, they must fulfill their organizational roles. Instead of authoritarian patterns of control, these managers exhibit as their major distinguishing characteristic an open approachability, a pattern with several behavioral aspects. Approachability manifests itself, first of all, in physical appearance. Managers with an enlightened style always dress in youthful, fashionable modes which, together with casual snatches of countercultural vocabulary, sharply differentiate them from other managers whose public images are primly conservative and circumspect. The youthful dress makes them appear relatively similar to the majority of clerks subordinate to them and therefore less forbidding. Enlightened managers are also publicly critical of the bank on certain, relatively safe issues. They often criticize, for example, branches' dress codes or the bank's traditional, though now changing, male managerial dominance, both of which are popular issues with female clerks. Finally, these managers develop and maintain public faces of concern for workers which contrast sharply with the abrasive or aloof visages which typify authoritarian or functional management. A principal aspect of such concern is their emphasis on developing morale-builders in their branches. Enlightened managers enthusiastically support a wide variety of morale-builders which at least temporarily ease workplace routine. In one branch, they strongly support a monthly "casual day" when dress codes are relaxed. In other branches, they note and remember their staff's birthdays; they plan staff pot-luck dinners; they encourage higher authorities to have as many staff parties as possible; they develop a staff choir to sing at the branch Christmas party with the stated hope of bringing everybody together. In short, they reduce, at least on some levels, the distance between themselves and their workers. As a result, workers often do view them, in workers' own words, as more "human," "approachable," "understanding," and "caring" than other bank managers. Workers are generally more amenable to the direction of enlightened managers. Often by casual suggestion or through more formal discussions called "counseling,"[10] these managers can implement policy.

However, as indicated throughout this book, the exigencies of clerical work as structured in the bank often do not make workers amenable to any managerial approach. In such cases, enlightened managers—simply to perform their own work, let alone further their ambitions—find themselves in situations where they must exert managerial authority more obtrusively and forcefully than they wish. They find such situations unpleasant and often respond by becoming very critical both of the bank and of workers. Privately, they criticize the bank's standardized work structure, its commercialism, and its strict discipline. They become angry as well at workers for, in their view, "making" them act like custodians when they want to see themselves as diplomats. In the hope of avoiding and preventing unpleasant situations from emerging at all, enlightened managers develop other, somewhat seamier patterns of controlling workers.

The key patterns here, as pointed out in workers' interviews, are private information gathering and quiet innuendo. Many workers report that enlightened managers select favorite workers, solicit information from them about other workers, and then use that information as a means of control. For instance, an in-mail clerk whose desk is adjacent to that of the assistant operations officer says:

I can sense that I'm always being watched here—by C. or J. [two other workers] and that whatever I do will get back to A. [the assistant operations officer]. A. often asks other people, "What does so and so do?" and then she uses that information. She keeps it to herself and then she'll be on the watch for particular things which that person is doing. Like when I was being trained by E. [still another worker], I always felt that she was going back and talking about me.

This experience is not idiosyncratic since several other workers under different but parallel managerial situations voice similar, though less detailed, remarks. An auditing clerk:

So then N. [the operations officer] and S. [another worker] went behind the pillar and began talking with one another. That really bothers me—I *knew* that they were talking about me, because then N. comes and tells me to take over [another worker's] desk. . . . I hate the atmosphere of people whispering to each other—about you.

Such experiences create a subtle atmosphere of suspicion, one which co-exists with enlightened managers' appearances of openness and with workers' favorable responses to that openness. The aura of suspiciousness at times adumbrates workers' perspectives and produces a mild para-noia—workers no longer know whom to trust. A bookkeeper, who earlier in her interview feels that her assistant operations officer is, in her own words, "open," "human," "considerate," and "trusting," says:

G. [a worker] said she heard P. [the assistant operations officer] talking to some of the other girls about how often I'm on the phone! For private calls! Hell, I had three calls the day before, all of them *very* short. G. said that the same thing happened to her. Then I have this paranoia—suppose G. was sent by P.? In any case, I think it's rotten that P. didn't come to me personally and tell me if there has been a problem. This thing with the phone . . . has really, really bothered me. A lot of it is that I'm afraid to get it all out in the open. Why? Because P. might say, "You're doing a terrible job." I think that I have these hidden springs of paranoia. Now my self-image is confused. I don't know whether I'm a good worker or a bad worker. I feel more and more like a resentful worker.

In practice, therefore, at least as workers experience it, the open ap-proachability of enlightened management is combined with less direct, indeed covert, methods of supervision which enforce discipline. An unintended consequence of these covert methods is workers' troubled resentfulness, directed precisely at the managers whom they trust more than any others in the bank.

The underside of enlightened management, when perceived by workers, clouds the public faces of these officers and calls their solicitude into question. As a result, workers under enlightened management often experience an ambivalent confusion. They view such managers as the best the bank has to offer, but there are times when workers are unsure whether their enlightened managers are entirely what they seem to be.

Typically, workers account for their ambivalence through negative comparison, justifying the acceptance of their present situations by contrasting enlightened officers with authoritarian or functional personnel. Often too—and this is an important pattern which was mentioned earlier—workers devise accounts for these authority figures. Thus, if the questionable actions of authority can be excused or justified, then one's own acceptance of that authority is mitigated. An auditing clerk:

I don't think that [the assistant operations officer] really knows that she is doing this [i.e., setting up a system where workers give her information]. See, one reason she doesn't want to come out and be rough with the girls is because of [another officer's] loud problems. [The reference is to an authoritarian officer of equal rank in a nearby division who regularly shouts at her workers.]

Here, the enlightened officer is granted an appeal to defeasibility on one hand—that is, she is presumed to be acting without harmful intention—and an appeal to difficult circumstances on the other. People in subordinate positions often excuse the disagreeable side of authority. In doing so, they express both their ambivalence towards authority and their concomitant unwillingness, because of their uncertainty and felt powerlessness, to alter their difficult situations.

Positive Rationales for Authority

Bank workers' experiences with authority are, however, more complex than indicated up to this point. As a counterweight to their negative experiences with and concomitant defensive accounts for the different types of authority in the bank, workers also express positive rationales legitimating authority. Although such rationales are generally derived from or conditioned by experiences with the specific types of personal authority treated above, these rationales assume a somewhat general form and become legitimations for the principle of workplace authority.

BUREAUCRACY AND THE PREMISE OF NECESSITY FOR AUTHORITY

One widespread rationale for authority among bank workers seems to be principally derived from workers' structural situations rather than from specific interaction with personal authority; this is a premise of necessity for hierarchical authority in the workplace. Bureaucratic structures, by their very stolidity, foster subjective perspectives where authority, among other things, seems necessary and indeed inevitable. As with any social institution, the already established organizational goals, the structures to implement them, and the authorities to facilitate them present themselves to workers as "givens." In lieu of visible and understood alternatives, the everyday realities of bureaucracy organize people's experiences. The organizational goal of maintaining operations is accepted as given, for instance, and authority becomes a necessary means to that end. A union clerk:

You have to have authority to run an office.

Again, in a common pattern, the organizational drive for efficiency is accepted as legitimate, and in light of that, hierarchical authority is postulated as essential. An auditing clerk:

Authority is very *necessary* in a work situation. . . . it's essential. I feel that the setup should be such that something given to a clerk should be done as quickly as possible.

Often, too, clerks point to the bank's existing structure of centralized decision making and responsibility as desirable and, with these premises, consider hierarchical authority essential to solve workplace problems. For example, an insurance clerk:

You need a center of control. There must be one man in charge. If there were no supervisor and we had a sudden problem which we could not solve, what would we do then? There's no authority vested in me or anybody else in the office to make a decision on our own. . . . If there is no *decisive* authority, then there will not be near unanimity of decision, and there will be problems.

Other workers, assuming and accepting the given structure of evaluation and promotion, point to hierarchical authority as essential to evaluate performance or to goad slackers. In short, authority is considered essential because without it, the things that authority is meant to insure would not get done.

Such tautological legitimations of authority reflect a resigned acceptance of existing conditions which evidences itself sporadically throughout workers' interviews. One worker's remarks, though singular in their content, point out dimensions of a fairly common experience:

There is *ample* supervision here. There are enough supervisors to control the situation in case there is something going on. No, there are not *too* many. . . . It seems to me that if you're working for an organization that rips people off, you have to know how to smooth over people to prevent an outbreak. That's what supervisors are for.

My own feelings? If I were *nihilistic*, I'd try to change the working conditions so that the employees were not so pressured. That would be really nihilistic to me though—to alter an organization like this. It's so well-designed to do this sort of thing. . . . The guy who put this whole thing together was a genius; it's like a finely tuned clock. . . . I think that the supervisors are *necessary* here.

In this view, expressed quite without irony, the organizational structure of the bank is legitimate by its very concreteness; authority is seen and accepted as the necessary guardian of that structure. Even though the structure is considered exploitative and its authorities defined as custodial, social change is considered destructive simply because it would alter the status quo. Workers often do not like the reality which they experience, but they accept it because in their view, which is shaped, indeed sometimes overwhelmed, by their organizational environment, it is the only reality there is. Bureaucracies like the bank, then, envelope workers and, perhaps even more thoroughly than other social structures, produce situations which people come to take for granted and accept as inevitable. Alternative ways of organizing work—where, for instance, authority is collective rather than hierarchical—simply do not occur to most workers.

There are other rationales for authority besides those stemming from a notion of necessity. The claim of knowledge is, as Lyman and Scott point out,[11] a common legitimating tool used by those in positions of power. Conversely, people in subordinate positions expect those in power to have greater knowledge about given situations than themselves. In the bank, particularly with managers of authoritarian or functional styles, workers positively legitimate authority as long as their superiors have or seem to have greater technical knowledge than they themselves do of bank work.

The importance of this legitimation for authority is evident in various ways. Workers often point to their authorities' presumably greater knowledge. Such presumed knowledge becomes identified with higher position and is seen as essential for everybody's performance of work. For instance, a utility clerk:

. . . a supervisor is *necessary*. Some things you don't know and you need help, and they know how.

Perhaps because it is considered necessary in the workplace, presumed knowledge elicits respect, an essential ingredient of legitimacy. A teller:

Generally with the officers, there's respect among the workers for them. I know I do. Why? Because they know more than I do and I respect anybody who knows more than I do.

Legitimating respect for presumed knowledge, however, demands that superiors at least *seem* knowledgeable. There are many cases in the data where workers perceive gaps in officers' knowledge. Almost invariably, this leads to a de-legitimation of authority, which, in a converse way, underscores the importance of knowledge or its appearance. For instance, a secretary:

I really get annoyed with people sometimes. Like T., the assistant manager, had customers at his desk yesterday; and I must have spent one-half hour at his desk trying to find out what I had to type for these people's accounts, and *he didn't know the answer.* That type of thing really gripes me. . . . They should just fire him.

In this case, neither the clerk nor the manager know the proper procedure; but in the clerk's eyes, the manager *should* know. Again, a general ledger clerk:

Knowledge is important. Once we had a supervisor who did not have a head on her shoulders. Often it's not what you know, it's who you know. She got where she was because of who she knew, and she didn't know anything. But if you go to such a supervisor and she says, "I don't know" to one of your questions, how much can you respect her?

Without the respect that perceived knowledge brings, authority figures become fair game for de-legitimating ridicule. A teller talks about her assistant operations officer:

It bothers me to have somebody who doesn't know anything supervising me. People here think that he's the biggest dummy around. Everybody calls him that.

Actual knowledge or its appearance in authorities is, then, pivotal in the organizational workplace for maintaining the structure of legitimacy. Workers will accept even abrasive or aloof authority figures if they seem to know more than workers. However, when that perception of knowledge is, for one reason or another, erased, workplace authority is undercut.

Interestingly, most local authorities in the bank know far less about the details of their subordinates' immediate work than do clerks themselves. However, except for de-legitimating cases such as those noted and except in certain negotiated cases,[12] most clerks do not discover this unexpected gap in knowledge. Rather, authority figures generally appear to workers to understand not only each individual job in the office but how all the pieces of work fit together. The reasons for such legitimating appearances of knowledgeability are both systemic and personal. As clerical work in the bank is increasingly routinized, supervisorial training stresses not the mastery of detail, but the general coordination of segmented parts. Because superiors do know something about each person's work, they often seem to be generally knowledgeable. On a personal level— and this judgment is based on interviews with and observations of managers—bank officers make every effort to master the appearance of knowledge, that is, the stagecraft of seeming to know what they actually do not know. Most commonly, they achieve this by sticking to their familiar general duties and by not allowing themselves to be drawn into the welter of details which make up clerical work. If they do not know the answer to a specific question, they usually throw the burden back on the worker and have her "research" a procedure in the *Standard Practices Manual.* By avoiding minutiae, officers successfully retain the appearance and the concomitant legitimacy of knowledgeability. When, in fact, authorities do try to delve too deeply into their subordinates' work, they run the risk of being found out and of having their appearances of knowledgeability stripped away. An NCR machine operator describes an encounter with a young operations officer, as yet unskilled in the stagecraft of authority, who compulsively delves into the details of her subordinates' work:

I get the feeling that she always has to know everything. She questioned me on the teller numbers which are on the checks, but [what she was pointing to] were really the nonreads [items rejected by the computer]. Right away I knew that she didn't know about the NCR machine, but she didn't want me to know that she didn't know.

There are few quicker ways of losing the appearance of knowledge-ability than of reaching for or pretending a grasp of details when one is equipped only for generalities. The maintenance of authoritative legitimacy demands, and usually gets from bank authorities, an appreciation of how to wear the mask of expertise.

THE QUEST FOR MANAGERIAL ATTENTION AND ASSOCIATION

The desire for attention from authorities is intrinsic to bureaucratic settings and is particularly important in legitimating authority. Desires for such attention are, in any context, external indications of the importance of authoritative others in shaping self-images.[13] Bureaucratic settings in particular, because of their hierarchical structures of status and authority, are important contexts where authority defines and is recognized as defining aspects of people's selves.[14] Essentially, bureaucratic hierarchies create upward-looking stances in those in subordinate positions, making them extra sensitive to the judgments of authorities, not least because such judgments determine the allocation of rewards. This natural condition of bureaucracy is exacerbated in organizations like the First Bank of Columbia, where organizational monopoly of power and authority prevents the emergence of all but the most marginal alternative forums for personal validation. In such situations, the attention of authorities becomes especially prized because it is crucial to people's ideas about themselves. Competition for attention, then, constitutes a social sharing of this prized evaluation and in itself validates the principle of workplace authority.

In bank workplaces, workers' desire for attention has several meanings. In its most rudimentary and widespread sense, it means a desire for recognition of work performed. This desire is usually expressed competitively and jealously when workers feel that their efforts do not receive a fair share of management consideration. In a more complex vein, workers, in their statements about ideal authority figures, often voice a desire for attentive authorities who care about them. This is a desire for personal consideration in an impersonal organizational context. In workers' present experiences, authorities often represent impersonality and thus become the focus of a desired alchemy in the workplace environment:

I find that the officers who are in training or new in the position are the most real people. . . . They *care* very much. I rarely if ever go to [the operations officer] for anything. I find him unfriendly and cold. When he asks you to do something, he never says "thank you" and never says "please." I don't think that's a good employer-employee relationship. What do I look for in a boss? I look, too much, for a friend. I expect him to *care* for the office. . . . K. [the assistant operations officer] seems to care about us. I guess I want someone who *cares* but who is knowledgeable.

What workers want therefore are considerate, personable authorities who seem, at least, to take an interest in workers as persons. This last point is particularly important, and many workers stress desires for managerial interest in them. A note teller:

The biggest thing that I don't like—I think—is lack of personal interest in employees on the part of supervisors. . . . *That would include some concern about the future.* I mean on the part of supervisors. . . . it's *personal interest* that I look for in a supervisor. Being open to complaints, knowing what your name is—dealing on a human level.

Only managers with an enlightened style of authority strike responsive chords in the many workers who want interested supervisors. Even there, however, as seen earlier, the underside of enlightened authority roles confuses workers and stimulates ambivalence, despite the public faces of concern which such managers carefully wear. Yet, although workers' desires for care are largely unfulfilled, the desires themselves legitimate authority because they predispose workers even further to its influence. Such desires strengthen the already firm prerogative of authority to give or withhold attention.

The final and most important meaning of workers' desire for attention is a widespread quest for the approval of authorities. Approval is a special kind of attention and is a primary social reward in a bureaucratic workplace; it provides prestige and a concomitant sense of personal well-being and it often leads to economic rewards. Approval by authorities sanctions behavior and thus reinforces and often alters people's self-images. In a variety of ways, workers' statements stress the importance to them of such approval. The most important manifestations of authoritative approval are the performance reports which, when favorable, are almost always a source of pride. A reconcilement clerk:

I got a beautiful performance report from W. [the operations officer]. . . . It was good to get that performance report because it's nice to know you're appreciated. . . .

Even disgruntled workers are, when they receive one, pleased by a favorable performance report, and not only because such reports mean increased money. Favorable official judgments of one's performance become important for people's selves, even when these same people deeply question their overall situations. Even casual compliments from supervisors are remembered and valued. A teller:

When I do my best, they notice. Mr. A. [the operations officer] told me once that he recognized that I was doing better than usual. That's nice.

Special assignments from superiors, though infrequent and usually small in scale, provide an unusual chance for approval, and chosen workers approach them eagerly. A teller talks about such an assignment from an assistant operations officer:

B. gave me a problem to figure out. He wants to see how I'll handle it. A company sent some bills with a BankColumbiaCard and B. returned it, but he sent too much money back and the company kept it. So I have to track down their account and take care of it. We'll just go right into their account and take their money. I mean, it's not much—$3.37.

As here, the desire for approval and especially being singled out by authority can lead to officiousness, a behavioral pattern that, through imitation, reinforces attentiveness to authority. In general, however, workers want and seek approval in both more passive and more ambivalent ways. Basically, they perform their work and want to be recognized for doing so. They will adjust their external behavior to get desired approval, but they generally do not remain constantly attentive to the desires of authority, except in some authoritarian situations where attentiveness is essential to avoid trouble. Perhaps because they recognize and resent both the scarcity of approval and what they see as its frequently inequitable distribution, they try to keep areas of themselves free from authoritative influences, even though they are often unsuccessful in doing so.

Workers' lack of success in this regard is evident in the corollary of the desire for approval, namely, the fear of disapproval, which, if anything, is even more pervasive in bank branches. Where approval bolsters self-images, disapproval calls these images into question. Uniting both is the desire for and fear of the opinions of authority about oneself. A bookkeeper describes an incident during which she was reprimanded:

Once I was talking to M. [another worker] and the phone was ringing; and P. [the operations officer] came up and said, "Answer the phone." I went on talking to M., while reaching for the phone, you know, trying to settle something, and he said again, "Answer the phone." Then he went back to his desk and then he came back and said, very loudly, practically yelling, "Answer the phone." I thought that was sort of rude. I felt bad about it, not because I didn't jump on it right away, but mainly because of what he thought about me. Another lady was sitting right there not doing anything, but he came to me probably because I was talking. I guess he thought I wasn't working. But he didn't know what we were talking about; and, in fact, it was about work.

Such concern with the judgments of authority, endemic wherever authority is hierarchical and centralized, implicitly legitimates authority precisely because it underlines, however unwillingly, superiors' already established institutional prerogative to influence identities.

In addition to desiring approval, some workers want and occasionally seek out informal associations with authority figures; these attitudes and occasionally concomitant behavior indirectly bolster authority relationships. One pattern here is the desire for camaraderie with authorities. A few workers look forward to branch parties and officer celebrations because, in their minds, they provide opportunities to mingle with officers and "to see them as people." Their desires in this regard coincide with managerial intentions, since one of the purposes of parties is to reinforce authority relationships by providing multidimensional settings for authority-worker interaction.[15] In this case, reinforcement and consequent legitimation takes place by a subtle diffusion, at least at the subjective level for some workers, of formal authority relationships.

A somewhat similar but more widespread pattern is the desire for various kinds of friendship with authority figures, a pattern which, in the bank, is principally true of younger female workers. Many such workers tend, in their interaction with authorities, to give those relationships familial or sexual overtones. Officers reciprocate and, quite often, initiate such byplay. Thus, female superiors are often regarded as older sisters and male authorities, depending on their ages, are regarded either with filial deference or with a coy flirtatiousness. Typically, familial images reinforce authority relationships because of their cultural resonances; it is not uncommon, for instance, to see younger workers behaving childishly in front of authority figures. Somewhat differently, sexual byplay seems to distract people from the underlying authority relationships of the workplace, emphasizing in the place of hierarchy the reciprocity of sexual give and take.

As a final point, in only a few cases do workers' positive legitimations of authority lead to a lasting identification with authority. Marginal identification does occur where, for instance, workers regularly adopt the viewpoint of authorities to explain workplace problems. Far more typical, however, are what may be called patterns of ambivalent non-alignment. Workers legitimate authority—account for their problems with the different styles of authority, assume the necessity of authority, presume authorities' greater knowledge, desire the approval of or association with individual authority figures—but, in general, they do not embrace authority. Despite workers' legitimations, there is evident throughout the data a wariness towards authority; one senses both in workers' remarks, which are often highly critical of authority, and in other patterns of behavior, a quiet struggle by workers, clearly not always successful, to keep a distance between themselves and the bank's officials. At the same time, however, neither do workers, as we have seen, identify on any permanent basis with their fellow workers. Rather, they find themselves for the most part caught in a shadowy noncommitment—wanting to please authorities, yet not quite trusting them; wanting some positive unity with their fellows, yet lacking perceived common grounds or the resources to shape such unity. The absence of firm commitments among workers only clouds the meaning of their actions to themselves. It does not impede the coordination of those actions by bureaucratic authorities acting in behalf of the organizational structure. In all likelihood, in fact, workers' ambivalence facilitates that coordination.

References

1. Writers in the field of industrial psychology have persistently pointed to stylistic differences in handling authority as an important organizational variable, though they have been almost entirely concerned with the impact of different styles of management on productivity. See, for instance, E. A. Fleishman, "Leadership Climate, Human Relations Training and Supervisory Behavior," *Personnel Psychology*, 6 (1953), 205–222; M. Patchen, "Supervisory Methods and Group Performance Norms," *Administrative Science Quarterly*, 7 (December 1962), 276–290; or A. S. Tannenbaum and W. H. Schmidt, "How to Choose a Leadership Pattern," *Harvard Business Review*, 36 (1958), 95–101. For a more sociological analysis, see Melville Dalton, *Men Who Manage* (New York: Wiley, 1959) and, especially,

John Brewer, "Organizational Patterns of Supervision: A Study of the Debureaucratization of Authority Relations in Two Business Organizations," in *The Sociology of Organizations*, edited by Oscar Grusky and George A. Miller (New York: Free Press, 1970), pp. 341–347.

2. Some writers argue that bureaucratic structure itself is the principal source of control in the workplace—through standardization, predictability, and so on—and that present-day managers are simply monitors. The power relations of bureaucracy are thus totally submerged and impersonal and consequently obscure to workers. In this perspective a focus on styles of control is irrelevant, since the only real source of control is the organizational apparatus. See Richard C. Edwards, "Alienation and Inequality: Capitalist Relations of Production in Bureaucratic Enterprises," Diss. Dept. of Economics, Harvard Univ. 1972, pp. 98–137. Edwards is quite correct in emphasizing the importance of the organizational apparatus in controlling workers and indeed in his structural appraisal of the manager's role as essentially that of a monitor. Even though later in his work, pp. 161–164, he recognizes the importance of local authorities, he still underestimates the various ways managers can fulfill their roles and only hints at the sharply different experiences workers have under different styles of management.

3. Brewer, "Organizational Patterns of Supervision," p. 342, notes that:
. . . the style of supervision which a superior adopts is the result of the *kinds of compliance* that he must elicit in order to perform his own role successfully. [Emphasis added.]
In this analysis, the most important worker responses in pressured situations (such as those mentioned in the text) are efficiency and productivity; these are not only norms to measure performance, but also norms to gauge compliance with direction by authorities.

4. In the present study, offices with authoritarian managers met or exceeded the bank's own productivity expectation which is a 95% index on a scale of 100, derived by dividing all the work task minutes in a branch by the total available man-hours, broken into minutes. However, since this study was conducted during the beginning of a tight labor market, classic "drags" on productivity such as absenteeism and turnover, which are related to types of supervision, were low. When the labor market contracts, workers are reluctant to leave their jobs no matter what kind of problems they have with supervisors. To get an adequate measure of the relationship between productivity and authoritarian supervision, indices of productivity should also be examined under slack labor market conditions when workers feel freer to move to other jobs. Also, Paul Blumberg's study of decentralized, participative work situations indicates that "with a consistency rare in social science," productivity increases in such situations. See *Industrial Democracy* (New York: Schocken Books, 1969).

5. Victor Vroom indicates that, contrary to beliefs of 20 years ago, there is substantial evidence that productivity is unassociated with workers' satisfaction. See "Industrial Social Psychology," in *The Handbook of Social Psychology*, edited by Gardner Lindzey and Eliot Aronson (Reading, Mass.: Addison-Wesley, 1969), V, p. 199.

6. There are, of course, notable exceptions to this observation. Some workers also become adept at using anger to gain their own ends, but they usually do so only against other workers, in which case the issue is simply a struggle of personal wills. If workers do display anger to those of higher rank, they always have some power basis with which to guard themselves, such as knowledge, length of service, presumed indispensability, and so on. Also, workers do not usually display anger under authoritarian managers, probably because of fear of retaliation.

7. Some young officers in lower-ranking authority positions display anger too often in adopting an authoritarian style, and its potential effectiveness is eroded since workers dismiss such officers as tantrum-prone.

8. Alvin W. Gouldner points out this same pattern of managerial excuse in *Patterns of Industrial Bureaucracy* (New York: Free Press, 1954), p. 165. He notes that bureaucratic structures provide managers with ready-made excuses. For example, a manager says, "I can't help [enforcing the rules]. It's *not my idea*. I've got to go along with the rules *like everyone else*." According to the data in this study, functional managers are most likely to use this excuse.

9. The human relations school of management, begun by Elton Mayo and carried through the Hawthorne experiments, finds its present day contemporaries using a variety of labels—participative management, the "X" or "Y" theories of management, and humanistic management, among others. The term "enlightened management" is an accepted inclusive label. In the bank, one finds represented only the more conservative exponents of this managerial tradition.

10. Counseling is a widely employed technique of industrial psychology which involves getting employees to talk about their workplace problems and even about related personal difficulties to supervisors or to professional psychologists. The bank eschews the use of professionals in this regard and assigns this task to its branch managerial personnel. As it happens, enlightened managers place the most emphasis on counseling as an important tool for their managerial work. This is probably because workers, who see enlightened managers as generally approachable, are more likely to respond to their efforts than to those of other managers. A recent pamphlet issued by the bank, entitled *Counseling Your Employes*, encourages all managers to use this technique and is a signal that approaches favored by enlightened managers are favored in some higher administration circles. We should note that in the bank's pamphlet, and in industrial counseling theory in general, the emphasis is on getting workers to air grievances and not necessarily on solving those grievances. The theory is that discussion and reformulation of problems will create subjective frameworks of acceptance and toleration. Some versions of counseling theory even advocate behavior modification techniques in the workplace to get workers to agree with management on a "mutual definition of desirable behavior." For a general treatment from the managerial perspective, see Allen J. Schuh and Milton D. Hakel, "The Counselor in Organizations: A Look to the Future," *Personnel Journal*, 51 (May 1972), especially p. 357. For a more critical perspective, especially about the role of social science in industrial manipulation, see Loren T. Baritz, *The Servants of Power* (New York: Wiley, 1960), pp. 163f.

11. Stanford M. Lyman and Marvin B. Scott, *The Drama of Social Reality* (New York: Oxford Univ. Press, 1975), pp. 116–117.

12. There are some cases where it is clear to both a superior and a worker that the worker alone has specialized knowledge essential for a job's performance. This could occur, for instance, when a newly transferred superior must supervise a job which did not exist at his old branch. Invariably in such cases, workers gain a measure of independence from control in return for accepting the authority figure on grounds other than knowledge.

13. See Hans Gerth and C. Wright Mills's interpretation of George Herbert Mead's social psychology in *Character and Social Structure* (New York: Harcourt, 1953), p. 95. They argue that authoritative others are "significant others whose appraisals sanction actions and desires" and that the appraisals of these others are the most significant aspects of a person's generalized other.

14. For an elaboration of this argument see Robert Presthus, *The Organizational Society* (New York: A. Knopf, 1962), pp. 136–148.

15. This judgment is based on interviews and conversations with a few managers. It is difficult to reconcile their view or, for that matter, the view of those few workers who look forward to parties with observed reality or with the perspectives of many other workers. Parties are generally joyless affairs conducted in a semi-frozen style. Officers do try to mingle with clerks, feinting at conversational topics which almost invariably revert back to work. Work is a subject, however, which does not bear too much discussion nor yield much humor. New topics are awkwardly suggested and dropped; pleasantries are exchanged. Occasionally a male officer will make advances towards an attractive female clerk. For their part, clerks generally feel on guard and stay to themselves or cluster in small groups where they watch and comment on other people's behavior. Still, the bank does consider parties important in keeping up morale and in reinforcing authority relationships and, at least with some workers, it succeeds.

Contrast this description of parties in the bank with the account given of similar affairs at the Uedagin, the Japanese bank studied by Thomas P. Rohlen in his *For Harmony and Strength: Japanese White-Collar Organization in Anthropological Perspective* (Berkeley: Univ. of California Press, 1974), pp. 97–100. Although the organizational purpose of parties in both banks is the same, it is quite clear that Uedagin's employees' experiences are very different. The key reason for this seems to be sharply differing cultural definitions of several aspects of the work role, including sociability towards co-workers, the relationship between work time and free time, and the scope and purpose of authority. Cultural values mediate bureaucratic arrangements and differentially shape the tone and meaning of those arrangements.

9 Work and Life

The organizational settings investigated in the last several chapters are not the only contexts important in shaping people's rationales for work. What Karl Marx called the reproductive sphere of human existence—people's lives outside of work—is also crucial to workers in legitimating their jobs. This chapter explores the links between the reproductive and productive spheres of bank workers' experiences. At one level, where in fact explicit legitimation of work does occur, the links are largely instrumental and grasping them involves examining the consumer goals towards which work is directed. Here, the "making" of "making a living" gains meaning from the "living." At other levels, however, especially in the use of free time, the links between work and life go beyond such instrumental connections. Work penetrates and shapes the quality of people's lives despite their efforts to suppress such a relationship. Another task of this chapter, therefore, is to examine this deeper connection between work and life and people's efforts to blur the relationship. The merely instrumental joining of work and life occurs within a context where the two worlds are already joined.

Work as a Means for Life

Bank workers regard their work as the means by which they purchase their lives outside of work. More exactly, the money which they earn makes life possible. This is a constant theme in workers' interviews. Even given all the wide-ranging and complex meanings of work analyzed in the last several chapters, work, in its most basic sense, means money which is deemed necessary for life. Workers' assertions of this meaning are generally very direct and explicit. For instance, a teller:

Why do I work? Because I need the money. I mean, I need it. . . . Why do other people work? Because they *have* to.

Again, a union clerk:

Why do I work? To make money. . . . Without money, you can't eat, can't travel and there's no other way to make money.

Also, an auditing clerk:

Why do I work? I work because we need the money. That's why I'm working. . . . Work means money.

Or a note teller:

I'm working here because I need a job, and I need money to survive.

Work is perceived as simultaneously necessary and instrumental. Through the medium of money, work becomes the only coin available with which to buy one's existence. Existence or survival is, of course, a socially defined concept, and workers work to sustain a certain way of surviving, one in accord with their past socialization as well as with their future aspirations. To understand the legitimating meaning of workers' lives for their work, we must examine how workers live within contemporary American society and how they want to live in the future.

CONSUMER PACKAGES AND IMAGES OF A NORMAL LIFE

Essentially, bank clerks work to gain and maintain a desired style of life, the material elements of which are immediately and instrumentally related to work. Most work for what David Riesman and Howard Roseborough call a standard "consumer package,"[1] that is, a basic set of consumer goods which have become culturally defined as essential starting points for a consumer career. The structural sources of these socio-cultural products can only be mentioned here. Briefly, the long-run economic choices of a society,[2] the advertising essential for the proper functioning of a mass consumer economy,[3] and the governmentally-sanctioned transfer to the public of the social costs of private profit,[4] all combine along with other influences to produce socially-sanctioned consumption necessities and choices for individuals. Through internalization which is continually reinforced by many elements in the social structure, these necessities and choices become symbolic desired goals of individuals. At the subjective level, then, consumer packages are clusters of desires, which are both imposed and induced, for culturally-approved items.

The basic consumer package which bank workers want is probably typical of that desired or already obtained by most American workers: a house, a car, and whatever accoutrements these items require. One of the perceived essentials for a house is furniture, and a great many workers report either desires for complete furniture sets or expenditures already made for them. In America, these are modest aspirations. Although some workers consider themselves ambitious for such desires, most, in a matter-of-fact way, define their consumption goals as average or normal. A payroll clerk illustrates a common sentiment:

I want a house. I want an average American life.

Again, a clerk-typist:

I want a nice house. . . . the essential things—a car, a house. The normal things, I guess.

Such normality is often equated with being comfortable, and this is valued in itself. A boarding clerk:

What kind of lifestyle do I want? I want a comfortable one. A home, normal things.

People's stress on the normality of their consumer desires is important because it suggests that consumer goods themselves do not motivate people to work; rather, workers feel that the acquisition of a certain consumer package will place them in the mainstream of American society.

Potential additions to the basic American consumer package are, of course, endless, and workers have a wide variety of additional consumer desires or actual acquisitions which cluster around the essential items. A large wardrobe, for instance, or recreational equipment are important to many workers; younger workers in particular mention travel as an important ingredient of their desired lifestyle. A very few workers, because of exposure to countercultural values, emphasize disaccumulation rather than constant accumulation of goods. But most workers develop new wants even as they obtain, and often before they obtain, the major elements of the standard package. These new wants become, in turn, new reasons for working. A lunch-time conversation between two married workers illustrates the expandability of consumer packages:

M. I always have the idea that after a while I'll stop working.

J. But the deadline keeps being extended!

M. After the house, then the car, then the boat, and on and on.

J. I think it's a very natural thing to obtain everything there is to obtain.

Consumption desires motivate work, but the fulfillment of these desires merely fuels more wants and perpetuates the cycle. Reciprocally related to people's work careers are consumer careers; together with other experiences, people try to piece together, out of the goods and experiences their work will buy, a satisfactory way of life.

Bank workers' salaries impede the ready actualization of consumption desires. Table III in the Appendix gives a complete listing of workers' earnings at all the levels in the bank's branch clerical hierarchy. By any American wage standard, their salaries are low; the average gross salary for a middle-level G4 clerk with one year's experience in the bank is approximately $490 a month or $3.11 an hour. Depending on grade and experience, many workers' salaries are considerably lower. Despite the desirable steadiness of their bank-derived incomes, almost all workers are bitter about their pay. Although their anger is most sharply focused on what they perceive to be the essential unfairness of their wage levels, workers also see their low earnings blocking their abilities to live the way they want to live. As might be expected, this creates considerable tension in their lives, although it does not vitiate their desires for consumer packages and for concomitant lifestyles. A young, single teller legitimates his work by his desired lifestyle, even as he points out the difficulty of being a *bon vivant* on a bank clerk's salary:

Why do I work? . . . I have a lifestyle that I have to maintain, and to support it within the framework of society, I have to work to maintain that lifestyle. I like a nice car, like to live in nice places, have a good tennis racket, have new tennis balls, go to the best restaurants, go to [resorts]. I really enjoy living life—going out and living it up, and you can't do that on $163 every two weeks. . . . They pay us shit. You know what I make? One hundred sixty-three dollars every two weeks. Three hundred twenty-six dollars a month take-home.

A married reconcilement clerk, whose husband is in a low-level service job, echoes the same sentiments:

I guess the biggest problem I have with the job is the *pay*. . . . For what we do, we get paid so rotten. By the time you pay for the babysitter—$30 a week—what do you have left? I bring home $378 a month *clear*. That's before the babysitter. . . . there are a lot of things that I would like; if I *had* the money I'd walk into a furniture store and buy a complete set of furniture. I window shop a lot; it's about all I can do. I never give up hope. I figure if you give up hope, if you don't have hope, you'll get really depressed. I just tell myself, "Maybe later." I never say, "No."

Single workers living alone or divorced women with children are in especially difficult economic circumstances. As noted in chapter 5, some of these workers make trade-offs and accept a lower standard of material living in return for a more intangible aspect of desired lifestyle such as independence. Some married workers are in relatively comfortable material situations because there are two income sources in the family. However, pooled incomes usually encourage greater financial obligations, especially mortgages, which involve people in new spending cycles at a higher level of consumption and therefore in new work obligations. In short, people work in order to live in the manner of their choosing, even though they often find that their work cannot provide them with the lifestyles they desire.[5]

It is here that consumer credit use becomes an important issue in bank workers' experiences. Most workers try to fill the gap between their desired lifestyles and their inadequate incomes by borrowing money in one way or another. Consumer debts are a recurring theme in workers' interviews—to cite only a few examples: a union clerk borrows $1,000 to buy furniture; a payroll clerk borrows $700 to buy clothes and a bass fiddle; a note teller purchases a complete stereo system on a credit card. Reflecting a national attitude,[6] workers are ambivalent about such borrowing. They are wary and distrustful of credit use, generally seeing it as a trap; but, at the same time, they cannot resist using it to buy the things they want. For its part, the bank encourages its workers' consumption motivations for work and their concomitant use of credit by lowering employee interest rates on loans and credit cards. Consumer loans are sold to workers for 3½ percent less than the going market rate; similarly, the employee BankColumbiaCard cuts interest rates on credit card purchases from 18 percent to 9 percent a year. The bank is highly successful in selling loans and credit card services to its workers. The great majority of this study's sample and, according to management figures, 80 percent of all bank employees take out consumer loans at the preferred rate, with many employees taking out multiple loans. A full 7 percent of the bank's multibillion dollar consumer loan portfolio consists of employee loans. If anything, clerks borrow more than officers. A similarly high percentage of workers have and use the employee credit card.[7] According to interviews with managers, the bank's strategy in this regard parallels its intentions in its administration of worker security benefits. The lower interest rates on employee loans and on credit card purchases return to the market level if workers quit the bank; thus, the bank can tie workers to itself for long periods of time, increasing the stability of its work force at a relatively low cost. Moreover, employees' low loan delinquency rates and continued tenure at the bank at low salaries more than compensate the bank for the small loss of interest which would be earned if the money were loaned at the market rates. The bank, in any case, still makes a profit. Although borrowed money at attractive interest rates does make desired lifestyles more accessible, it is workers, ironically, who end up paying the bank to live as they choose.

THE USES OF FREE TIME

Perhaps an even more reliable clue to the texture of people's lives is their use of free time. Even though free time is not necessarily instrumentally related to work as is consumption,[8] still, people's everyday activities reveal the deepest meanings of the lives they work to sustain.

Bank workers' experiences of free-time activities bear striking resemblances to their workplace experiences. Many workers feel pressure outside of work which closely parallels their reaction to the often harried work pace in the bank. Particularly for female workers in traditional sex roles, household and child-care chores consume a great deal of their off-the-job time and therefore limit their genuinely nonobligated time. In these cases as in the case of people who are less harried, many seem directionless in their use of available nonobligated time. Such directionlessness matches the aimless quality of people's drift into and tenure with the bank. In their lives in general, at home as at work, workers are often unsure of what they like to do; some even have difficulty recounting concretely how they spend their free time. A general ledger clerk, when asked to describe the areas of meaning in her life outside work, says:

There's nothing really in particular. Whatever more or less happens.

A machine operator appraises how she spends her evenings:

I've gotten to the point where I don't really care for TV. No, I don't read; well, I read sometimes. I really don't enjoy reading that much. [Pause.] When it gets right down to it, I lead a pretty dull life. [Laugh.]

A teller talks about her life outside work:

I don't really have that many outside activities. . . . I don't belong to clubs or anything. I feel that I'm a shallow person because I don't have any outside interests. I don't really *do* anything except go to work and come home.

Such states of drift and seeming inertia are closely related to passivity in the use of free time; in general, workers do not speak of self-directed free-time activities. Reading habits are good indices of people's use of free time, since reading is a self-directed activity accessible to everyone. When asked, only a few bank workers claim to read at all. Of those that do, most read popular magazines or light fiction. Although workers with some college do tend to read slightly more than those with less formal education, nonreading is a pattern which generally cuts across education-al lines. Significantly, the most common explanation for not reading is a stated inability to keep one's mind on the materials at hand. Instead of engaging in self-directed activities, most workers rely on external stimuli which distract rather than fasten the mind. Many, for instance, report shopping as a recreational activity, not to obtain anything in particular but as a way to spend time. The great majority of workers, of course, depend upon television to fill their evenings, as probably do most Americans. Some are avid watchers, viewing a regular schedule of shows for several hours each night. Most workers, however, are unhappy with their reliance on television but continue to watch it anyway. An auditing clerk typifies this pattern:

TV? I find myself sitting in front of it quite often. You must of heard of it called an "idiot box." I don't like to spend my time there but I do. The first thing that I look for is a movie. Like something that I haven't seen before. I usually turn it on every night but usually just for background.

Again, a teller:

TV? I don't really watch it. There's not much that I enjoy. We watch it about two to three hours a night. I don't really get into the programs.

For most people, television is an easy distraction from work and personal cares. Even though it is unsatisfying, it at least fills time or provides a comforting backdrop to other activities. For many workers, television is also an acceptable way of spending time with one's family because it provides a common focus of attention and an inexpensive framework for communal life. However, in mediating and structuring people's experi-ences of their free time so that they are passive participants in a process over which they have little control, television is paradigmatic of other key dimensions of workers' use of free time. Moreover, structured passivity is probably at the root of a great deal of the expressed uneasiness which runs through most workers' statements about how they spend their hours outside of work.

There are some partial exceptions to the patterns of drift and passivity in free-time use. Some workers who evidence these general patterns also stress the importance to them of more active endeavors. These are generally compensatory activities of one sort or another where people seek personal expressions and rewards in their free time which are unavailable in their work. On the whole, with the exceptions of a few workers who engage in satisfying community activities and of other workers with hobbies who will be considered shortly, workers' compensatory free-time activities have a somewhat escapist character. While these activities demand active participation, they are unlikely, given workers' circumstances, to lead to long-run personal satisfaction. While various spiritual interests or devotion to the occult are not uncommon here, active recreational pursuits—particularly participant sports—best exemplify escapist compensation. A utility clerk, for example, discusses the central role assigned to softball in his life:

I play softball. I'm a fanatic. Success for me is reaching the finals. I don't think about work and success. I think about success and softball. Like when you do win, you know that your efforts are worthwhile. . . . I usually play ball six nights a week from early spring to November. Now [December], I have nothing to do at night between now and April, and I get depressed because I have nothing to do. I really enjoy it. People tell me that you better get something else, but I feel that I can play decent ball even when I'm 35. I don't see anything wrong with my batting eye yet.

Other workers, women as well as men, point to bowling, or tennis, or to other sports as significant bases of meaning in their lives. These workers try to make their sources of enjoyment, interest, and recreation into the value centers of their lives; they want to experience somewhere the activity, the achievement, the exhilaration, or, in the case of more esoteric pastimes, the mystery which their work cannot bring them. But no matter how much time they spend on the diamond, or in meditation, or in other rewarding pursuits, these activities cannot provide them with a salary or with a lasting social identification; neither can this time equal the amount of time they spend at work. Despite the growing importance of free-time activities in American society, they can be, for most men and women, only a subplot to the real dramas of their lives, even though people may try to place such activities in center stage.

In a similar yet somewhat different way, some workers point to their personal hobbies as important sources of meaning in their lives. These workers emphasize the importance of doing something constructive with their free time. They find in writing, drawing, sewing, crocheting, interior decorating, or other handicrafts arenas for expressing their creativity, which is not called into play in their jobs. Like sports, these activities are compensatory. They differ from sports, however, because hobbies are another form of work and, as such, have the potential for giving people the experience of being productive in a way that purely recreational activities cannot. However, in a final structural parallel between bank workers' jobs and their use of free time, discussions with workers who have hobbies reveal very frustrating experiences of fragmentation and consequent lack of productivity. Fragmentation is the feeling of life being broken into little pieces, and it closely parallels the frustration which highly segmented work creates. Indeed, segmentation at work probably causes fragmentation outside of work. Routinized, segmented work erodes the energy, mental discipline, and ability to concentrate which are the prerequisites for creative expression. The experience of fragmentation cripples workers who want to be productive outside of their jobs. Workers with hobbies are often discouraged with their free-time efforts. They cannot, after work, summon up the energy to pour themselves into further, even though different, work. They leave their jobs in a state of restless agitation, as do most bank workers; after settling themselves and attending to necessary chores, they discover that the evening, the only possible time during the work week for creative work, is almost gone. Their tiredness is not conducive to serious efforts in any case. Their weekends are better, but too short to complete projects, the accomplishment of which could encourage new efforts. After a period of time, and as a defensive measure because of their lack of visible success or progress in a hobby, workers begin to denigrate their interests or to relegate them to decidedly secondary places in their lives. Other people's opinions are important here. Since many people refuse to value unpaid work, workers feel no sense of social worth in their efforts. Projects remain unfinished, and new hobbies are started. The same cycle repeats itself, increasing discouragement and a sense of being scattered, making what could be creative work into another form of distraction and, for many, of debilitation quite similar to that which the lack of recognition and success at work creates.

With the partial exceptions of some compensatory activities, workers' free-time experiences mirror their work experiences. This is not to say that workers are consciously aware of the parallels noted here; generally speaking, their awareness of work's impact on life assumes other forms. Still, whether workers are aware of it or not, these data suggest, as Martin Meissner has shown in another study,[9] that the structural forms of people's work reach far beyond the workplace.

The lives that bank workers work to sustain are then clearly problematic in themselves. Nonetheless, the lifestyles constructed from real and desired consumption and from uses of free time remain important legitimations for work. Workers, however, often focus so closely on lifestyles that the relationship between work and lifestyle is blurred, if not forgotten. This point emerges very strongly in workers' definitions of success. Success for bank workers—insofar as the idea has meaning at all—consists mainly of the accomplishment of one's personal, private goals; it means attaining the consumer goods one desires and finding interesting things to do in one's free time, usually within a familial context which provides for workers' basic social needs. In short, success means being happy within a personally chosen and socially accepted way of life. A union clerk's definition of success is typical of that of most bank workers:

Success? It's all those things I told you about put together: (1) taking care of all your bills; (2) getting a nice home and things we need for it; (3) having wonderful kids; (4) save up money for their education; (5) enjoy yourself with your husband and have what you need. That's success.

Some workers, those who are more acutely aware of the traditional meanings of success in America, reject the word altogether, although they retain the concept of reaching some goals. Wealth, mobility, prestige, influence, and the material symbols of success remain desirable but remote and therefore inapplicable to their own lives. A note teller comments on this:

I use this word "success" very infrequently, and I think about it very little. It's hard for me to define success. As long as I'm happy—you know, a lot of people in office and clerical positions don't feel that they can experience success; they don't feel that they are in a position to experience it. So they don't think about it. Because it doesn't relate to them somehow.

Instead of basing success on occupational achievement, people think in terms of being happy or having what they need and want. The only connection between work and being happy is a monetary one, and that impersonal mediating relationship seems to obscure the deeper intrinsic connections between work and the rest of life. Despite the parallels and connections between the two worlds, some of which are directly experienced, most workers try to keep them separate. Here, work is only the necessary instrument to obtain money which buys a way of living. The problem is that work is much more than that and, more to the point, workers know that it is, despite their efforts to compartmentalize their work from their life.

Compartmentalization and Awareness of the Impact of Work on Life

Through compartmentalization people attempt to keep different areas of their lives, and particularly the emotional problems which arise from those areas, segregated from one another. Although this psychological phenomenon is by no means restricted to modern societies, it is probably particularly widespread in such complex bureaucratic social orders where people must each day play several different, often contradictory roles. The segregation of the emotions associated with different roles allows each role to be performed without the possible encumbrance of emotions from other roles. Compartmentalization is one psychological counterpart of the segmentation and general rationalization which marks all bureaucratic systems. In a bureaucratic society, therefore, compartmentalization is "functional;" and the ability to compartmentalize is often extolled as a personal and indeed public virtue. Individuals' reasons for dividing their psychological lives into segments do not, of course, depend upon such definitions of their behavior as functional, although this may be the case.

Nowhere is compartmentalization more evident in our society than in people's attempts to separate their work from the rest of their lives. Many social observers report this phenomenon.[10] It is safe to say that, with the exception of some craftsmen, some professionals, and some upper-level management executives, most American workers under present working conditions in this country try to keep the worlds of work and of free time psychologically apart and, in the process, try to place a higher value on their free-time activities.[11] Almost all bank workers evidence this pattern. Their reasons for compartmentalizing are probably indicative of those of other workers in similar situations. Briefly, since they find their work extremely troublesome and generally unrewarding, they separate it from the other areas of their lives where they hope to find some personal fulfillment. Although work is seen as instrumentally necessary for life, it is defined at this level as an impediment to happiness and as something, therefore, which must be kept separate and contained.

The extent to which workers can successfully compartmentalize work from life varies. A few workers claim to be able to block out all thought of their jobs upon leaving the bank. For instance, a boarding clerk when asked about the impact of her job on her life says:

Oh, this doesn't affect my life at all. . . . You can just leave it here. I never think about it.

Again, a bookkeeper:

Well, there's very little connection really. I come here at 8:15 A.M. and I leave at 5:00 P.M., and I forget it when I go home. . . . I just think about other things at home. I don't think about work. No, I don't have to deliberately *not* think about it. I just don't.

These workers seem able to keep sharply defined barriers erected between the different parts of their lives. In most cases, they define their work as a job which plays a decidedly unimportant part in their lives. An auditing clerk:

I don't think that it's that important to me. I mean my work. It's like a separate thing to me. I don't think about it after work. I mean, here you have your problems and worries, and out there you have problems and worries. They are different. I think that it should be that way. I don't think that work is that important.

Definitions of work as unimportant devalue work and simultaneously isolate it as a social role from the other roles of one's life. Precisely through such neutralization of the work role, these workers are able to establish a kind of balance in their lives. The balance may be a precarious one; it is certainly one that depends upon a continued devaluation of work and a rigorous suppression of its latent importance. More than once during field work, workers who claim successful compartmentalization responded to probes into these areas with warning statements, like the response of a general ledger clerk:

You are making me think about things that I don't want to think about.

Successful compartmentalization may require not only definitions of work as unimportant, but lives which are consciously unexamined.

Although they attempt compartmentalization, most bank workers are continually aware of the impact of work on their lives. The most immediately felt effect of clerical work is that it tires people out and undercuts their free time. Highly rationalized office work, though not physically onerous, nonetheless puts a deep strain on people by its overt and subtle pressures for production. A clerk from a country with more traditional modes of production tells how and why bank work affects his life:

[When I first came here and] I heard that it was only eight hours a day, five days a week—a 40-hour week—I thought, "This is going to be easy." But then I found that the work load was so metered, your time was so programmed, that they wring everything out of you while you are at work. When I leave here, I can't do anything. I've heard that all the work—the amount of it—is audited and then put into a computer, and if it's not enough then they don't take on new hands, or they may lay off old ones. Everything is metered. I had never seen that before. And it's hard to get used to. I understand now why in my country people don't have high blood pressure. They're not under this constant pressure at work.

Many other workers speak of a similar exhaustion or, in a common phrase, of being "wiped out" by their work. Their personal exhaustion is one result of the bank's continual efforts to cut costs. Even though they produce no concrete commodities, clerical workers in commercial enterprises constitute a new type of production worker in a capitalism increasingly geared towards services;[12] their work, therefore, is a special target for intensive rationalization. Job-induced tiredness affects people's moods outside of work as well, and many workers attribute crankiness to such exhaustion. A teller contrasts her moods after she began working at the bank with her previous experiences:

. . . I'm really tired now. Almost all the time, I'm tired. I'm also getting really bitchy—really moody. I was never like that before. I don't like to let my job interfere with my life.

The social strains of the workplace also spill over into people's lives and produce an enervating tension akin to the tiredness caused by production pressures. Again and again in the data, workers talk about the constant strain both of living with the hidden social tensions and quiet resentments of the bureaucratic workplace and of adapting their public faces to fit the commercial and social requirements of their jobs. They also speak about how they must, when they get home, talk out the tensions, often yelling to "blow off steam." When this can be done, such externalization of work tensions through language is considered a healthy coping response. But workers also indicate that the tensions cannot always be aired. Mates and friends tire of hearing the same complaints, and sometimes the small annoying antagonisms of the clerical work world seem petty even to workers. Many work-derived tensions are, therefore, suppressed, and flash out in sudden bursts of anger usually directed at family because an emotional display at work could have serious consequences. Here, workers' awareness of the impact of work on life is often latent and reveals itself in the juxtaposition of their comments. Despite an extricating appeal to defeasibility where action is separated from intention, a safe-deposit clerk's statement points out the semi-conscious connection which many people make between the maintenance of a necessarily guarded public face at work and the eruption of tensions in the home:

We get quite a few people here . . . with special complaints. On a heavy day, we'll get 10 to 15 people an hour. It's one window nobody really wants to get on. It's a hectic window. Everybody has problems. . . . But I never lose my patience. I don't think that I've ever been angry at anyone in the last 10 years. [Pause.] Except when I'm home. There I blow up at the least little thing. I don't understand why I do that.

The tiredness and social tension of rationalized commercial work are experiences which seep under the barriers erected between work and life and shape the quality of people's lives.

Workers also see their jobs intruding on their lives in other ways, subtly demanding their unwilling attention. Several workers claim, for instance, that they are constantly reminded of their work during their free time by external factors over which they have no control. The proliferation of First Bank of Columbia branches, the bank's extensive advertising campaigns, and even the presence of companies which the bank services insistently remind them of their organizational affiliation and of their jobs. A machine operator:

The job really affects the rest of your life. You begin to think about nothing else. Like when I'm driving and I see a certain sign, you know, of another company, I'll think, "Oh, yeah, they have an account at our bank." It's stupid, but it's there in your mind. Even though you try to leave it behind, it's always there. . . . You can't help but have your work affect you. Whether you like it or hate it, it has to affect the rest of your life.

Even without external stimuli, the sheer amount of time people spend working creates psychic baggage which cannot easily be placed aside. Many clerical workers worry about technical details of their jobs—about mistakes which they have made or might make or about the amounts of money which they must handle every day. Some workers report that they dream regularly about aspects of their work, often waking up wondering whether they processed items correctly or behaved in the socially appropriate fashion. In short, despite efforts at compartmentalization, factors both extrinsic and intrinsic to the workplace keep thrusting work into at least the edge, and often the center, of people's consciousness.

Perhaps most important of all, a great many workers sense that their jobs are damaging their selves, an experience which cannot easily be compartmentalized. Within the overall context of this study, which has repeatedly focused on the issue of work and self, these perceptions of self-damage are ambiguous since workers are ambivalent about their work. Workers define many aspects of their jobs positively and see themselves as benefitting from them. However, the negative side of their ambivalence constantly asserts itself, often in expressions of a sense of unfulfilled potential and a corresponding sense of being stifled. A teller, for instance, says very bluntly:

[My] work stifles my real self.

Very few workers claim that their jobs aid their self-development, and many feel that their work not only stands between them and what they could be but also is leading them in directions not of their choosing. One worker comments on this in talking about the sources of meaning in her life:

You mean, what's my thing in life? I don't know. [Long pause.] I don't really know what would make me happy. Let's put it this way. I know it's not working at a job like this. . . . On an intellectual level, I feel like I'm on a steady decline. If I did this for the rest of my life, I'd become exactly what I don't want to be.

In this view, shared in various ways by many, work in the bank is an oppressive weight which smothers self-expression and negatively shapes identity. Almost no one wants to participate consciously in activities perceived to be self-damaging. By mentally dividing their lives into self-contained spheres, people can try to minimize the general impact of problems in any one sphere. But despite such attempts at segregating emotions, people know that trouble at work affects the rest of their lives. While compartmentalization is imperative if people are to continue working, it is also impossible in such contexts. A payroll clerk:

I really try hard to keep the bank out of the rest of my life. As soon as I leave here, that's it. I know it's not healthy to chop up your life into little segments, but I'd have to quit if I didn't. . . . But I'll admit that it's done things to my psyche— chopping up my life, doing things that are not important to me—that's not good at all.

The work-related sense of self-damage, of unfulfilled potential, can be temporarily suppressed but it cannot be permanently contained. Nowhere is the deep ambiguity of bank workers' entire situation more evident than here. These workers work at jobs they feel ambivalent about in order to live in a style of their choosing; yet if they are to enjoy that life, they must try to cordon off the scores of hours a month they spend at their jobs. Still, their work and what their work does to them reach beyond the functionally useful barriers which they erect to get through their days. Despite all the legitimations which they fashion for their work, many of them feel that, at best, their jobs leave their selves unemployed.

References

1. David Riesman and Howard Roseborough, "Careers and Consumer Behavior," in David Riesman, *Abundance for What?* (Garden City: Doubleday, 1964), pp. 114-115.

2. In the United States, the most fundamental long-run economic choice, of course, has been for the capitalist premise—namely, the organization of the economic order around the principle of private profit and property. This premise has decisive ramifications in every sphere of the economic and, indeed, entire social order. On the basis of that premise, particular economic choices are made which, while they immediately further the interests of particular business or professional classes, have profound and frequently destructive impacts on vast numbers of other people both in the present and future. The American decision to shape a transportation network based on the automobile instead of on public transit is a classic case. See Emma Rothschild, *Paradise Lost: The Decline of the Auto-Industrial Age* (New York: Random House, 1975). The organization of a health-care system controlled by professionals who are also entrepreneurs is another. See Barbara and John Ehrenreich, *The American Health Empire: Power, Profits and Politics* (New York: Vintage, 1971).

3. There is a plethora of books on the advertising industry and its decisive impact on American society. Among the most interesting are: Frank S. Presbrey, *The History and Development of Advertising* (Garden City: Doubleday, Durant & Co., 1929); E. S. Turner, *The Shocking History of Advertising!* (New York: Dutton, 1953); and Martin Mayer, *Madison Avenue U.S.A.* (New York: Harper, 1958).

4. This is the economic notion of "external diseconomies," which are economic costs which someone must bear for social problems created by the normal operations of private industry. These costs can be small ones, such as people's increased laundry bills due to nearby industrial pollution, or large ones, such as the long-term results of illness and medical bills caused by the same pollution. External diseconomies are sanctioned by government through the lack of effective preventive legislation and through inadequate enforcement of existing legislation.

5. During periods of rapid inflation people's lifestyles are, of course, eroded no matter how hard they work. Towards the end of the field research for this study, rapid inflation began to occur in the American economy and many workers complained of necessary cutbacks even in essentials like food.

6. See Lewis Mandell, *Credit Card Use in the United States* (Ann Arbor: Institute for Social Research, Univ. of Michigan, 1972). Of the respondents to this study, 75% consider credit cards a temptation to which they do not want to yield, yet half of them use credit cards anyway.

7. Within their income bracket, bank workers are probably anomalies regarding credit use. Generally speaking, credit card ownership and use decline as income level declines. It is usually harder for people with lower incomes to get credit cards in the first place. However, the bank's encouragement of consumer spending through credit use enables all bank employees to borrow money, whatever their income levels.

8. Generally, in their own minds, people "have" rather than "work for" free time. However, many free-time activities demand consumer items such as television sets, stereos, sports equipment, and automobiles. At another level, therefore, these activities are also instrumentally related to work.

9. Martin Meissner, "The Long Arm of the Job: A Study of Work and Leisure," *Industrial Relations*, 10 (October 1971), 239-260. In this very able study of industrial workers, Meissner found that work experiences carry over into free-time activities. Workers who experience constraints of various sorts at work engage less than other workers in free-time activities where discretionary judgments and planning are required. Workers who are socially isolated at work reduce, in their spare time, their exposure to situations where they have to talk.

10. See, for instance, Adriano Tilgher's general treatment of the separation of work and life in an industrial society in *Homo Faber*, translated by Dorothy Canfield Fisher (Chicago: Henry Regnery, 1958), pp. 159-163. Robert Dubin analyzes more empirically the assigned significance of work and life among industrial workers in "Industrial Workers' Worlds: A Study of the Central Life Interests of Industrial Workers," in *Social Problems*, 3 (No. 3, 1956), 131-142; and C. Wright Mills in *White Collar* (New York: Oxford Univ. Press, 1951), pp. 235-238, analyzes the "big split" between work and life among white-collar employees.

11. Robert Blauner's data suggest that this is not the case for printers and other craftsmen who control their working conditions. See *Alienation and Freedom* (Chicago: Univ. of Chicago Press, 1964), pp. 35–57. Similarly, Louis Orzack in a study of professional nurses found a dominant attachment to work which cut across other phases of their lives. See "Work as a 'Central Life Interest' of Professionals," *Social Problems*, 7 (Fall 1959), 125–132. Finally, Joseph Bensman's portrait of the advertising executive points out the narcissistic compulsiveness of work for many top executives. See "The Advertising Man and His Work," in *Dollars and Sense* (New York: MacMillan, 1967), pp. 9–68.

12. For a good general description of the transformation of American capitalism into a service-oriented economy, see Victor Fuchs, *The Service Economy* (New York: National Bureau of Economic Research, 1968).

part four

CONCLUSION

10 Bureaucratic Work and Social Order

However tangled, ambiguous, and troubling bank workers' experiences of their work may be, they live their public lives steadily and quietly. Their accounts and motives for work help produce social order in their lives, and it is on this central sociological process that I wish to refocus attention in this final chapter. In analyzing people's legitimations for work, this book has had as its basic concern the subjective mechanisms by which people fashion order out of the underlying conflicts in their world and, in doing so, help reproduce and maintain the social structure. Workers' accounts for their problems on the job help them shape truces with alienating work situations and enable them to continue working; their asserted motives for work explain the world to themselves and to others and provide positive rationales for the work that they do. Moreover, it is important, both personally and socially, that this fashioning of order happens within workers' work roles, for these roles are clearly crucial parts of their lives and, taken collectively, help form part of the economic basis of society itself. Since people's conscious realities are conditioned by their social situations, a full understanding of workers' legitimations for work has also meant an examination of the power contexts within which the legitimations are asserted. The most important context for understanding bank workers' constructions of their world is the organizational apparatus of the First Bank of Columbia. Although I have examined other aspects of these workers' lives as they relate to and are affected by work, I have spent the most time unraveling the bank's bureaucratic intricacies as they influence workers' experiences. For these workers, and for millions of other white-collar workers, the key social structure which unites and shapes their meanings for work, including their legitimations for what they do, is precisely the *bureaucratic* dimension of their work world, that is, its highly rational, standardized, hierarchical, segmented, and impersonal character. Moreover, as we have

170

seen, elements of bureaucratic work experiences spill over into other areas of workers' lives. The final task of this book is to examine, in a structural way, how the specifically bureaucratic character of their work shapes bank workers' experiences and underpins their own making of social order.

Bureaucratic Work and the Routinization of Personal Experience

The bureaucratic work in which bank workers are engaged shapes their life experiences, at least in their public roles, into orderly and stable patterns. Such personal stability is not a principal organizational goal of the First Bank of Columbia, but is, rather, a by-product of the bank's bureaucratized operation which has, as we have seen, quite different aims. I want to detail the main ordering influences which bureaucratic work has on bank workers.

1) *Bureaucratic work routinizes and ritualizes workers' lives and shapes stable patterns of behavior and, at the same time, circumscribed world views.* Because of its continuous regularity, bureaucratic work, more than most other forms of work, shapes workers' experiences of time and their daily activity as well in a very orderly fashion. Such work engages workers constantly in socially-approved, purposive action. The very rationality of such action infuses workers' outlooks with a markedly steadfast character because their work gives them a measure of social respectability which places them in the mainstream of a work-oriented society. The act of regularly working in a social context becomes for many workers a ritual which has, despite their ambivalence towards what they do, great emotional import in their lives. Regularized work faithfully performed, even when disliked, becomes a fixed point of reference and a comforting framework in many workers' lives; it comes to represent desirable constructive activity and an important, if vague, measure of personal progress, both of which are emotional counterweights to personal drift. Most important, the bank's bureaucratic work context, with its well-defined system of rewards, offers workers financial and concomitant emotional security, even if modest and perhaps ultimately illusory, in return for at least external conformity to organizational rules. Over a period of time, then, engagement in bureaucratic work regularizes workers' experiences in their public world. In the process, such regularization narrows workers' visions about their lives and about social arrangements, creating a kind of myopia where alternatives do not even occur to them, let alone seem feasible. In fact, present realities, both personal and social, come to be seen as inevitable and intractable. Finally, insofar as bureaucratic work reaches beyond the workplace and shapes workers' experiences outside of work, it routinizes their free-time activities as well. Free time comes to mirror work time.

2) *Bureaucratic work brings workers into daily proximity with and subordination to authority; among the images of reality which workers gain from such contact are confusing but nonetheless stabilizing perceptions of their own experiences.* Authority guarantees all social institutions, and subordination to workplace authority secures the personal routine which bureaucratic work shapes in workers' lives. Bank workers are involved, day after day, in subordinate relationships to authority in the workplace. Generally speaking, workplace authority is the most important type of authority in workers' adult experiences. In fact, some of the data of this study suggest that, in borrowing familial images to strengthen itself, workplace authority appropriates and becomes a partial substitute for even the most rudimentary form of social authority, at least with younger workers. Most workers remain deeply ambivalent about workplace authority. However, because they are isolated from other workers, because authority figures are the arbiters of material and social rewards at work, and because it is socially appropriate to do so, workers do comply with managerial wishes, although in most cases not wholeheartedly. Such external compliance demands, however, that workers always take account of authorities' perceptions of the world and of workers themselves. In the absence of any social basis for workers to assert or even form counterviews, inherently conservative official versions of reality and self, even if not wholly accepted, become over a period of time important, though ambiguous, influences on workers' interpretations of their experiences. More than anything else, managerial perspectives so internalized confuse workers' own interpretations of even their alienating experiences; such confusion characteristically produces an ambivalent indisposition to remedial action.

3) *Bureaucratic work situations foster individualistic and semi-isolated perspectives and approaches to the personal problems which result from rationalized work; while such individualism and semi-isolation are often enervating, they are also socially stabilizing.* Despite bureaucracy's hallmark of standardization and the ethos of teamwork characteristic of the First Bank of Columbia, the bureaucratic aspect of bank work is an individualizing and isolating social structure. Bureaucratic work in the bank separates people from each other even while it coordinates their actions to perform tasks. Part of this separation between workers stems from the standardized and segmented shape of bureaucratic work and the consequent absence of meaningful, unifying common tasks. The major part of this separation, however, is caused by personal and social antagonisms and suspicions which emerge from workers' competition for scarce rewards—especially money, status, managerial approval, and advancement—and from workers' personal and social attempts to gain, at other workers' expense, some control through negative comparison over the making of their workplace identities. Competition for rewards, competing status claims, and concomitant animosity are intrinsic to bureaucratic structures, but are especially evident in work situations such

as those in bank branches where great work and social pressures are placed on workers.[1] Since workers in the bank are so separated from one another, they most often do not perceive common bases for the problems which arise from their rationalized work. Rather, problems are defined and accounted for as private troubles, and workers generally pursue individual settlements of them, usually within already established frameworks for action. Habits of defining and accounting for or otherwise settling problems individually rather than collectively make workers' worlds of meaning highly individualistic, indeed somewhat privatistic. Their semi-isolation is personally alienating but socially integrating, at least within a bureaucratic context, because private coping is inherently ambiguous and leads, in time, to a psychological inertia which reinforces habituation to routine.

It is within this context that bank workers come to live with their work. Like many people in our society, they are involved in work which they do not control; in fact, because of their structural positions, the organizational and social framework of the bank seems intractable to them. But these workers are not defeated nor reduced to despair by such perceived intractability, although they often come close to these experiences. Rather, they account for and cope with their troubles as best they can and make their situations tolerable if not enjoyable; in such ways, they try wherever possible to extend the parameters of their individual control over their own immediate situations at work, even if this only means distancing themselves from their actions. As it happens, such fashioning of separate truces helps reproduce and maintain the very mode of organizing work which is so problematic for them; as is often the case, the struggle for individual rather than collective survival is the basis of an alienating social order. Finally, the same bureaucratic structure which prohibits workers from achieving self-direction in their work and which narrows their visions of the world and of themselves also gives them positive reasons to keep on working. It provides workers with stable, rational, and predictable patterns of regularized activity which are socially and authoritatively approved and, at least to a small extent, are emotionally comforting. Moreover, it anchors regularity with the promise if not the substance of security in an insecure society. Perhaps more than anything else, this helps workers come to terms with their world.

Reference

1. Research by Stuart M. Klein on production workers suggests that work pressure—that is, for faster production—is the key variable in prohibiting "social-supportive" or "cohesive" behavior in blue-collar work situations. Instead, work pressure enforced by authorities leads to "competitive and intragroup conflict behavior." See *Workers Under Stress* (Lexington, Ky.: Univ. of Kentucky Press, 1971), especially pp. 100–101. Work pressures are also an important factor in shaping the divisiveness among bank workers, but more important are the various types of social pressures which are especially characteristic of white-collar work.

Appendix

SALARY RANGES AND PERFORMANCE EVALUATIONS

Table III below charts the bank's salary structure for the clerical grades G3 through G7; the highest two clerical grades, G8 and G9, are reserved for executive secretarial positions and are not found in the branches. As noted in the text, the overwhelming majority of branch clerks are in grades G3 through G5.

Table III also presents the timetable for work-performance evaluations. Salary increases are geared to performance reports which evaluate a worker's overall performance as satisfactory, superior, or outstanding. The dollar amount of raises depends upon these ratings, as shown by the increase pattern at the far right of Table 3. Operations officers make these evaluations *semi-annually* until a worker reaches her *performance control point*, the approximate midpoint of her grade. The performance control point itself is divided into satisfactory, superior, and outstanding categories, each with a corresponding salary figure. A worker's most recent performance report evaluation determines her *performance control point* rating and salary. After reaching the *performance control point*, the worker is reviewed and receives raises only once a year until she reaches her *performance maximum* salary level, also geared to her latest evaluation. There is no salary progression beyond this level unless the worker changes her grade level. By providing semi-annual evaluations and, if work performance is judged satisfactory, semi-annual raises until the grade-midpoint is reached, this system seems aimed at fostering an illusion of rapid progression during a worker's early days in a grade. However, once a worker passes her grade-midpoint, salary increases slow to once a year.

Table 3

CLERICAL SALARY RANGES AND INCREASE PATTERNS
(for Grades G3 through G7)

Grade	Minimum	Performance Control Point			Performance Maximum			Increase Pattern		
		Sat.	Sup.	Out.	Sat.	Sup.	Out.	Sat.	Sup.	Out.
3	$420	$465	$480	$495	$555	$570	$590	$ 20	$ 25	$30-35
4	450	510	525	545	610	635	660	20	25	30-35
5	480	555	570	590	680	705	730	20	25-30	35-40
6	555	630	645	665	755	780	805	25-30	35-40	45-50
7	605	690	705	725	800	850	880	25-30	35-45	50-55

Note: Sat. = Satisfactory
Sup. = Superior
Out. = Outstanding

Bibliography

Abegglen, James C. *The Japanese Factory*. Glencoe, Illinois: Free Press, 1958.

Anon. "Retail Banking Enters New Phase." *Bankers Monthly*, 84 (August 15, 1967), 20 f.

Argyris, Chris. *Organization of a Bank*. New Haven: Labor and Management Center, Yale Univ., 1954.

———. *Personality and Organization: The Conflict Between System and Individual*. New York: Harper, 1957.

Aronowitz, Stanley. *False Promises*. New York: McGraw Hill, 1973.

Bankers Trust Company. *1970 Study of Industrial Retirement Plans*. New York: Bankers Trust Co., 1970.

Bardht, Hans P. *Industriebürokratie: Versuch Einer Soziologie des Industrialisierten Burobetriebes und Seiner Angestellten*. Stuttgart: Enke, 1958.

Baritz, Loren. *The Servants of Power*. New York: John Wiley and Sons, 1960.

Barum, Daniel J. *The Final Plateau*. Toronto: Burns and MacEachern, Ltd., 1974.

Baxter, William F., Paul H. Cootner, and Kenneth E. Scott. *Retail Banking in the Electronic Age: The Law and Economics of Electronic Funds Transfer*. Montclair, N.J.: Allanheld, Osmun & Co., 1977.

Bell, Daniel. "Labor in the Post-Industrial Society." *The World of the Blue Collar Worker*. Edited by Irving Howe. New York: Quadrangle-New York Times, 1972.

———. *Work and Its Discontents: The Cult of Efficiency in America*. Boston: Beacon Press, 1956.

Benét, Mary K. *The Secretarial Ghetto*. New York: McGraw Hill, 1972.

Bensman, Joseph. *Dollars and Sense*. New York: MacMillan, 1967.

Bensman, Joseph, and Robert Lilienfeld. *Craft and Consciousness*. New York: John Wiley and Sons, 1973.

Bensman, Joseph, and Bernard Rosenberg. "The Meaning of Work in Bureaucratic Society." *Identity and Anxiety*. Edited by Maurice Stein, Arthur J. Vidich, and David M. White. New York: Free Press, 1960, 181–197.

Bensman, Joseph, and Arthur J. Vidich. *The New American Society*. Chicago: Quadrangle, 1971.

———. "Social Theory in Field Research." *Sociology on Trial*. Edited by Maurice Stein and Arthur Vidich. Englewood Cliffs, New Jersey: Prentice-Hall, 1963, 162–172.

Berg, Ivar. *Education and Jobs: The Great Training Robbery*. New York: Praeger, 1970.

Berger, Peter, ed. *The Human Shape of Work*. New York: MacMillan, 1964.

Berger, Peter, and Thomas Luckmann. *The Social Construction of Reality*. Garden City, New York: Doubleday-Anchor, 1967.

Bendix, Reinhard. *Work and Authority in Industry*. New York: John Wiley and Sons, 1952.

Berlin, Ronald S. "Towards a General Analytic Framework for the Study of Status Inconsistency." Unpublished Paper (mimeo), Dept. of Sociology, Univ. of Pittsburgh, April 17, 1970.

Blau, Peter. *Bureaucracy in Modern Society*. New York: Random House, 1956.

——. "Presidential Address: Parameters of Social Structure." *American Sociological Review*, 39 (October 1974), 625–628.

Blau, Zena S. *Old Age in a Changing Society*. New York: New Viewpoints, 1973.

Blauner, Robert. *Alienation and Freedom: The Factory Worker and His Industry*. Chicago: Univ. of Chicago Press, 1964.

——. "Work Satisfaction and Industrial Trends in Modern Society." *Class, Status and Power*. Edited by Reinhard Bendix and Seymour M. Lipset. 2nd ed. New York: Free Press, 1966, 473–487.

Blum, Alan F., and Peter McHugh. "The Social Ascription of Motives." *American Sociological Review*, 36 (February 1971), 98–109.

Blum, Albert A. "The Office Employee." *White Collar Workers*. Edited by Albert Blum, et al. New York: Random House, 1971.

Blumberg, Paul. *Industrial Democracy: The Sociology of Participation*. New York: Schocken Books, 1969.

Bonjean, Charles M., and Michael D. Grimes. "Bureaucracy and Alienation: A Dimensional Approach." *Social Forces*, 48 (March 1970), 365–373.

Braude, Lee. *Work and Workers*. New York: Praeger, 1975.

Braverman, Harry. *Labor and Monopoly Capital: The Degradation of Work in the Twentieth Century*. New York: Monthly Review Press, 1974.

Brewer, John. "Organizational Patterns of Supervision: A Study of the Debureaucratization of Authority Relations in Two Business Organizations." *The Sociology of Organizations*. Edited by Oscar Grusky and George A. Miller. New York: Free Press, 1970, 341-347.

Burke, Kenneth. *A Grammar of Motives and a Rhetoric of Motives*. Cleveland: World, 1962.

Burns, R. K. "The Comparative Economic Position of Manual and White-Collar Employees." *Journal of Business*, 27 (No. 4), 257–267.

Caplow, Theodore. *Principles of Organization*. New York: Harcourt, Brace and World, 1964.

Chaney, Laura K. *The Way Up: A Guide for the Office Worker*. New York: Vantage Press, 1960.

Chapman, John M. *Concentration of Banking*. New York: Columbia Univ. Press, 1934.

Chapman, John M., and Ray B. Westerfield. *Branch Banking*. New York: Harper and Bros., 1942.

Chinoy, Ely. *Automobile Workers and the American Dream*. Boston: Beacon Press, 1965.

Collins, Charles W. *The Branch Banking Question*. New York: MacMillan, 1926.

Corey, Lewis. *The Crisis of the Middle Class*. New York: Covici-Friede, 1935.

Cressey, Donald R. *Other People's Money*. Glencoe, Illinois: Free Press, 1953.

Crocker Bank. *Skills of the Labor Force in California*. San Francisco: Crocker Bank, One Montgomery Street, 1973.

Crozier, Michael. *The Bureaucratic Phenomenon*. Chicago: Univ. of Chicago Press, 1964.

——. *The World of the Office Worker*. Chicago: Univ. of Chicago Press, 1971.

Dahrendorf, Ralf. *Class and Class Conflict in Industrial Society*. Stanford, California: Stanford Univ. Press, 1959.

Dalton, Melville. *Men Who Manage*. New York: John Wiley and Sons, 1959.

Davis, Louis E., Albert B. Cherns, and Associates. *The Quality of Working Life*. 2 vols. New York: Free Press, 1975.

DeGrazia, Sebastian. *Of Time, Work and Leisure*. Garden City, New York: Doubleday, 1964.

De Maria, Alfred T., Dale Tarnowieski, and Richard Gurman. *Manager Unions?* New York: American Management Association, 1972.

Dibble, Vernon. "Occupations and Ideologies." *American Journal of Sociology*, 68 (September 1962), 229–241.

Dreyfuss, Carl. *Occupation and Ideology of the Salaried Employee*. 2 vols. Translated by Eva Abramovitch. WPA Project #465-97-3-81. New York: Dept. of Social Science, Columbia Univ., 1938.

Dubin, Robert. "Industrial Workers' Worlds: A Study of the Central Life Interests of Industrial Workers." *Social Problems*, 3 (No. 3, 1956), 131–142.

Durant, H. W. *The Problem of Leisure*. London: Routledge & Sons, Ltd., 1938.

Edwards, Richard C. "Alienation and Inequality: Capitalist Relations of Production in Bureaucratic Enterprises." Doctoral Dissertation, Dept. of Economics, Harvard Univ., 1972.

Ehrenreich, Barbara, and John Ehrenreich. *The American Health Empire: Power, Profits and Politics*. New York: Vintage, 1971.

Engelhard, Erich. *The Salaried Employee*. Translated by E. E. Warburg. WPA Project #465-97-3-81. New York: Columbia Univ., 1939.

Erickson, Kai. "Notes on the Sociology of Deviance." *The Other Side*. Edited by Howard Becker. New York: Free Press, 1964, 9–21.

Ericson, A. S. "International Comparison of White-Collar Working Conditions." *Monthly Labor Review*, 80 (November 1957), 1351–1355.

Fallada, Hans. *Little Man, What Now?* New York: Simon and Schuster, 1933.

Flannery, Mark J., and Dwight Jaffee. *The Economic Implications of an Electronic Money Transfer System*. Lexington, Massachusetts: D. C. Heath, 1973.

Fleishman, E. A. "Leadership Climate, Human Relations Training and Supervisory Behavior." *Personnel Psychology*, 6 (1953), 205–222.

Ford, Robert. *Motivation Through the Work Itself*. New York: American Management Association, 1969.

Fournet, G. P., *et al.* "Job Satisfaction: Issues and Problems." *Personnel Psychology*, 19 (Summer 1966), 165–183.

Fraser, Ronald, ed. *Work: Twenty Personal Accounts*. Harmondsworth. England: Penguin, 1968.

———. *Work 2: Twenty Personal Accounts*. Harmondsworth, England: Penguin, 1969.

Friedlander, Frank. "Comparative Work Value Systems." *Personnel Psychology*, 18 (1965), 1–20.

Friedmann, Eugene, and Robert J. Havighurst. *The Meaning of Work and Retirement*. Chicago: Univ. of Chicago Press, 1954.

Friedmann, Georges. *The Anatomy of Work*. Translated by Wyatt Rawson. New York: Free Press, 1961.

Fuchs, Victor R. *The Service Economy*. New York: National Bureau of Economic Research, 1968.

Garson, Barbara. "Luddites in Lordstown." *Harper's* (June 1972) 68–73.

Gerth, Hans, and C. Wright Mills. *Character and Social Structure*. New York: Harcourt, Brace and World, 1953.

Ghiselli, E. E., and C. W. Brown. *Personnel and Industrial Psychology*. New York: McGraw Hill, 1955.

Givant, Michael. "Alienation From Bureaucratic Work: Classical Theory and Empirical Research." Doctoral Dissertation, Dept. of Sociology, City Univ. of New York, 1971.

Glaser, Barney G., and Anselm L. Strauss. *The Discovery of Grounded Theory: Strategies for Qualitative Research*. Chicago: Aldine, 1973.

Goffman, Erving. *Asylums*. Garden City, New York: Doubleday-Anchor, 1961.

———. *The Presentation of Self in Everyday Life*. Garden City, New York: Doubleday-Anchor, 1959.

Goldthorpe, John, *et al. The Affluent Worker in the Class Structure*. Cambridge, England: Cambridge Univ. Press, 1969.

———. *The Affluent Worker: Industrial Attitudes and Behavior*. Cambridge, England: Cambridge Univ. Press, 1968.

———. *The Affluent Worker: Political Attitudes and Behavior*. Cambridge, England: Cambridge Univ. Press, 1968.

Gooding, Judson. "The Fraying White Collar." *Fortune* (December 1970) 78 f.

Goodwin, Leonard. *Do the Poor Want to Work? A Social-Psychological Study of Work Orientations*. Washington, D.C.: Brookings Institution, 1972.

Gouldner, Alvin W. *Patterns of Industrial Bureaucracy*. New York: Free Press, 1954.

Gross, Edward. "Cliques in Office Organizations." *Readings on Economic Sociology*. Edited by Neil Smelser. Englewood Cliffs, New Jersey: Prentice-Hall, 1965.

Halper, Albert. *The Little People*. New York: Harper, 1942.

Hamilton, Richard F. "The Marginal Middle Class: A Reconsideration." *American Sociological Review*, 31 (April 1966), 192–199.

Harrington, Alan. *Life in the Crystal Palace*. New York: A. Knopf, 1958.

Heilbroner, Robert L. *The Economic Problem.* Englewood Cliffs, New Jersey: Prentice-Hall, 1968.

Heron, Alexander. *Why Men Work.* Stanford, California: Stanford Univ. Press, 1948.

Herrick, Neal Q., and Robert P. Quinn. "The Working Conditions Survey As a Source of Social Indicators." *Monthly Labor Review,* 94 (April 1971), 15–24.

Herzberg, Frederick. *Work and the Nature of Man.* Cleveland: World, 1966.

Herzberg, Frederick, B. Mausner, R. Peterson, and D. Capwell. *Job Attitudes: Review of Research and Opinion.* Pittsburgh: Psychological Service of Pittsburgh, 1957.

Herzberg, Frederick, Bernard Mausner, and Barbara B. Synderman. *The Motivation to Work.* New York: John Wiley and Sons, 1959.

Hodge, Robert W., Paul M. Siegel, and Peter H. Rossi. "Occupational Prestige in the United States: 1925-1963." *Class, Status and Power.* Edited by Reinhard Bendix and Seymour M. Lipset. 2nd ed. New York: Free Press, 1966, 322-334.

Homans, George. "Status Among Clerical Workers." *Human Organization,* 12 (Spring 1953), 5–10.

Hoos, Ida R. *Automation in the Office.* Washington, D.C.: Public Affairs Press, 1961.

——. "The Sociological Impact of Automation in the Office." *Management Technology,* 1 (December 1960), 10–19.

Howton, F. William. *Functionaries.* Chicago: Quadrangle, 1969.

Hughes, Everett C. "Dilemmas and Contradictions of Status." *American Journal of Sociology,* 50 (March 1945), 353–359.

——. *Men and Their Work.* Glencoe, Illinois: Free Press, 1958.

——. "Work and Self." *The Sociological Eye, Book II: Selected Papers on Work, Self, and the Study of Society.* Chicago: Aldine-Atherton, 1971, 338-347.

Kahn, Robert. "The Meaning of Work: Interpretation and Proposals for Measurement." *The Human Meaning of Social Change.* Edited by Angus Campbell and Philip E. Converse. New York: Russell Sage Foundation, 1972, 159–203.

Kanter, Rosabeth Moss. "Women and the Structure of Organizations: Explorations in Theory and Behavior." *Another Voice.* Edited by Marcia Millman and Rosabeth Moss Kanter. Garden City. New York: Doubleday-Anchor, 1975, 34-74.

Ketch, David, Richard Crutchfield, and Egerton Ballachey. *Individual in Society.* New York: McGraw Hill, 1962.

Kilborn, Peter T. "White-Collar Unemployment: No Drop in Sight." *The New York Times,* Business and Finance Section (February 23, 1975) 1 & 9.

Kirsch, Barbara A., and Joseph Lengermann. "An Empirical Test of Robert Blauner's Ideas on Alienation in Work as Applied to Different Type Jobs in a White Collar Setting." *Sociology and Social Research,* 56 (January 1972), 180–194.

Klein, Stuart M. *Workers Under Stress.* Lexington, Kentucky: Univ. of Kentucky Press, 1971.

Kohn, Melvin I. "Bureaucratic Man: A Portrait and an Interpretation." *American Sociological Review,* 36 (June 1971), 461-474.

Langer, Elinor. "Inside the New York Telephone Company." *New York Review of Books,* 14 (March 12, 1970), 16 f.

——. "The Women of the Telephone Company." *New York Review of Books,* 14 (March 26, 1970), 14 f.

Lederer, Emil. *The Problem of the Modern Salaried Employee: Its Theoretical and Statistical Basis.* Translated by E. E. Warburg. New York: Columbia Univ., 1937.

Lindesmith, Alfred R., and Anselm L. Strauss. *Social Psychology.* New York: Dryden Press, 1949.

Lockwood, David. *The Black-Coated Worker: A Study in Class Consciousness.* London: George Allen and Unwin, Ltd., 1958.

Lyman, Elizabeth. "Occupational Differences in the Value Attached to Work." *American Journal of Sociology,* 61 (September 1955), 138–144.

Lyman, Stanford M., and Marvin B. Scott. *The Drama of Social Reality.* New York: Oxford Univ. Press, 1975.

——. *A Sociology of the Absurd.* New York: Appleton-Century-Crofts, 1970.

Macarov, David. *Incentives to Work.* San Francisco: Jossey-Bass, 1970.

Mack, Raymond. "Occupational Ideology and the Determinate Role." *Social Forces,* 36 (October 1957), 37–50.

Malewski, Andrzej. "The Degree of Status Incongruence and Its Effects." *Class, Status and Power.* Edited by Reinhard Bendix and Seymour M. Lipset. 2nd ed. New York: Free Press, 1966, 303–308.

Mandell, Lewis. *Credit Card Use in the United States.* Ann Arbor: Institute for Social Research, Univ. of Michigan, 1972.

Mannheim, Karl. *Man and Society in an Age of Reconstruction.* London: Kegan Paul, Trench and Trubner, 1940.

Marx, Karl. *Economic and Philosophic Manuscripts of 1844.* Edited and introduced by Dirk J. Struik. Translated by Martin Milligen. New York: International Publishers, 1964.

Marx, Karl, and Friedrich Engels. *The German Ideology.* New York: International Publishers, 1947.

Mayer, Martin. *Madison Avenue, U.S.A.* New York: Harper, 1958.

McHugh, Peter. *Defining the Situation: The Organization of Meaning in Social Interaction.* New York: Bobbs-Merrill, 1968.

Mead, George Herbert. *Mind, Self and Society.* Chicago: Univ. of Chicago Press, 1934.

————. *On Social Psychology: Selected Papers.* Edited by Anselm Strauss. Chicago: Univ. of Chicago Press, 1956.

Meissner, Martin. "The Long Arm of the Job: A Study of Work and Leisure." *Industrial Relations,* 10 (October 1971), 239–260.

Merton, Robert K. "Bureaucratic Structure and Personality." *Reader in Bureaucracy.* Edited by Robert K. Merton, *et al.* New York: Free Press, 1952, 361–371.

Michels, Robert. *Political Parties.* Glencoe, Illinois: Free Press, 1915.

Michigan University Survey Research Center. *Survey of Working Conditions.* Washington, D.C.: U.S. Employment Standards Administration, 1971.

Mills, C. Wright. "The Cultural Apparatus." *Power, Politics and People.* Edited by Irving Louis Horowitz. New York: Oxford Univ. Press, 1967, 405–422.

————. "Mass Society and Liberal Education." *Power, Politics and People.* Edited by Irving L. Horowitz. New York: Oxford Univ. Press, 1967, 353–373.

————. "Situated Actions and Vocabularies of Motive." *Power, Politics and People.* Edited by Irving L. Horowitz. New York: Oxford Univ. Press, 1967, 439–452.

————. *The Sociological Imagination.* New York: Oxford Univ. Press, 1959.

————. "The Sociology of Stratification." *Power, Politics and People.* Edited by Irving L. Horowitz. New York: Oxford Univ. Press, 1967.

————. "The Unity of Work and Leisure." *Power, Politics and People.* Edited by Irving L. Horowitz. New York: Oxford Univ. Press, 1967. 347-352.

————. "The Unity of Work and Leisure." 347–352.

————. *White Collar.* New York: Oxford Univ. Press, 1951.

Morse, Nancy C. *Satisfactions in the White Collar Job.* Ann Arbor: Survey Research Center, Institute for Social Research, Univ. of Michigan, 1953.

Morse, Nancy C., and Robert S. Weiss. "The Function and Meaning of Work and the Job." *American Sociological Review,* 20 (April 1955), 191–198.

Nadler, Paul. "The Territorial Hunger of our Major Banks." *Harvard Business Review,* 52 (March-April 1974), 87–98.

Nairn, Tom. "The Nightwatchman." *Work: Twenty Personal Accounts.* Edited by Ronald Fraser. Harmondsworth, England: Penguin, 1968, 34-54.

Nance, Harold W., and Robert E. Nolan. *Office Work Measurement.* New York: McGraw Hill, 1971.

Neal, Arthur G., and Solomon Rettig. "Dimensions of Alienation Among Manual and Non-Manual Workers." *American Sociological Review,* 28 (August 1963), 599–608.

O'Connor, William, and Charles J. Coleman. "Unionization: What's Ahead for Banks?" *Magazine of Bank Administration,* 49 (May 1973), 15–19.

Office Management Association. *Electronics in the Office: The Practical Application of Electronic Computers and Data Processing Machines to Clerical Work.* London: Office Management Association, 1958.

Oppenheimer, Martin. "White Collar Revisited: The Making of a New Working Class." *Social Policy,* 1 (July-August 1970), 27–32.

————. "The 'Y' Theory: Enlightened Management Confronts Alienation." *New Politics,* 6 (Winter 1967), 33–48.

Orzack, Louis H. "Work As a 'Central Life Interest' of Professionals." *Social Problems,* 7 (Fall 1959), 125–132.

Palmer, Gladys. "Attitudes Toward Work in an Industrial Community." *American*

Journal of Sociology, 63 (July 1957), 17–26.

Parker, Stanley R. *The Future of Work and Leisure*. New York: Praeger, 1971.

————. "Work and Non-Work in Three Occupations." *Sociological Review*, 13 (No. 1, 1965), 65–75.

Parsons, Talcott. *The Social System*. Glencoe, Illinois: Free Press, 1951.

Patchen, M. "Supervisory Methods and Group Performance Norms." *Administrative Science Quarterly*, 7 (December 1962), 276–290.

Pennings, J. M. "Work-Value Systems of White Collar Workers." *Administrative Science Quarterly*, 15 (December 1970), 397–405.

Polanyi, Karl. *The Great Transformation*. Boston: Beacon Press, 1944.

Presbrey, Frank S. *The History and Development of Advertising*. Garden City, New York: Doubleday, Durant and Co., Inc., 1929.

Presthus, Robert. *The Organizational Society*. New York: A. Knopf, 1962.

Riesman, David, and W. Blomberg. "Work and Leisure: Fusion or Polarity?" *Research in Industrial Human Relations*. Edited by C. M. Arensberg, *et al*. New York: Harper, 1957.

Riesman, David, and Howard Roseborough. "Careers and Consumer Behavior." *Abundance For What?*, by David Riesman. Garden City, New York: Doubleday, 1964.

Roche, William, and Neil L. MacKinnon. "Motivating People With Meaningful Work." *Harvard Business Review*, 48 (May-June 1970), 97–110.

Rogers, George W. "The Economic and Social Development of the Office Worker in the United States." Master's Thesis, Univ. of California, Berkeley, 1943.

Rohlen, Thomas P. *For Harmony and Strength: Japanese White-Collar Organization in Anthropological Perspective*. Berkeley: Univ. of California Press, 1974.

Rothschild, Emma. *Paradise Lost: The Decline of the Auto-Industrial Age*. New York: Random House, 1975.

Roy, Donald F. " 'Banana Time': Job Satisfaction and Informal Interactions." *Human Organization*, 18 (Winter 1959-1960), 158–168.

Schuh, Allen J., and Milton D. Hakel. "The Counselor in Organizations: A Look to the Future." *Personnel Journal*, 51 (May 1972), 354–359.

Schutz, Alfred. "Acting and Planning." *On Phenomenology and Social Relations: Selected Writings*. Edited by Helmut R. Wagner. Chicago: Univ. of Chicago Press, 1970.

————. "On Multiple Realities." *Collected Papers I: The Problem of Social Reality*. The Hague: Martin Nijhoff, 1962.

Seeman, Melvin. "On the Meaning of Alienation." *American Sociological Review*, 24 (December 1959), 599–608.

————. "On the Personal Consequences of Alienation in Work." *American Sociological Review*, 32 (April 1967), 273–285.

Seligman, Ben B. "On Work, Alienation, and Leisure." *American Journal of Economics and Sociology*, 24 (October 1965), 337–360.

Sennet, Richard, and Jonathan Cobb. *The Hidden Injuries of Class*. New York: Random House, 1973.

Shepard, Jon M. *Automation and Alienation: A Study of Office and Factory Workers*. Cambridge, Massachusetts: MIT Press, 1971.

————. "Functional Specialization, Alienation and Job Satisfaction." *Industrial and Labor Relations Review*, 23 (January 1970), 207-219.

————. "Functional Specialization and Work Attitudes." *Industrial Relations*, 8 (May 1969), 185–194.

Sheppard, Harold L., and Neal Q. Herrick. *Where Have All the Robots Gone? Worker Dissatisfaction in the 70's*. New York: Free Press, 1972.

Slater, Philip. *The Pursuit of Loneliness*. Boston: Beacon Press, 1970.

Strauss, Anselm L. *Mirrors and Masks: The Search for Identity*. Glencoe, Illinois: Free Press, 1959.

Sturmthal, Adolf, ed. *White Collar Unionism in Seven Countries*. Chicago: Univ. of Illinois Press, 1967.

Sykes, A. J. M. "Some Differences in the Attitudes of Clerical and Manual Workers." *Sociological Review*, 13 (No. 3, 1965), 297–310.

Tannenbaum, A. S., and W. H. Schmidt. "How to Choose a Leadership Pattern." *Harvard Business Review*, 36 (1958), 95–101.

Taviss, Irene, ed. *The Computer Impact*. Englewood Cliffs, New Jersey: Prentice Hall, 1970.

Taylor, Frederick W. *The Principles of Scientific Management.* New York: Harper and Bros., 1911.

Terkel, Studs. *Working.* New York: Random House, 1974.

Tilgher, Adriano. *Homo Faber: Work Through the Ages.* Translated by Dorothy Canfield Fisher. Chicago: Henry Regnery, 1958.

Torbert, William R., with Malcolm P. Rodgers. *Being for the Most Part Puppets: Interactions Among Men's Labor, Leisure, and Politics.* Cambridge, Massachusetts: Schenkman Publishing Co., 1973.

Turner, A. N., and A. L. Miclette. "Sources of Satisfaction in Repetitive Work." *Occupational Psychology,* 26 (1962), 215–231.

Turner, E. S. *The Shocking History of Advertising!* New York: Dutton, 1953.

United States Senate Committee on Labor and Public Welfare. *Work In America: A Report of a Special Task Force to the Secretary of Health, Education and Welfare.* Washington, D.C.: Government Printing Office, 1973.

———. *Worker Alienation, 1972.* Washington, D.C.: Government Printing Office, 1972.

Vaughan, James, and Avner Porat. *Banking Computer Style.* Englewood Cliffs, New Jersey: Prentice Hall, 1969.

Veblen, Thorstein. *The Instinct of Workmanship.* New York: W. W. Norton and Co., 1964.

Vidich, Arthur J. "Introduction." *The Method and Theory of Ethnology: An Essay in Criticism,* by Paul Radin. New York: Basic Books, 1966.

Vidich, Arthur J., and Joseph Bensman. *Small Town in Mass Society: Class, Power and Religion in a Rural Community.* Revised ed. Princeton: Princeton Univ. Press, 1968.

Vidich, Arthur J., and Maurice R. Stein. "The Dissolved Identity in Military Life." *Identity and Anxiety.* Edited by M. Stein, A. Vidich, and David M. White. New York: Free Press, 1960, 493–505.

Vogel, Ezra F. *Japan's New Middle Class.* Berkeley: Univ. of California Press, 1971.

Vroom, Victor. "Industrial Social Psychology." *The Handbook of Social Psychology.* Edited by Gardner Lindzey and Eliot Aronson. Reading, Massachusetts: Addison-Wesley, 1969, V, 196–268.

———. *Work and Motivation.* New York: John Wiley and Sons, 1964.

Walker, C. R. "The Problem of the Repetitive Job." *Harvard Business Review,* 28 (No. 3, 1950), 54–58.

Weber, Max. "Bureaucracy." *From Max Weber.* Edited and translated by Hans Gerth and C. Wright Mills. New York: Oxford Univ. Press, 1968, 196–244.

———. "Class, Status, Party." *From Max Weber.* Edited and translated by Hans Gerth and C. Wright Mills. New York: Oxford Univ. Press, 1968, 180–195.

———. "The Meaning of Discipline." *From Max Weber.* Edited and translated by Hans Gerth and C. Wright Mills. New York: Oxford Univ. Press, 1968, 253–264.

———. *The Theory of Social and Economic Organization.* Translated by A. M. Henderson and Talcott Parsons. New York: Free Press. 1947.

Weiss, Robert S., and Robert L. Kahn. "Definitions of Work and Occupation." *Social Problems,* 8 (Fall 1960), 142–151.

Whitehill, A. M., Jr. "Cultural Values and Employee Attitudes: United States and Japan." *Journal of Applied Psychology,* 48 (No. 1, 1964), 69–72.

Whyte, William F. *Human Relations in the Restaurant Industry.* New York: McGraw Hill, 1948.

———. *Money and Motivation.* New York: Harper and Bros., 1955.

Whyte, William H., Jr. *The Organization Man.* Garden City, New York: Doubleday-Anchor, 1956.

Wilensky, Harold L. "Varieties of Work Experience." *Man in a World of Work.* Edited by H. Borow. Boston: Houghton Mifflin, 1964, 125–154.

———. "Work, Careers and Social Integration." *International Social Science Journal,* 12 (Fall 1960), 543–560.

Yavitz, Boris. *Automation in Commercial Banking.* New York: Free Press, 1967.

Index

184

The Author

Robert Jackall is Assistant Professor of Sociology at Williams College, Williamstown, Massachusetts and Research Associate at the Center for Economic Studies in Palo Alto, California. He is presently engaged in research on collective work organizations and in a study of bureaucracy and the ethics of managers. He is the author of several essays on work and workers.